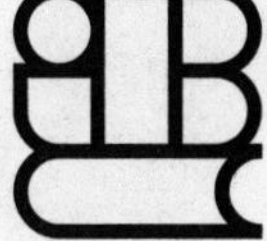

Improving the Environment for Learning

Janet Donald

Improving the Environment for Learning

Academic Leaders Talk About What Works

Jossey-Bass Publishers
San Francisco

Jossey-Bass Web address: http://www.josseybass.com

Manufactured in the United States of America on Lyons Falls Turin Book. This paper is acid-free and 100 percent totally chlorine-free.

Library of Congress Cataloging-in-Publication Data

Donald, Janet Gail, date.
Improving the environment for learning : academic leaders talk about what works / Janet G. Donald. — 1st ed.
p. cm. — (The Jossey-Bass higher and adult education series)
Includes bibliographical references and index.
ISBN 0–7879–0832–0
1. Universities and colleges—United States—Administration. 2. Learning. 3. College teaching—United States. 4. Educational change—United States. I. Title. II. Series.
LB2341.D66 1997
378.1'07—dc21 96–44482

FIRST EDITION
HB Printing 10 9 8 7 6 5 4 3 2 1

The Jossey-Bass
Higher and Adult Education Series

Contents

Preface

The knowledge era has created new challenges for universities. The demand for new knowledge, ways of organizing it and applying it, and the production of expertise have become central to economic wealth and social well-being. Universities have traditionally been both treasuries and exchanges for knowledge or learning, but in their policy-making and governance procedures, university administrators and planners have paid comparatively little attention to the learning environment. Measurements of university effectiveness tend to ignore the context of learning, focusing instead on the selection and performance of staff and students.

In universities, great effort has been expended in developing management and evaluation techniques, but the environment in which such techniques are intended to be implemented has not been investigated. Performance indicators appear precise and valid; their application is specific, their measurement simple. Their use allows responsibility to be allocated, and the solution of management problems appears feasible. Environments, on the other hand, are complex and frequently messy. The complexity can be conceptualized most fundamentally as a system, but problems within systems rarely have simple and immediate solutions.

The learning environment consists of the entire setting in which learning takes place—the campus and the social milieu, the disciplines that provide the knowledge environment, the students and the arrangements made for them, the teaching and learning process, and the assessment of learning, instruction, and programs.

The most frequent response in postsecondary institutions to the complexity of the learning environment is to create committees of stakeholders, that is, all those who might have some responsibility for the solution of problems. Committees, in their turn, produce policies but cannot directly implement practices based on the policies. The very fluidity and multidimensionality of the university environment that allows experts in so many different fields to function in juxtaposition but without expectation of synchrony, prevents a paradigm or action schema from developing. Without such a paradigm, coming to an agreement—or even communicating about the functioning of the university—becomes a herculean task.

Mission statements are the most frequent response to the need for agreed-upon operating principles. Such statements are welcome, to the extent that they provide context and guidelines for academic leaders to work within. But they are rarely translated and realized at the most basic level of the university—the classroom. At this level, organizational mission statements may be inappropriate, since they deal with aspects of education that surround but do not directly affect student learning. For example, mission statements often respond to community needs for access or economic development and are less frequently focused on the specific development of students.

For this and other reasons, university students may not receive a clear message about expectations of their intellectual development in the midst of a learning community. Other factors impeding reception of this message include students' own social and developmental needs and the increasing decentralization of programs, hence a limited relationship of them to the institution as a whole. If educational coherence and coordination are lacking within a university, students may come to a realization of what learning and an intellectual life are late in their undergraduate careers, if at all.

This book offers ideas or benchmarks about how to improve the postsecondary learning environment and is the result of conversations with academic leaders about the quality of learning in universities. Benchmarks are optimal practices that can be applied to bring about organizational improvement. The book is grounded in the immediate experience of academic leaders in postsecondary administration and in a cross-section of academic disciplines. It is intended for academic decision makers who have the task of ensuring accountability and instituting improvement in their universities and colleges.

Over the last decade, pressures from within and outside the institution on higher education administrators have frequently prevented them from providing leadership in fostering student learning. The underlying theme in *Improving the Environment for Learning* is that academic leaders' energies need to be refocused on the tasks that support and enhance learning. In the book, insights and methods that others have found useful in dealing with these tasks, accountability, teaching and learning improvement, and the plight and promise of the postmodern university are described.

To accomplish these objectives, I interviewed academic leaders in four premier research universities—the University of Arizona, Northwestern University, Pennsylvania State University, and Syracuse University—to determine their perspectives on what impedes and what could be done to improve the learning environment. The four universities are research universities with highly regarded higher education centers—two public and two private—in the United States. Although all are research universities, they serve as models within their states, nationally and internationally. Thus, they could well serve as benchmark universities for other postsecondary institutions. Certain problems, needs, and solutions addressed by the respondents from these universities may not fit the experiences and environments of some universities and colleges, but the respondents quoted in this book are concerned with educational issues in the broader sense. Those interviewed include administrators at all levels, faculty developers, and professors from across disciplines. The advice and discussion collected in the interviews thus reflect a vast range of experience in and knowledge of academe at diverse levels of administrative and scholarly functioning. Interviews call upon people's perceptions and yield ideas rather than a set of quantifiable data, but the respondents' concerns and strategies for dealing with them reflect an understanding of the ecology of higher education.

The conversations I had with these academic leaders led me to re-examine my previous research and to recall other conversations with acknowledged experts in the field of higher education in the last twenty years. During that time, I have been privileged to be a visiting member of the Center for Studies in Higher Education, University of California, Berkeley, the Center for Research in Teaching and Learning at the University of Michigan, and the Center for Educational Research at Stanford University, and I have visited a cross-section of American universities, including the University of California at Los Angeles, Harvard University, the University of Maryland, the University of South Carolina, and the University of Texas. Conferences have taken me to other campuses in the United States. My work in the field of higher education, particularly in evaluation and in teaching and learning, has acquainted me with most of Canada's universities and many of its colleges.

In addition, I have garnered insights and perspectives internationally from sojourns at the Universities of London, Cambridge, and York in the United Kingdom, the Universidad Autonoma de Mexico, the École Polytechnique Fédérale de Lausanne, and the Eidgenossische Technische Hochschule in Zurich, the National University of Singapore, Tsukuba University in Japan, and Monash University in Australia. My work in faculty development with the United Nations Educational, Scientific, and Cultural Organization (UNESCO) since 1985 introduced me to Charles University in Prague, the Universidade de Aveiro in Portugal, the Centre Europeen pour l'Enseignement Superieur in Bucharest, the Universidad de Habana in Cuba, the Université de Paris, and the Association of African Universities in Ghana. In conversations with professors, administrators, students, and faculty developers, the need for developing an environment that is conducive to learning for the twenty-first century is clear. The challenges facing universities in these divergent milieux and the resources available to deal with the challenges vary immensely, but the universities have one thing in common. They are all looking for better ways to discover and share knowledge.

Overview

In each chapter of the book, academic leaders talk about their concerns and the improvements they think can be made to the learning environment. The words of faculty, administrators, and members of higher education centers who were invited to speak about the problems they see and potential solutions to them, are used to portray a complex milieu with multiple perspectives. In Chapter One, I explain the nature of the study, the challenges facing universities in the twenty-first century, and the redefinition that will be needed to improve the learning climate. Chapter Two focuses on the role of the disciplines and their effect on the quality of learning. In Chapters Three and Four, I examine student selection and access, especially questions of quality and diversity and ways of fostering students' motivation for learning. In Chapters Five and Six, I explore instructional improvement methods that are focused on student learning, then projects undertaken by institutions to support the improvement of teaching. In Chapters Seven and Eight, I broach the use of assessment to define tasks and measure learning and teaching, then turn to faculty responsibilities and rewards. The final chapter returns to the theme of educational challenges facing colleges and universities and institutional assessment to improve learning.

This book is based on research funded by the Québec Fonds pour la Formation de Chercheurs et l'Aide à la Recherche and the Social

Science and Humanities Research Council of Canada. I wish to express particular appreciation to the academic leaders who participated in the study that forms the basis of the book, and especially my hosts at the four institutions, professors Sarah Dinham of the University of Arizona, Bob Menges of Northwestern University, Jim Ratcliff of Pennsylvania State University, and Bob Diamond of Syracuse University.

January 1997 JANET DONALD

Montreal, Quebec
Canada
E-mail address: donald@education.mcgill.ca

The Author

Janet Donald is professor of education in the Department of Educational and Counselling Psychology and the Centre for University Teaching and Learning at McGill University. She earned her B.A. degree (1962) and M.A. degree (1963) in honors psychology at the University of Western Ontario, and her Ph.D. degree (1968) in educational theory at the Ontario Institute for Studies in Education. Before joining McGill University in 1973, she was coordinator of psychology at Vanier College. She was director of the Centre for University Teaching and Learning at McGill from 1982 to 1993.

Donald's research activities have included studies on postsecondary learning and teaching, as well as evaluation and institutional research. Her current research is on knowledge acquisition in higher education, the quality of postsecondary learning and teaching, students' conceptualizations of learning, and fostering higher-order learning. Recent publications include articles and chapters on professors' and students' conceptualizations of learning in different disciplines, disciplinary differences in knowledge validation, the evaluation of undergraduate education, and the role of higher education centers in improving the academy.

Donald was president of the Canadian Society for the Study of Higher Education in 1990–1991 and won the Distinguished Researcher Award given by that society in 1994. She is national coordinator for Canada for the UNESCO Staff Development Workgroup in Higher Education and is on the Program Advisory Council of Improving University Teaching and the Editorial Board of *Assessment and Evaluation in Higher Education*.

1

Frameworks for Improving Learning

In the twenty-first century, the global economy and the knowledge or information era will increasingly depend upon effective postsecondary educational practice to provide knowledge and expertise.

Among social institutions, universities are highly successful. They are recognized as being enormously important to a nation's well-being (Rosenzweig, 1994) and are seen as the channel of opportunities around the world (Pelikan, 1992). At the same time, universities face immense challenges. Asked to fulfill expanding roles with fewer resources, they are being called to account for the resources at their disposal (Ashworth and Harvey, 1994; Kells, 1992; Piper, 1993; Woodhouse, 1995). Forces external to universities—government, the press, and the public—exhort them to change their financing, their organization, and their goals, to do more with less, and to do it better. Inside the university, administrators, faculty, and students evaluate each other and demand change.

For any institution to adapt to new circumstances, judgments about purposes and priorities must be made. Making wise judgments in complex social institutions such as universities requires insight into the multiple components and relationships in these institutions. Often, the judgments that are made—for example, to increase the number of students per staff member or to make across-the-board cuts—appear not only counterintuitive but dangerous to the learning environment. The centrality of learning is lost in the exigency of expenditure reduction. The real need is for a new pragmatism in which the practical consequences of university policy are tested. Academic leaders, particularly those who have had responsibility for the nurturance of higher education, whether through long experience, administrative roles, or special duties in their institutions, have a great deal of expertise that has not yet been shared about how universities might be administered to optimize learning.

Origin of the Book

This book originated in a study of academic leaders' perspectives on what impedes and what could be done to improve the quality of learning. As interview sites I chose major research universities because they are the most praised and often the most criticized postsecondary educational institutions; they bear the heaviest burden of scholarship and general advancement. I selected both public land grant and private institutions in the United States to ensure that each major type of institution was represented. Universities function on a continuum that stretches from quasi-public service to the unfettered pursuit of knowledge; the legal status of a university brings it closer to one pole or another (Cabal, 1993). Private institutions tend to be specialist—focused, coherent, and selective—as opposed to public, and hence generalist, institutions that are broad, open, and ambiguous (Levy, 1992). Sampling public and private universities allowed the perspectives of leaders in each to surface.

During the first four months of 1994, I visited a public and a private university in the eastern United States—Pennsylvania State and Syracuse; a private university in the Midwest—Northwestern—and a public university in the Southwest—the University of Arizona. Each university was founded in the latter half of the nineteenth century; each is a research university according to the 1994 Carnegie classification, and is a member of the Association of American Universities, indicating that they are leading recipients of federal financial support of academic science. The universities are also noteworthy because they have centers of higher education and instructional development that were created in the late sixties or seventies to investigate and respond to issues of higher education policy and practice. These universities recognized early the need to devote resources to the study of postsecondary education and its improvement. Their foresight has on innumerable occasions allowed them to guide other postsecondary institutions to better practice.

The University of Arizona

A public land grant university, the University of Arizona was established in 1885 and is located in Tucson, in the southwest United States, with over 37,000 full- and part-time students. Its role in the Arizona university system is as "a major comprehensive research university, competitive with the best public universities in the nation" (Arizona Board of Regents, 1982, p. 7). It is the flagship university in one of the fastest-growing states, where approximately 94 percent of postsecondary enrollment is in public institutions (Arizona Board of Regents, 1990). As the state's land grant university, it had an early emphasis on agriculture, mining, and engineering, and it houses the state of Arizona's colleges of medicine and pharmacy. Respondents at the University of Arizona described the focus of its identity as being one of the top fifteen to twenty research institutions in the country.

The university's strategic plan for 1990–1995 consisted of seven directions: (1) improving undergraduate education, (2) strengthening research, the creative arts, and graduate education, (3) expanding community outreach and public service programming, (4) ensuring access for underrepresented groups, (5) emphasizing affirmative action goals and programs, (6) responding to future enrollment demands, and (7) enhancing resources. The multiple directions in the strategic plan are interrelated but at times competitive, according to respondents.

The university has two centers concerned with postsecondary education. The Center of Higher Education, founded in 1977, was set up as a graduate program, with the goal of providing institutional analysis for state administrators in higher education. One of its principal areas of study is student experience of higher education (student persistence and the effect of college on students); the two most recently hired faculty members are experts in the area of community colleges and student affairs. The mission of the more recently opened (in 1990) University Teaching Center is to support instruction on the campus. This center is responsible for providing audiovisual services and for classroom renovation and modernization. It houses a teaching evaluation service, oversees the provost's teaching improvement awards for faculty who want to redesign courses or design new ones, and sponsors teaching awards that recognize faculty across the campus who have contributed to teaching.

Pennsylvania State University

The eastern public university chosen for the study, Pennsylvania State University, was founded in 1855 and designated as the land grant college of the Commonwealth of Pennsylvania in 1863. It operates as a university system, with the flagship campus at University Park in the center of the state. According to the university catalogue, Penn State in 1994–95 had a student body of over 68,000, over 5,000 faculty, more than 5,000 undergraduate courses, and more than 3,000 graduate courses. There were 36,000 students at the University Park campus, 30,000 of whom were undergraduates. There are twenty-two additional campuses throughout the state, including seventeen Commonwealth Campuses that are similar in function to community colleges. The president of the University Park campus is the president of the system, and the faculty senate makes policy that governs the entire system.

The university mission statement declares three traditional responsibilities: education, research, and service (*Penn State Catalogue*, 1994–95, p. 13). Its educational mandate is inspirational. It focuses on introducing students to "the collective knowledge, wisdom, and experience of human society." This is to be accomplished by motivating students to acquire intellectual discipline and to consider the values that will guide their future. The research mandate stresses the university's public responsibility to promote scholarship, creativity, and the advancement of knowledge. The service mandate of the university is oriented to contributing to economic and societal vitality, both public and private, through its expertise.

The Center for the Study of Higher Education (CSHE) at Pennsylvania State University was founded in 1969 as one of the first research organizations established specifically to examine postsecondary policy issues. It is an interdisciplinary research organization concerned with higher education policy and practice that seeks to inform and be informed by the major policy debates of the field and to engage policy leaders, analysts, and federal, associational, state, and institutional leaders in the reexamination of principles, programs, and practices (*Center*, 1992, p. 7). The center reports to the vice president for research and houses the National Center on Postsecondary Teaching, Learning, and Assessment, a consortium of six research universities studying these issues.

Northwestern University

Northwestern is a private university founded in 1851 and located in Evanston, Illinois, on the west shore of Lake Michigan. It has some 12,000 students, of whom more than one-third are graduate students (*Peterson's Competitive Colleges 1996–1997*, 1996). According to respondents at the university, what gives the university its considerable prestige is the volume and quality of the research engaged in by the faculty. It is a decentralized university in which most administrators have been faculty members, and respondents say that deans are responsible for everything in their schools.

In 1988, a task force on the undergraduate experience focused several of its recommendations on curriculum and teaching, and in 1991 a university committee on the evaluation and improvement of teaching described the environment for teaching in the following manner: "Although high valuation of teaching is a definite part of the Northwestern culture, teaching is not yet a highly valued part of the Northwestern system" (*Northwestern Observer*, 1991, p. 5). The university participated from 1988 to 1993 in a project involving seven universities and designed to influence the attitudes and priorities of campus leaders regarding teaching. This study, entitled *Focus on Teaching Project*, was headquartered at the other private university selected for this study—Syracuse University. A result of the increased attention to teaching at Northwestern is the recent creation of a center devoted to the support of teaching in all undergraduate schools.

The university has two centers concerned with postsecondary teaching and learning. The Center for the Teaching Professions, founded in 1969 and originally funded by the Kellogg Foundation, serves the university as a research and development center in higher education and reports to the dean of the School of Education and Social Policy. The director of this center chaired the committee on the evaluation and improvement of teaching and the *Focus on Teaching Project* at Northwestern. This center is also part of the National Center on Postsecondary Teaching, Learning, and Assessment, and so has links to the Center for the Study of Higher Education at Pennsylvania State University. The more recently opened (in 1992) Searle Center for Teaching Excellence reports to the provost and provides service to the campus in promoting effective teaching. This line of reporting means that there is major responsibility from central administration for the Searle Center and that it has central administration support and attention.

Syracuse University

The eastern, private university chosen for the study, Syracuse, was founded in 1871 and is located in the city of Syracuse in upper New York State. It has a history of strong support for the improvement of academic courses and programs. The university enrolls over 10,000 undergraduate students and nearly 5,000 graduate students in degree programs in the arts and humanities, the physical sciences and mathematics, architecture, visual and performing arts, management, engineering, information studies, computer science, and education.

The Center for Instructional Development was established in 1971 to support Syracuse University faculty in the improvement of academic courses and programs. It reports to the vice chancellor of the university. The center enjoys an international reputation and received the 1989 Award for Outstanding Practice in Instructional Development from the Association for Educational Communication and Technology. It is also part of the National Center on Postsecondary Teaching, Learning, and Assessment at Pennsylvania State University. Since its inception, more than one hundred projects have been undertaken with departments representing the entire campus. These projects include the redesign and evaluation of new and existing courses and curricula. In addition, the center provides evaluation and research support to programs and services offered by other areas of the university such as new faculty and student orientation programs, the teaching assistant program, residence life, and student services.

One respondent noted that in some ways the center is also an applied institutional research agency, doing studies of attrition, holding focus groups of first-year students to explore their perceptions of the university, or designing the mail registration system for incoming new students so that 90 percent of entering students get their first or second choice of courses. Staff at the center involve themselves in an array of activities and assume that the mission and activities will change frequently. Of particular importance to this study is the campuswide effort to improve the quality of students' undergraduate experience that took place beginning in 1989. By 1995, the university's decision to transform itself into a student-centered research university had led to a university-wide policy on learning, to the establishment of mentoring programs and funds for the development of programs, and to a substantial change in attitudes across schools and colleges toward the mission of the university (Diamond and Adam, 1995).

A review of the universities selected for the study shows that the private and public universities differ in two major respects—the private universities are approximately one-half the size of the public, and their long-standing higher education centers are devoted more to teaching than to policy analysis. They are similar, however, in being established research universities. In addition, all of the universities have academics in the field of higher education who are linked to a center in another of the universities.

From the four universities, chosen because of the contribution they have made to improving postsecondary education, I interviewed thirty-two academic leaders who were selected as respondents based on their understanding of their university and of higher education more broadly. One of my university hosts noted that if credit were to be awarded to the participating universities, it should be for having thoughtful people who are wrestling with insoluble problems. A wide variety of knowledgeable people agreed to be interviewed. Sixteen were administrators: one chancellor, one vice president, one assistant vice chancellor, and one vice provost, three associate deans, three department chairs, two program directors, and four center directors. Of the sixteen administrators, twelve were also professors, out of a total of twenty-three professors interviewed. The respondents came from the following fields: art history, biology, economics, education, educational psychology, engineering, history, human development, humanities, mathematics, physical education, physics, political science, religious studies, speech, and the visual and performing arts. Thus, the sciences, social sciences, humanities, and the professions were represented in the sample. Eleven women participated. The number of respondents with backgrounds in higher education or faculty development was eighteen—seven administrators, six professors, and five faculty developers.

In a series of individual, semistructured interviews, I invited the academic leaders to discuss topics related to the quality of learning in their institution. These included student learning issues, student selection, responsibility for learning, and motivation for learning. Other areas of interest were how the disciplines respond to these issues, the effect of different methods of inquiry and their relative primacy in developing knowledge, and the effect of postmodernism and constructivism on university epistemology.

Since assessment has become a major issue in universities, due both to external demands for accountability and to recent attempts in some to organize the curriculum around learning outcomes or competencies, I asked respondents for their perspective on assessment and its use in defining university tasks, as well as on broader evaluation issues such as performance indicators and procedures. In discussions with members of higher education centers (fourteen of the respondents), I gathered information on the role of their center, along with its history, goals, activities, and resource base. Toward the end of the interviews, the conversation turned to the future—the anticipated operation of the university, conceptual frameworks for the twenty-first century, and the most important issues in higher education from the perspective of the respondents.

Each person responded to the list of topics in terms of what was critical or most important to his or her conceptualization of the university; hence, the responses were highly individualistic. All interviews except three (given confidentially to provide context) were tape-recorded and transcribed, and a report on the interview was sent to each respondent for editorial comment, which was included in a final report to each. The reports were then coded, and a composite report of the views expressed in each university was produced and sent to the host at each institution for editorial review. Analysis of the results yielded certain commonalities across universities and respondents, but the most striking characteristic of the results was the mosaic of interpretations.

Respondents' comments highlight perspectives and benchmarks, that is, best practices or aspects of an optimum learning environment. Evidently, the setting in which learning takes place and the role of the disciplines in providing knowledge supply the backdrop for their comments. Students, the teaching and learning process, and the assessment of learning, of programs, and of instruction are central to the discussion. The quotations from the interviews allow complex interrelated issues to be presented in a manner that does not oversimplify them, yet provides provocative insights into the dilemmas postsecondary educators face. The issue stimulating much of the discussion is how higher education fits into and contributes to the society that houses it. This leads to the question of which roles a university can and should fulfill within its larger community and how universities might redefine their goals and priorities.

Responsibilities of the University to Society

At the end of the twentieth century, with dwindling government funding and global economic imperatives, universities are increasingly being asked to operate using an economic model in which the important considerations are students and the job requirements of society. Universities have a multitude of roles, however, on a continuum of interaction with the larger community, ranging from universal to local. At the most universal end of the continuum, a university—as the intellectual or nerve center of a learning society—influences society through knowledge construction (Newman, 1976; Pelikan, 1992; Shils, 1983). As a center for research and technological advance, the university plays a more direct role through application of that knowledge (Cole, 1994). As critic of society or guide to the nation for the betterment of humankind, the university is explicitly involved in the development of society (Organization for Economic Cooperation and Development, 1982; Shils, 1983).

Each role has a different focus and implies a particular organization and set of criteria for evaluating outcomes. For example, as the intellectual or nerve center of a learning society in which the university is a source of intellectual leadership, control, or energy, the role is predominantly epistemological. As an intellectual center, systems of meaning, theories, models, and methods for organizing information assume precedence. Knowledge is its own end (Newman, 1976; Pelikan, 1992). The justification for a university, then, is that it unites young and old in the imaginative consideration of learning, and the task of the university is to weld together imagination and experience (Whitehead, 1929). The criterion for success is significant knowledge, and the function of the university is to stimulate inquiry and reflection. This role renders the university autonomous, or at least relatively independent of society in its operation, yet intimately connected with it for the ultimate well-being of society.

As a center for research and the development of technology, the university fulfills both epistemological and economic roles. A center for research suggests a professor-centered arena where success depends on research grants and publications. In a discussion on the dilemmas of choice facing research universities, Cole (1994) points out that academic leaders recruit and support scientists and scholars who have made or are apt to make seminal discoveries—those who define fields and specialities. The emphasis is on the production of new knowledge. Corollary to this emphasis, however, is the application of knowledge through technology or marketing: expertise is the defining criterion. In this role, the university has a contract with society to supply expertise in the form of problem solution or the next cohort of experts, and the public has a direct stake in the outcomes. One respondent noted that the current emphasis on expertise has led to increased demand for postgraduate programs.

> Universities are special places in providing the advanced expertise for society. The need for expertise makes the master's degree the fastest-growing degree, and the doctoral degree an unspoken but

> nevertheless valued piece of training that extends beyond just perpetuating the professoriate. That makes the university subject to far more public scrutiny, as well as giving it far more public importance than it had when it enrolled 2 or 3 percent of the population. It is not necessarily more valued.

As a guide to society for the betterment of humankind and as critic of society, the university plays a sociopolitical role. In the role of societal guide or critic, the focus is on wider issues, and the criterion for success is societal change and development. The extent to which a university acts as social conscience, if not social critic, has varied from one era to another. A concrete example of how societal issues have been dealt with in the curriculum was provided by a respondent:

> The curriculum provides a special "time out" function in society, where you work through difficult and troubling issues. The first socially troubling issue that comes to mind is the Vietnam War, which had a myriad of courses that emerged in higher education institutions in the United States. Those courses were taught largely by people who became young faculty after or during the Vietnam War and attracted students who were concerned about the social consequences of the war. There was an enormous up curve of student and faculty interest and passion, and we are now on the down curve. If you want to think about it in terms of a product life cycle, what function did that play? From my vantage point, it provided an avenue for investigation of a very troubling and unresolved social issue.

The function of the university as social conscience is also linked to its epistemological role, which requires determining what knowledge is significant and what criteria are used in making judgments. Troubling issues in society can be resolved only if inquiry is encouraged and time is allotted for reflection. Sutton (1994) makes the argument that the old reverential regard for universities rested on dual faith in the essential roles of highly educated people and of the advancement of knowledge for the betterment of the human condition. In developing countries, this is the primary role of many universities (Cabal, 1993), where professors and students conduct their postsecondary programs by attempting to solve local problems.

The roles for universities as intellectual centers, research producers, and societal developers overlap. Advocates of one or another role are more likely to divide along disciplinary lines than according to type of institution. The role of a university is affected, however, by whether it is private or public. Land grant universities were expressly designated to respond to local or state needs. Private universities, unless heavily endowed, depend upon tuition and therefore student and parental support. Public universities receive over half their revenue from state and local appropriations, while private universities receive a minimal (1.3 percent) amount (Stadtman, 1992). Tuition and fees average 17.5 percent of revenues in public universities, while in private universities, over half the revenue is from tuition and fees, and another quarter comes from private gifts, grants, and endowment income. Endowment may allow students and faculty to pursue intellectual aims, but memorable from my interviews with students at Stanford University in 1987 was their self-definition as leaders in making the world a better place, on or off the North American continent. Widely apparent in discussions with the academic leaders in this series of interviews, seven years later, was the demand being placed on universities to shift priorities and to respond to local needs. This was described by one respondent in terms of the broad range of expectations the larger community has of institutions of higher education.

> We have to have counseling services on campus, because our kids don't go to the counseling service in the community if they have problems. We have to have vocationally relevant undergraduate

> degree programs because of the economy or because that is the current trend, but also we expect students to understand the implications of Aristotle for being an accountant. So, society is asking higher education institutions to do everything. I see expectations that research universities have to have poison control centers that people can call up when their kid swallows dishwasher soap from under the sink, because that is what the university is supposed to be. Land grant schools have the obligation to extend knowledge, in this case, about poison, to the general community. And yet we are also asking the university to acquaint first-year students with the notion of Aristotelian concepts of knowledge and to think about that as it relates to their own evolving intellectual lives. I think that is an impossible task for higher education today.

In some locales, society has turned to the university as the major resource for social problem solving, as well as for intellectual development. Society has thus placed not only the responsibility for developing the next generation vocationally and intellectually on the university's shoulders but also the burden of its well-being. Which roles a university can and should fulfill in a given community require closer examination.

The University Redefined as a Social Institution

What can realistically be expected of universities today? The growth in the importance of universities to their communities in the last half century has led to a thicker web of reciprocities between higher education institutions and the local environment (Lane, 1992). Higher education institutions reflect their local communities in the sense that the structure of the community is a frame of reference for the identification of the mission and to some extent a constraint on the mission of the institution. To illustrate, the transition in universities from elite to mass education responded to a public need but created a new set of pressures and required major adaptations on the part of universities. According to Lane, the community does not shape the destiny of the institution and is more frequently symbiotic with it, but its particular interests may at times conflict with the more universalistic orientation of the university. For example, the principle of academic freedom may lead universities to support research findings that a community would judge politically incorrect and socially harmful. The respondents described a mosaic of approaches to the redefinition of the university. Four criteria can be discerned to determine the nature of the mission a university undertakes.

The Criterion of Exclusive Competence. *To discriminate the nature of a university's mission within the larger community, one important criterion is whether some other social agency can respond to the problem or whether only the university is equipped to deal with it.*

By accepting the transfer of resources from a community, locally or more broadly, the university commits itself to deliver certain services to the community. Public universities in particular may feel inundated by demands to respond to a wide variety of needs, more so when the resources that are required to respond exceed those the university has. When resources to the university are being cut back at the same time, a redefinition of role that affects how the university operates becomes imperative. One respondent noted that this redefinition is going on at several levels.

> What can we salvage? What should we salvage? What do we need to ascribe to someone else? The public is redefining their expectations of the university. Policy makers, those people who provide funding to the university, are reexamining that, not only within light of their own value system but in light of what the constituency argues the university should do.

Research universities have come to represent the epitome of intellectual leadership, and in the past half century have been given corresponding freedom to define their role. This has also made them targets. The deconstruction of society, especially the breakdown of or emancipation from social norms, has left the university in the position of being one of a very few (along with judges and politicians) icons to be examined. Previously left to its own devices, perhaps because it was assumed that the university, of all institutions, knew what it was doing, or possibly because its intellectual resources were not valued to the same extent in the pre-knowledge era, the research university is now under scrutiny.

> One of the criticisms being leveled at any research university is that the focus and the emphasis is too much on research and not enough on providing a quality education to undergraduates or serving the needs of the larger community. I think that those charges are to some extent accurate, but they dismiss what the university really does for a community. This is a very complex place, and there are a lot of things that affect its operation. The operational load of this university, like others, was based on a time when there was access to a lot of resources so that we could follow different directions. In the process of doing that, not only did we overextend ourselves but we created certain expectations that we were not able to meet for a variety of reasons. I think now we need to say, "What are those expectations, and which ones can we adequately meet, and which ones can we not meet and maybe are the province of some other group?"

It is imperative to analyze what roles other social agencies can fulfill, as a means of limiting the pressure to fulfill all of society's needs and thus diverting attention from what is most critical for the university to accomplish. The advancement of knowledge is the most central mission to a university. The constituency a university serves imposes certain conditions on its operation.

The Criterion of Constituency. *The nature of the constituency of a university and the extent to which that constituency is also the provider* *of resources has increased in importance in determining the mission of the university. Fewer resources are being made available to postsecondary institutions through government and other official channels, making tuition a more important resource. The threat of dwindling resources has led postsecondary institutions to be more accountable and to restructure—to do more with less, or to decide what has to go.*

It was clear in the interviews that the resources made available to universities through official channels have decreased. Many respondents spoke about the problem of resources, some relating it to poor administration generally, both at the state and university level. Others focused on how to live with reduced resources.

> There will be more cuts coming. We are at a point where we cannot do more with less. That means making strategic choices about what we're going to keep, what we are good at. I think institutions are very reluctant and not very good at making those kinds of choices—getting a faculty to give up its Ph.D. program, even though it's mediocre, is very difficult; closing down an office or a division, or combining units, is painful. We have some years of rough sledding ahead of us.

Parents are making choices based on the relative costs and benefits of different educational systems and on their childrens' likely need to pursue graduate studies. They are choosing undergraduate schools that offer the best educational value for the price and are examining how much attention students are receiving in them. An administrator explained how parents make these decisions:

> One man astounded me one night when I was on the road for the university. He said, "I've sent three of my youngsters to the university, and two have gone to the local community college, and one has gone to a community college in a neighboring state. Now don't tell me that the education at the university is better, because you certainly don't have to be a genius to succeed in American higher education.

> What you really have to do is work hard and develop a sense of commitment." I said that I did not disagree but asked why that would not make a university degree a better one. He said, "Because you don't work the folks hard enough; you don't provide them with feedback on a regular basis like the kids are getting at the community college." The parent was not hostile; he was just making an observation.

If parents are scrutinizing the value of their educational dollar, down to the point of examining how closely students are supervised, professors also recognize the costs and benefits of an education and inform students to that effect. The question of the efficient use of resources has filtered into the classroom, affecting how one respondent in a private university approaches the issue of student investment of time and money.

> I tell first-year students, "You could buy this education at this institution, or you could buy a McDonald's franchise, or you could buy a duplex and rent it out. I don't know which one is going to make you happier, but you made this choice. Think about it that way, because this is an enormous investment, an enormous price to pay. And I want you to figure out how much it costs to come to this class today, if you add up your tuition and divide by the number of courses taken and then by how many times they meet."

The benchmark suggested here is readily quantifiable. If a student is paying $25,000 a year for tuition and living expenses, and takes ten courses during the year, each course costs $2,500. If a course meets three times a week during a term of fifteen weeks, each class costs that student approximately $55. Although we might question the extent to which students will be motivated to study based on being made aware of the per dollar cost of their education, the fact that a university professor has discussed the subject of education with students in economic terms tells us that we are in an era of closely watched resources.

The effect of the threat of dwindling resources is twofold. It has provoked a need to be more accountable, that is, to prove that society is being served efficiently and effectively, and it has revealed the need to restructure, so that there is a better match between financing and performance.

> There is an increasing stranglehold on state or federal aid. . . . [L]egislatures are not supporting institutions of higher learning to the extent that they used to. Most colleges and universities are, ostrich-like, waiting for somebody better to be elected, or they are waiting to get a more articulate spokesperson for themselves who can better lobby with the legislature. It circles right around to assessment and performance indicators. A lot of the reason we are not getting money is that people in government think we have not been terribly responsible with the money we have received.

Changes in sources of funding are changing the ways universities think about their missions. An obvious effect is to consider what the likely sources of funds will be in the future. One respondent considered that for both public and private universities, the straightened financial situation constitutes a wake-up call for colleges and universities to ask the question, Why are we here?, and in answering that question to establish goals and procedures for meeting them to accompany the budgetary adjustments that will need to be made.

> When asking why we are here, we end up, in the private universities, asking, Where does our source of money come from? Depending upon the university, probably 60 to 80 percent of it or more comes from tuition. What follows from that is the question, How can we be a place where students are willing to pay these exorbitant charges to get an education? So through the back door, the significant educational issues will be confronted in a way we haven't seen.

The constituency, ever more knowledgeable, is gaining greater voice in the directions a university takes. Accountability becomes immediate.

The Criterion of Equity. *The sociopolitical criterion of equity or equal opportunity evoked an expansion and diversification of postsecondary institutions available to the population at large. Equity must be balanced with the intellectual mission of the university.*

In the past four decades, when governments made resources available in response to societal needs, the university expanded to satisfy them. Now that continuing government cutbacks have become a reality, some means of determining what needs have priority is essential. A pivotal test case of what a university can be expected to do within society, or whether some other social agency can respond to the problem, is the question of access to postsecondary education.

If the enunciated role of education is to be available to its citizens, postsecondary education will be evaluated against the criterion of how well it aids a broad spectrum of students. If on the other hand, the university is envisioned as a center of expertise, as this respondent suggests, it is unlikely to meet the equality of opportunity criterion. It also affects how knowledge is perceived.

> We like to use education as a way of trying to overcome our inequities in society, and we haven't been too successful at doing that. In fact if anything, the effect of education is to increase inequality in society. That is not the way people talk, but that is what is happening. The more that a hard science conception of knowledge predominates, the more we are going to maintain a very conventional, traditional notion of learning and quality—there are some people who are experts and have knowledge, and other people need to come to them to get that knowledge. This is opposed to the view that everybody has knowledge, and instead of students coming into the insti-

> tution and learning from faculty and learning from the institution and becoming socialized into a big community, we might see the university and faculty benefiting and changing as a result of the influx of new kinds of students.

Postsecondary educational institutions have responded to the political challenge of equity or equal opportunity by expanding the number and kinds of institutions available to the population at large. This has, however, increased the heterogeneity, and hence the complexity, of postsecondary education. The variety of competing demands on postsecondary institutions—for the development of human capital, for the solution of social problems, for the production and dissemination of new knowledge, and for economic prosperity based on a competitive position in the knowledge economy—has led to an expansion of postsecondary education within and across institutions. The various demands require a different ordering of priorities within postsecondary institutions or among them, leading to differentiated patterns of learning. Within an institution, this increases the need for a clear mission statement and an equally clear statement of how that mission will be undertaken.

The Criterion of Fostering Intellectual Development. *A fourth criterion reflects the university's responsibility for the advancement of learning by the next generation. Fostering intellectual development is one of the most essential missions of the university.*

In *The American University: How It Runs, Where It Is Going,* Barzun (1993) suggested that learning is hard, continuous, attentive work whose essence is the convening of studious minds better than our own, who compel us to change ours. One aim that universities have more clearly than any other social institution is to foster intellectual development. Students enter universities seeking meaning and wanting to learn, but students have competing aims. Some may have only vague notions about what advanced or higher-order learning is and may be content to let knowledge wash over them. Our research has shown that in some programs, for example science and engineering, the great majority of students have chosen to attend a university in order to learn and to develop reasoning skills (Donald and Denison, 1996b). But students are also interested in career preparation and in meeting new people. They have diverse goals that, at times, compete for their attention. The way in which success is counted, however, is in credits and grades, not in learning. Students quickly intuit that grades are the medium of exchange. The accounting procedure in higher education has thus led to a distortion in students' educational goals that may only be rectified by major administrative and programmatic changes. One respondent approached the problem in the following manner.

> The question that I think really needs to be asked is, What is an education? It isn't just a matter of sitting in a seat and getting credits and thinking you've learned something. They talk about grades, because those of us who are supposedly encouraging learning talk about how many units you have, and what are you majoring in, and do you have your requirements yet, instead of saying, What's the big issue in the United States today? How can we solve this problem? We talk too much as if there's a price and you're getting a certain poundage for your money. How can we change that culture to not only allow students but to encourage students, and how can we recognize an educated person and award a degree? If we could more accurately measure quality of learning and more accurately examine in order to determine an educated person, some young people coming from rich intellectual environments at home, in high school, could acquire a degree in one of the liberal arts in maybe two and one-half years. Others starting behind might be expected to take five, but we would have different ways of determining what they've accomplished.

Finding ways to ensure students' intellectual development is a theme that runs through this book. A further challenge comes from the demands of the global economy. According to Skolnikoff (1994), the education of American students, to be able to function effectively in an integrated world, has become a major charge on American universities, especially on universities that are themselves significant participants in the international community. The question we are led to ask is, then, How can higher education institutions ensure that they are providing an environment in which students learn to think and to become participants in the larger world?

Frameworks for Improving the Environment for Learning

The relationship between society and the university appears noticeably strained. Internationally, politicians note that educational and science policy are not popular portfolios for politicians, as industry withdraws from the national arena and scientists insist on pursuing their specialized research (Trutmann, 1995). This situation has led many governments to make decisions based on cost-benefit considerations and to fund based on outputs. In turn, this kind of thinking has led to examination of the way universities operate and, specifically, how they make decisions. Higher education experts have approached the problem from various perspectives, from the sociological to the managerial. At the broadest level, the question is of self-conception or identity (Clark, 1995). The way that an institution defines itself determines how it will be managed, and self-definition is the first step toward the deliberate design of institutional change. Clark considers a knowledge of the disciplines and how they operate to be a critical need for designing institutional progress.

A second step in the process of improving the learning climate is to clarify the university mission and set priorities within the university. In a study of thirty-five research universities, Taylor and Schmidtlein (1995) found setting priorities to be an important environmental issue in strategic planning, along with the previously mentioned issues of declining resources, changing demographics, increasing competitiveness, and decreasing public esteem. Internal issues bearing on strategic planning included changing cultures and attitudes, reallocating resources, dealing with a decrease in the infrastructure with an increased emphasis on curriculum and teaching, and the effective utilization of faculty. As one respondent pointed out,

> Institutions have to define what their goals and priorities are. Most don't. The focus of efforts in the faculty reward system has to agree with this statement. The priority statement has to get more specific as you move to the departments, and the departments and schools and colleges have to become more accountable so that all the pieces mesh together. This is going to have major ramifications on structure, organization, and role of administration so that we're going to be far better at what we do than what we are now. Right now, I don't think we're educating particularly well, or doing service well; a lot of the research we do or articles we write are insignificant. When you have 90 percent of the publications in some fields never being cited in a five-year period including by the author, it tells you it isn't particularly important.

Another approach to improving the learning climate at the macro-institutional level is to view postsecondary education as a multinational knowledge industry in which the relationship between knowledge and information is critical, and relearning and economic productivity enter the equation as objectives (Peterson, 1995). This approach requires an international, interdisciplinary stance and a different planning process. An immediate effect of taking this approach is the need to develop an information strategy that brings staff, professors, and students on-line. An investment in computer facilities and networking and in policies that assist professors and students in their use of computer facilities follows, as specifically as equipment rental to students of laptop computers with modems (Sporn, 1995).

Two internal processes for redefining the university are *reengineering* and *benchmarking*. These approaches operate at more specific levels and so are closer to institutional practice. For example, the reengineering process at the Massachusetts Institute of Technology is designed to fundamentally change the way work is performed to achieve radical performance improvements in speed, cost, and quality (Bruce, 1995). The basic principle underlying the reengineering process is that it must reduce work. MIT has instituted reengineering procedures in its administrative work processes, including facilities maintenance, management reporting, student services, and research proposals to reduce overhead on research grants. The process requires adroit management. One respondent described the need for improved administration.

> If I see one desperate need out there, it's to start educating our administrators to be administrators. One university has a very effective program that has all their chairs and program directors meeting regularly. Too many campuses have revolving chairs. We don't have the leadership we need in colleges and universities. Too many administrators don't know enough about the things they need to know to do their jobs well. For change to occur the whole academic community must be involved.

Reengineering does not need to be limited to administrative work processes. The major complaint among faculty is that they are overworked. The application of reengineering to the academic's work week could alleviate the stress many of the respondents were experiencing.

Benchmarking is a strategy for organizational learning that examines performance and the processes that lead to high performance. A benchmark is a point of reference to which practices can be compared and evaluated—a process of evaluating the products, services, and work processes of organizations that are recognized as representing the best practices for the purpose of organizational improvement (Blumenstyk, 1993; Spendolini, 1992; Stralser, 1995). In performance benchmarking, performance in one's own institution is compared with that of a similar institution considered to be more effective. Differences in performance—performance gaps—have been documented in a wide variety of areas in postsecondary education: staff-student ratio, annual alumni giving, retention, cost per student, or learning outcomes.

Once performance gaps have been identified, benchmarking consists of learning about the processes that enable the more effective institution or program to perform and adapting those processes to one's own institution. The steps of the process consist of three planning steps: determining what to benchmark (often areas where most complaints arise), forming a team that includes members who will be able to implement changes, and deciding on the most effective institutions in the areas to be compared. The team collects data through observations, interviews, and note taking and through documents such as performance statistics. It then analyzes the data, redesigns operations, and monitors the performance of the modified processes.

If the quality of learning is at issue, some of these frameworks for improvement may be considered more appropriate than others, but all may serve as potential processes for improving the academic climate. An administrator recapitulated.

> There is a major concern for the social ambiance of the American university and the issue of whether that ambiance drives an enhancement of the academic climate or frustrates it. Most of us would agree that we have not achieved a level of support between social ambiance and the academic climate that we would like to see. Although I have refused to enter into some mechanical social engineering projects that I have seen at other campuses. . . . there are things we could do as administrators and faculty and students to create a climate . . . that is more supportive of the academic venture.

Throughout the book, quotations from the academic leaders interviewed in the study on the learning environment may raise questions or problems that need to be solved. Important for improving the environment for learning, many quotations describe benchmark practices that can be considered and applied. At the end of Chapters Four through Eight, benchmark practices are summarized for immediate reference.

Summary: Frameworks for Improving Learning

The university has many potential roles—as a center for research, a guide to the nation for the betterment of humankind, critic of society, and intellectual center of a learning society. Each role implies different criteria for evaluating outcomes. To discriminate the mission of the university, one important condition is whether some other social agency can respond to the problem or whether only the university is equipped to deal with it. The constituency and equity must also be considered. A particular aim of universities is to foster intellectual development. Approaches to improving the learning climate include engaging in self-definition, clarifying the university mission and setting priorities, viewing postsecondary education as a multinational knowledge industry, reengineering procedures to reduce work, and using benchmarks or best practices that have been successful in other institutions.

In the following chapters, academic leaders talk about the issues of greatest importance to them and the ways they see improvements can be made to the learning environment. The underlying question that guides this book is, What characteristics of institutions of higher education enable students to learn? In the next chapter, the central mission of the university—the advancement of knowledge—and its effect on the learning climate is examined.

2

The Role of the Disciplines in the Quality of Learning

Disciplines represent ways of thinking and are the primary source of identity for faculty.

The advancement of knowledge is the central mission of the university. In response to that mission, the university is organized on the basis of generally accepted knowledge boundaries or disciplines. In this chapter, the focus is on the effect of the disciplines in advancing knowledge and enabling learning. In medieval universities, learning was grouped in the trivium—grammar, rhetoric, and logic—and the quadrivium—arithmetic, music, geometry, and astronomy. After completing the trivium and quadrivium, students advanced to the faculties of theology, law, or medicine. Departments—the current organizational counterparts to the medieval divisions of learning—are the gatekeepers to disciplines. They make decisions about who will be allowed to enter, and they provide ratification and commendation of their members. The department allows the discipline to operate as the core culture for faculty members and to serve as the primary unit of membership and identification (Clark, 1987b).

Disciplinary Structure and Function

Academic disciplines provide the basic building blocks of higher education by giving cognitive and social focus for research and a framework around which teaching is organized (Becher, 1992).

Within disciplines, however, increasing specialization and accompanying fragmentation have led to the perception that it may no longer make sense to think of a discipline as a unitary and coherent domain but rather as a family that provides local metaphors or models (Leary, 1992). Thus, although social cohesion is assumed within the constituent departments of a university, with accompanying representation in university governance, department members may not recognize or experience epistemological cohesion.

Disciplines have traditionally provided homes within the larger learning community, because they determine the domain or parameters of knowledge; that is, the theoretical or conceptual structures and the mode of inquiry that guide learning. A discipline is expected to possess a specialized body of knowledge or theory with a reasonably logical taxonomy so that gaps or incoherences in knowledge can be recognized (Dressel and Mayhew, 1974).

> There is a vocabulary and a grammar to any conversation, and a discipline is in part a language and a grammar providing different knowing patterns, as any language would, and causing musicians and mathematicians to argue at faculty meetings.

Disciplines are also expected to have techniques for theory testing and revision and a sense of sequence that enables scholars to predict where they should look next (Dressel and Mayhew, 1974; King and Brownell, 1966). Disciplines are defined epistemologically by their distinctive sets of concepts and propositions, their logical structure—in theory, generalizations or models, the truth criteria by which the propositions are assessed, and the methodology employed to produce the propositions (Donald, 1986; Hirst, 1974; Kuhn, 1970; Toulmin, 1972).

Disciplines meet these expectations to varying degrees. The physical sciences are the best exemplars and because of this are described as "well structured" or "paradigmatic" (Frederiksen, 1984;

Kuhn, 1970). To the extent that a discipline does not meet the criteria, it is considered to be "soft," "unrestricted," or "less well structured"; content and method are more idiosyncratic (Becher, 1989; Biglan, 1973; Frederiksen, 1984). In less well-structured disciplines, as in the social sciences and humanities, complexity is regarded as a legitimate aspect of knowledge; "unrestricted" refers to the fact that the field of phenomena is relatively unlimited. The least well-structured areas of study are more often referred to as "fields of study," and are characterized as having ill-defined parameters or boundaries, and as lacking a logical structure of knowledge and a generally accepted methodology (Dressel and Mayhew, 1974). Applied areas of study are sometimes described as fields, because the phenomena they study are relatively unrestricted, and the methods are diverse.

The degree of coherence or structure within a discipline and the principal methods of inquiry could be expected to affect what is learned and how it is learned. The discipline, to a large extent, determines the learning objectives of courses and programs, the kinds of pedagogical and learning strategies utilized, and the methods of evaluation employed. Members of well-structured or paradigmatic disciplines have a high level of agreement on the knowledge structures and modes of inquiry in use and are thus more likely to be aware of the content of various courses in a program. Professors then are more likely to reinforce the knowledge structures and modes of inquiry in the different courses in the program. The convergence in a discipline can extend to the use of a standard textbook. For example, Halliday and Resnick's *Fundamentals of Physics* (1988) in its several editions is recognized as the introductory physics textbook in courses throughout the world. Epistemological, linguistic, and curricular convergence are found in physics, in contrast to other disciplines in which agreement on the principal concepts is not as readily found (Donald, 1986, 1987a; Goldman, Schoner, and Pentony, 1980).

The Epistemological Role of Disciplines: The Validation of Knowledge

Disciplinary convergence means that a scholarly community can claim a high level of validity or authority. In a series of forty-eight cross-disciplinary studies of professors nominated as expert researchers and teachers in the physical sciences (physics and engineering), social sciences (psychology and education), and humanities (English literature and language), I asked the professors how they validate knowledge in their discipline (Donald, 1995). Analysis of interview data from the studies revealed three major criteria for validation—consistency, coherence, and precision. Consistency with the external world was the criterion most frequently mentioned by the professors (a majority in each discipline) as a criterion of validity in judging their own work and that of others in their discipline. Examples of consistency included reliability over time, situations, or persons and thus proof by means of replicability, objectivity, or agreement. Coherence or internal consistency was described in terms of testing a model or an interpretation. Precision, accuracy, or specificity was sometimes assumed but was also employed as a screening device for information. The similarity across disciplines in the use of consistency as a criterion for validity suggests a common meeting ground and acceptance of a measure that establishes authority or eminence.

A further test of validity lies in the processes used to validate knowledge. In the cross-disciplinary study, the representatives of the physical and social sciences spoke more often of using empirical evidence as a means of validating their work than professors in the humanities (Donald, 1990). Professors in these disciplines did not differ significantly in the kinds of validation processes or criteria they used. The differences across disciplines in the validation processes used were greatest between the social sciences and the humanities. Social science professors reported using empirical evidence and conceptual frameworks or models more than humanities professors, who reported greater use of precision as a validation criterion. Broudy (1977) suggests that because the humanistic disciplines are concerned with phenomena that do not have immediate referents, humanistic truth involves something other than logical or scientific validity. Although not easily described, the differences across disciplines are authentic.

> In what faculty do, in the way that faculty approach things, in the way the work they do can be documented, in the terminology they use, there are major differences among disciplines, far more than I ever anticipated. They won't agree conceptually; they can't agree on so many things.

How do these findings affect the operation of a discipline and its department in the university? The validation criteria and processes in a discipline determine its method, its development, and its status. The natural sciences are described as combining high reliance on experience with systematic theorizing, while the humanities are said to rely on experience but not on a specific code of reasoning (Thompson, Hawkes, and Avery, 1969). According to Thompson and others, disciplines relying on both experience and systematic theorizing have a double-checking procedure for eliminating error and can therefore claim a high degree of validity. Social scientists have been trained to discern and formulate patterns that can be expressed in general terms and can therefore create models that can be tested and verified (Rosenberg, 1979). Precision of methodology confers status, which may in turn influence a choice of methods. Within groupings of disciplines, some are more well structured than others and may lay claim to greater validity and hence, resources.

The Sociological Role of Disciplines: Identity and Control of Resources

Disciplines are the central source of identity for faculty within the university (Becher, 1989). Traditions, practices, and rules of conduct integrate a disciplinary community but also set it apart from others and demand loyalty to the norms of the particular scholarly group. As well as differing in their epistemological composition, disciplines differ in their state of organization of research and publications, including peer review mechanisms and professional organization. Established disciplines, that is, those that defined themselves as scholarly communities early in the history of universities, are more likely to have secure funding sources and procedures and prescribed methods for publishing, for example, a series of journals dealing with different aspects of the discipline. One way a "young" discipline can become established is to produce a manual describing how to publish. An example is the American Psychological Association's *Publication Manual* (1994), now in its fourth edition. Disciplines may owe their place in the disciplinary hierarchy as much to their sociological establishment as to their modes of inquiry and validation processes.

Established disciplines may be sociologically convergent, that is, have long-established and clear procedures governing group behavior, even though their epistemological methods are more or less varied. History and English literature, for example, were established relatively early as disciplines. History, although not characterized by a dominating theoretical structure, is considered to be convergent because historians see themselves as members of a community of scholars (Becher, 1989). Professors of English literature, on the other hand, prize divergence and may not close ranks in interdisciplinary debates, perhaps relying on their disciplinary longevity and size for clout. Newer disciplines, particularly the social sciences but also many of the biological fields, may find it more difficult to further their collective interests because they have not gelled as disciplinary communities. Having a set of diverse communities within the university, with a variety of points of convergence and divergence among them, creates organizational complexity, if not political strife. As one respondent commented, the effect of the disciplines is widespread and powerful.

> The university still operates on a feudal model. Each discipline often thinks that that discipline could be hermetically sealed and that there is no crossover.

This isolation leads to inequalities within the scholarly community. Disciplines form a political hierarchy based on claims of validity, utility, and longevity. The place of a discipline in the political hierarchy is reflected in an accompanying control of institutional policy and resources. Members of the three major disciplinary groups—the natural or physical and life sciences, social sciences, and humanities—have widely differing perspectives of the role of their discipline in the university.

One respondent explained why representatives of different disciplines hold the views they do.

> The sciences and engineering will be the engines of the university of the twenty-first century. In a recent study I interviewed university administrators about resource allocation. When I asked department heads in the sciences how they thought they would fare in future allocations within the university, since the university has faced some severe cuts, they said, "We're not too worried." In physics, the head said, "We're not a first-class physics department; we're probably second class, but we're not worried because you cannot have a first-class research university in the twenty-first century without a first-class physics department." The biology head said the same thing. When I talked to people in the social sciences and humanities, in history, sociology, and English, even though that is where the university is strongest and historically has been strongest, none of them said that.

The resources under the command of a discipline because of its place in the political hierarchy also affect the learning climate. Some disciplines have histories of rich endowment, just as some universities have. Other disciplines, usually the newer and less well-structured ones, lack organization and control of resources. For example, the natural sciences have a well-organized research grants system, which means that a larger percentage of natural science professors are funded, and funded at higher levels, than are professors in the social sciences and humanities. Although one could argue that the kind of research undertaken in the natural sciences requires more funding, the result is that support and incentives are higher in these disciplines. Kudos in the form of disciplinary recognition or more general honors (for example, Nobel prizes) are also more frequent in these disciplines. This halo extends to the place of the sciences on campus, so that members of these disciplines are more likely to be listened to and to create and govern university policy. Although prominent scientists may be as politically naive as any other focused researcher when it comes to university policy, since their well-funded research supports the infrastructure of the university, they have greater voice in its governance. Given the increased social and economic dependency on sciences and technology in the knowledge era, rifts are now occurring, where before the ground was merely uneven. Two respondents described this phenomenon.

> Most institutions are in some process of reorganization, and the biggest issue that I see in that reorganization process is the pattern of winners and losers that appears to me to be reinforcing past patterns. That ultimately detracts from the quality of learning, although quality is usually not framed in those terms.

> The culture and practices of higher education everywhere have been too greatly influenced by the natural sciences. For instance, the definition of scholarship, the conditions for promotion, the whole understanding of a faculty member's role, all are dictated mainly by the scientific community and its needs and understandings. To give just one example, theory and abstraction are held in too high a regard and professional experience and practice in too low a regard.

The Effect of the Disciplines on the Organization of Curriculum

Based on the assumption that a given field or domain is the perquisite of experts in the domain, universities have not, as a rule, attempted to institute procedures to regulate the curriculum in any discipline. In general, curriculum remains a forbidden field for review or evaluation by others in the academy. Disciplinary or scholarly control of curriculum is rarely yielded, which tends to prevent cross-disciplinary understanding and development.

Curriculum is protected by close association with academic freedom. The right to teach or study a subject without fear of reprisal or hindrance includes choice of course content. The exception to disciplinary control occurs when approval is needed for a new course or program, but reviews of new courses or programs tend to be general and not rigorous (often only a calendar description of a course is required or the titles of courses in a program). Only in certain fields, usually professional, is the curriculum examined on a regular basis; even then, examination is done within the field, when programs undergo regular reviews for accreditation.

At the more specific level of program administration, course outlines may be filed within a department and may be examined as part of departmental review. However, cross-disciplinary, in-depth curriculum analysis of the vocabulary and methodology of a course or program does not occur in a normal review process. The effect is to preclude avenues of curriculum development and alignment that might lead to a rationalization of courses and programs, particularly across disciplines. The assumption of expertise thus tends to prevent cross-disciplinary understanding and development. The assumption in several disciplines that there is no longer a canon or paradigm also works against coherence and coordination within and across disciplines. Specialization within a discipline leads to linkages off campus rather than in-house, and technology, particularly since the introduction of the Internet, is now in place to make off-campus linkages even stronger.

> There is recent work that says that collegiality on U.S. campuses is a myth. At one level, people are friendly and collegial and all in this together, but in most departments, there are usually only one or two persons at the most who share your research interests, so you really cannot talk to a group of colleagues who understand exactly what you do. Your colleagues in your area of specialization are usually off campus.

Attempts to reform the curriculum show the extent to which disciplines are open to the perspectives and methods of other disciplines. When the Association of American Colleges called upon faculty members to participate in curricular change in the liberal arts curriculum, general education, and the undergraduate major, the disciplines responded in terms of their disciplinary membership. Differences across disciplines occurred not only in matters of disciplinary substance but in organizing schemes, their relationship to other disciplines, and attitudes about what is worth studying and how it should be studied (Lattuca and Stark, 1993). Whether in physical science and mathematics, social sciences, or humanities, national task forces of faculty recommended local variation and autonomy. Emphasis on connectedness with other disciplines was minimal in the physical sciences and increased across disciplines to the point of being assumed in the humanities, another example of restricted versus unrestricted disciplinary tendencies. But disciplinary differences affect the learning climate more directly.

Differences Across the Disciplines in Learning Goals

In the study undertaken by the Association of American Colleges on curricular change, the learning goals emphasized differed according to disciplinary area (Lattuca and Stark, 1993). In the physical sciences, while respondents readily addressed the integration of knowledge and skills, thought it possible to sequence learning, and expressed belief in scientific method, they found a critical perspective unfamiliar. In the social sciences, the potential for sequencing learning was acknowledged, and a critical perspective was considered important. Humanities representatives objected to sequencing learning and stressed a critical perspective. The physical scientists acknowledged the importance of student research opportunities but noted that such experiences were often unavailable to undergraduates because of a lack of resources and student interest. In the social sciences and humanities, more general oral and written communication skills were deemed important, as were critical reading and lifelong learning. In another study, the development of communication skills was emphasized by professors in the humanities, while engineering, mathematics, and science teachers emphasized facts, principles, and problem solving (Franklin and Theall, 1995). Thus, both curricular and more general learning goals are affected by the disciplinary ethos.

The most extensively used and researched method of evaluating the quality of learning employs students' ratings of what is taught and their satisfaction with it. In a study of disciplinary differences in course objectives and in students' perceptions of what they learn and of how they are taught, Cashin and Downey (1995) found differences in the kinds of course objectives emphasized by professors across disciplines. Moreover, students reported making progress in learning what the specific discipline emphasized. In general, research examining disciplinary differences in responses on student rating questionnaires shows that although differences in ratings do not tend to occur in course organization or planning, humanities instructors are rated significantly more positively in faculty-student interaction and communication skills than are physical science and mathematics instructors (Centra, 1993; Marsh, 1984).

Differences in favor of the humanities have been shown to extend to overall ratings of the amount learned, the instructor and the course, and course integration (Franklin and Theall, 1995). This is consistent with findings in studies of faculty role differences—most faculty engage in research, but significantly more faculty in the humanities than in the sciences aspire to be good teachers (Milem and Astin, 1994). Taken together, these studies suggest that the learning experience of students in various programs differs in much more than curriculum. The surrounding disciplinary culture and the specific learning outcomes create distinct learning climates. This calls for a closer examination of the learning climate in different disciplinary groups.

Physical and Life Sciences

The dominance of the sciences on campus creates a more consistent and supportive environment for those in the physical and life sciences. For example:

> In the university, the rationalist model still prevails, and that would mean that the promotion and tenure committee is dominated by people, whether they are physicists or speech scientists, who employ traditional scientific paradigms and see no other avenues toward illuminating our understanding of the physical and human world.

Due to the momentum of discovery, the sciences are also the site of greatest differentiation within the university (Kruytbosch, 1992). The most common form of differentiation is into increasing complexity—physics, the most fundamental science, can be apportioned into as many as eighteen divisions, from classical mechanics to medical physics (Rothman, 1992). Another form of differentiation is reconfiguration based on empirical evidence. To illustrate, the shift in departmental nomenclature from meteorology to atmospheric and oceanic sciences resulted from recognition of interactions between oceanic phenomena such as water temperature and atmospheric events such as hurricanes. A third form of differentiation is the emergence of new disciplines such as computer science from electrical engineering, with additional input from mathematics, logic, and psychology.

The biological sciences have tended to differentiate and coalesce in slightly different form, as research has led to new points of interest (Mcgregor, 1992). Biologists talk of proliferating disciplines; departments—recapitulating mitosis—multiply and divide in relatively brief cycles. Medical sciences have differentiated into a set of disciplines, essentially research-oriented, that range on a research continuum from pure to applied, and have a history of funding in research institutes. Cole (1994) notes that the dependence of research universities on federal government financing has changed academic and financial relationships within universities by leading to enormous growth in the health science divisions, altering the size of health science relative to the arts and sciences and other professional schools.

The most general findings about the physical and life sciences are their continuing growth and differentiation into subfields that may or may not later coalesce, and their definition through research. The nature of the research problems that are being investigated drives their disciplinary organization. What does this mean for the learning climate?

Two of the fields identified in the comparative study of what is taught and what students learn across disciplines (Cashin and Downey, 1995)—mathematics (because it is foundational to the physical sciences) and biological sciences—serve as examples for the kind of learning that occurs in the physical and life sciences. The course objectives weighted more highly by professors in these fields than by professors in others were gaining factual knowledge and learning fundamental principles, generalizations, or theories. Students in biological sciences reported making greater progress in gaining factual knowledge than others, but students in mathematics reported making less. Students in both fields reported learning fundamental principles, generalizations, or theories to the same extent as students in other areas.

Mathematics professors rated learning to apply course material to improve rational thinking, problem solving, and decision making higher than other professors, but biological science professors on the whole rated it as less important than the norm. Students in mathematics rated their progress in learning to apply course material to improve rational thinking, problem solving, and decision making the same as students in other courses, but biological science students rated their progress lower than the norm. Overall in these courses, the most important learning objectives were basal-level—gaining factual knowledge and learning fundamental principles, generalizations, or theories. Students did not report learning that exceeded the norm, except for biological science students learning fundamental principles.

Students reported that the amount of work and the difficulty of the subject matter exceeded the norm in these courses, however, and that they worked harder on these courses than on others. They also reported fewer teaching methods involving students. Mathematics professors were reported to display less enthusiasm than professors in other fields and were less clear about communicating content and purpose. Biological science professors were rated average in these areas. The overall effect on students was that in the mathematics courses, students' attitudes were slightly more negative toward taking further courses or having positive feelings about the field of study as a result of having taken the course than were students in other courses. Biological science students' attitudes matched those of students overall. The gist of these results is that the emphasis on knowledge apparent in the physical and life science domains is conveyed into the teaching milieu, but at a cost to students' attitudes and involvement, as Tobias (1990) has affirmed. The difference is more pronounced in the mathematics courses than in the biological sciences.

Social Sciences

The general culture of the social sciences is intermediary to the physical sciences and humanities but closer to the physical sciences in its methods and validation processes. Pelikan (1992) points out that, like the physical and biological sciences, the social sciences proceed by the collection of precise data obtained through controlled observation; they have also come increasingly to rely on research that is primarily quantitative. Pelikan deplores the distinction that has arisen between hard (as mathematical as possible) and soft social sciences, those more closely related to the humanities in presuppositions, methods, and values. In his view, social scientists have been driven to use hard science methods that may not be appropriate to answer important questions in their fields. As one respondent noted:

> Some methods of inquiry are more highly rewarded than others. Within a lot of disciplines in the social sciences, there are alternative methods of inquiry that are emerging and in some cases being validated, but I don't think within the university as a whole they have any effect at all or are highly regarded.

As in the physical and life sciences, the social sciences have been characterized by growth and fragmentation. They are also characterized by having developed primarily in North America, within a logical empiricist and pragmatic philosophy. The institutionalization of the social sciences began at the end of the nineteenth century (the American Economic Association was founded in 1885 and the American Psychological Association in 1892), but internationalization has occurred in the latter half of the twentieth century, so that most countries now have national associations or are linked in international associations (Scott, 1992). Internationalization has also led social scientists to recognize that social science knowledge is time- and culture-dependent. Thus, the quest for a unifying theory that characterized early development in the social sciences has been abandoned, and attempts to gain agreement about theoretical perspectives, core methods, or concepts have been diluted to bootstrapping efforts in which an eclectic approach is advocated and local metaphors are employed.

Learning in the social sciences has likewise been transfigured from a generalist approach through an introductory text that related questions in the field, to a specialized approach in which the serious student can claim a close working knowledge with only a limited sub-area within one specific domain of specialization (Scott, 1992). One respondent, an economist, regretted the effect of this fragmentation.

> To talk about disciplinary differences, I will draw an image from Adam Smith and the division of labor, where different people work on different parts of the process and then they combine their efforts, and the whole is greater than the sum of the parts. I think the disciplines in research universities have divided up the labor but have lost touch with the notion of integrating the independent effort into something that is greater than the sum of the parts. People do a Ph.D. in economics without a clue about the political context of any country in the world other than the U.S., what is the social psychology of all the fundamental assumptions that drive the logic, and whether they make any sense.
>
> People become tribes; there is an article published in the *Western Economic Journal* in 1975 called "Life among the Econ" that I always have my students read. It's about how the social sciences have become different tribes. The Econ tribe lives in a barren land to the north, worshiping totems called "modls," that have no obvious value. If they ever talk to members of other tribes—for example, Sociogs—they run the risk of being banished from the tribe. One of the reasons that I find the history of economic thought so interesting is that if you go back far enough, to Adam Smith, there is no division. He was a moral philosopher who would never have thought of separating economics from the political and social dimensions of existence.

Specialization and fragmentation have contributed to a loss of identity in the social sciences, but a more serious threat has been questioning of the validity of social science research. The deconstruction of the social sciences, most notably in anthropology where ethnographic authority was critiqued, has cost the social sciences as areas of study. The instability created by the self-critical stances taken in some social sciences has led to an overall questioning of the value of these disciplines and a consequent loss in bargaining power.

> The notion that among social scientists there may be paradigm wars or paradigm evolution means that they get short shrift.

In spite of the turbulence evident in theoretical and methodological debate in these areas, there appear to be some consistencies. Sutton (1994) points out that however disturbed some parts of the social sciences may be by the new skepticisms, relativisms, and resistances to authoritative doctrine, there is also the academic ideology of disciplined and critical inquiry, which provides a binding sense of shared purpose. Progress in the social sciences, according to Scott (1992), will depend upon debate colored with tolerance and respect for differences of opinion, in a climate where scholars are free to pursue lines of reasoning and approaches to study to their logical conclusions. What does this mean in terms of the quality of learning in the social sciences?

In the study of disciplinary differences in what is taught and in students' perceptions of what they learn (Cashin and Downey, 1995), two social science fields were identified—psychology and education. The course objectives weighted more highly by psychology professors were similar to those of the mathematics and biological science professors—gaining factual knowledge and learning fundamental principles, generalizations, or theories. As might be expected, psychology professors were most different from other professors in the greater weight they awarded to discovering the implications of course material for understanding oneself. Education professors, in accordance with their career orientation, assigned greater importance to developing specific skills, competencies, and points of view needed by professionals in the field.

Psychology students concurred with their professors by stating that they had gained factual knowledge and learned fundamental principles and by giving greater relative weight to their progress in discovering the implications of course material for understanding themselves. Students in education reported greater progress on several fronts. They agreed with their professors about developing specific skills, competencies, and points of view needed by professionals in the field. But they also reported progress in learning to apply course material to improve rational thinking, problem solving, and decision making, in developing skill in expressing themselves orally and in writing, and (as for psychology students) in discovering the implications of course material for understanding themselves. Thus, if progress for psychology students was primarily with basal-level objectives—gaining factual knowledge and learning fundamental principles—education students reported more progress than average on a wide variety of objectives.

Students in psychology courses reported few differences from other students in rating instructional behaviors but did report that they had a higher amount of reading for their course. Education students were notable in their reports of the greater use of teaching methods involving students, and they were generally more positive about their professors' teaching habits. Psychology professors were rated the same as other professors in most areas and slightly negatively in comparison on their examination procedures. General attitudes toward both fields were more positive as a result of students' having taken the course than in other courses. These findings are consistent with those of Franklin and Theall (1995), who found that education and social and behavioral science students rated their instructors as more effective than did those in science and mathematics.

Humanities

Asked what the most important questions were in higher education, a humanities professor's reply was in close agreement with those of professors in other fields:

> The greatest problem that confronts us all is the increasing fragmentation and specialization, which is something that we really cannot do very much about. The English department clearly is breaking up into warring camps. There is fragmentation on the microscopic scale.

Once recognized as the focal point of the university, the humanities now appear to be on the defensive; the onus is on them to prove their utility and relevance compared to the sciences (Weiland, 1992). A relatively small proportion of government funding for research goes to the humanities, and Weiland suggests that many departments in the humanities are small and, having a limited future, are being rationalized or concentrated into area studies. The exploration of particularities, as opposed to generalities, translates for professors in the humanities into welcoming complexity, noting diversity, and accepting that many things cannot be proven through replication (Austin, 1992; Becher, 1989). Scholars tend to work independently, professional societies tend to be weaker, and publication rates are slower, all of which makes it more difficult for professors to establish a reputation.

At the same time, student demand for the humanities and their appreciation of them, as shown in elevated ratings of instruction, continues. The humanities address more of students' academic career goals than do the physical and social sciences. According to Rhodes (1994), these include the ability to listen, read, and analyze with comprehension and to write and speak with precision and clarity in the expression of disciplined thought. Higher-order goals extend to the ability to reason effectively, the ability to engage people of different cultural perspectives, an appreciation of modes of thought and expression of the disciplines, sensitivity toward the ideas, values, and goals that have shaped society, and some sense of the moral implications of actions and ideas. The emphasis on personal interpretation that characterizes the humanities, as opposed to an emphasis on public verification and the expansion of knowledge (Snow, 1959), makes the humanities immediately relevant to the undergraduate.

As an example of the humanities, English language and literature was examined in the comparative study of what is taught and learned across disciplines (Cashin and Downey, 1995). The course objectives weighted more highly by professors in English language and literature were developing skill in oral and written expression, gaining a broader understanding and appreciation of intellectual-cultural activity, and developing creative capacities. English language and literature professors attached considerably less importance to gaining factual knowledge and learning fundamental principles than professors in other disciplines.

Students in English language and literature reported making greater progress than did other students, on average, in all the learning objectives. They concurred with their professors in developing skill in expressing themselves orally and in writing, but they also noted progress in discovering the implications of course material for understanding themselves, developing specific skills, competencies, and points of view needed by professionals in the field. Progress in learning to apply course material to improve rational thinking, problem solving, and decision making, as well as in learning how professionals in the field go about gaining new knowledge, was reported. Students judged that their professors stimulated their learning and were more positive about examinations but did not, on the whole, register more positive general attitudes about taking further courses. Humanities courses on the whole are, however, given the highest ratings among disciplines for instructor effectiveness (Franklin and Theall, 1995; Murray and Renaud, 1995).

Crossing Disciplinary Boundaries

The differences across disciplines in what students say they are learning are profound. How can students be helped to achieve a broader set of learning outcomes, particularly higher order outcomes? The question for academic leaders attempting to create a meaningful curriculum for the twenty-first century is how to bridge disciplinary boundaries or how to communicate across them. Postsecondary associations such as the Association of American Colleges (1991) have challenged faculty to achieve curricular coherence, help students develop a critical perspective, and connect learning across fields.

> What we discovered in our interdisciplinary humanities where we do literature, philosophy, and art history is that the strongest support we got from the student body was from the honors students, who said, "This is the one place where I am asked to think."

Unfortunately, since the challenge of interdisciplinarity and the research backing it have been documented in higher education publications, few university scholars will be aware of it. In our studies of learning across disciplines, we found that disciplinary specialization means that journals addressing more general issues such as curriculum review and development are not read by members of disciplines or referenced across fields.

In response to the challenge to connect learning across disciplines, another problem arises. Interdisciplinary programs have always been subject to departmental criticism on the ground that they are less rigorous than the source disciplines (Kennedy, 1994). Such programs threaten department autonomy. Interdisciplinary programs are also hampered by the perception that interdisciplinary degrees are less marketable (Blaisdell, 1993). They are therefore politically and economically vulnerable. Another argument leveled against them is that students need to learn about individual disciplines in order to be able to become interdisciplinary in their thinking.

> Discussion about interdisciplinarity often downplays the value of disciplinary learning, to be quite literal about it. One learns from a discipline ways of thinking and knowing, and one cannot be too efficient at being interdisciplinary until one is disciplinary.

Interdisciplinary programs often arise when a gap is perceived between disciplined research and undisciplined problems (Blaisdell, 1993; Rose, 1986). Some of the most important scientific and scholarly discoveries of the past decades have taken place on the borders between two or more disciplines rather than inside them (Pelikan, 1992). Also in their favor, programs based on interdepartmental agreement, such as human ecology or science and technology studies, encourage cooperation among faculty, which in turn is essential for program development. More pertinent to improving the learning climate, high-quality interdisciplinary courses have been found to develop students' critical thinking ability and the ability to synthesize or integrate (Newell, 1994). Enlarged perspectives and creative and original thinking result from these courses. Blaisdell (1993) recommends that administrators make integration easier by easing barriers to cross-listed courses, nurturing interdisciplinary course development, offering courses with integrative goals for graduate as well as undergraduate students, and redirecting institutional rewards to encourage curriculum and pedagogical innovation. One approach to finding meeting points between disciplines so that learning is coherent and meaningful is to focus on general education requirements.

General Education

The concept of general education has its origin in the Greek term *paideia*, which means growth in experience as well as in knowledge of general principles (Pfinster, 1992). Although general education has found its expression primarily in the liberal arts colleges of North America and has had less common focus than in the original foundational trivium and quadrivium, it is also an important part of the undergraduate curriculum and has been described as representing the philosophy of an educational institution (Ratcliff, 1992). General education is also a focal point for curriculum adaptation and development. In a discussion of general education in her university, a humanities professor suggested looking at the future needs of students as a starting point.

> There has got to be a new look, and I'm not at all sure that those of us in the academy are capable of . . . sufficient objectivity, that we can really look at our students and say, "What is it they are going to need twenty years from now?" One of the things that I think is needed is for us to drop our loyalties to our specific areas of interest and be able to look at them and say, "Is there some new way that we can help them gain what it is they are going to need?" This is with the understanding that we are not going to know for sure.

Curriculum analysis and development in general education programs provide both disciplinary and interdisciplinary learning experiences. They thus introduce students to new ways of thinking. For courses given within an individual department or discipline, the aim is to provide both a conceptual framework of the discipline and its methods of thinking.

> The goals of general education are to provide breadth and an intellectual awakening that the world is full of different kinds of knowledge that are structured quite differently. To be an educated person is to have some sense of this breadth of knowledge. At our university, we have two kinds of general education courses. Breadth courses are survey courses—the introduction to sociology, for example—a view of the discipline from five miles up, where you see . . . the general areas of interest, the lay of the land, how research questions or knowledge are advanced or integrated or applied in the context of the discipline. Then there are depth courses in which you take a particular kind of sociology, say the sociology of the family, and . . . use a particular topic within the field to demonstrate everything that you would see from five miles up. Here, the students have to take a specified number of depth and breadth courses, but most of them are survey courses.

One way of accomplishing the goal of general education is to bring together representatives from different disciplines to plan interdisciplinary courses based on broader academic goals such as the purpose of learning.

In the general education committee, an astronomer and I often found ourselves on the same side of the discussion, and so we were assigned the task of designing an interdisciplinary course in science and humanities, called "Twentieth-Century Science and the Arts." It was fascinating for us and the students. We used as the textbook for the first semester a novel called *White Noise* by Don Delillo (1985). We chose it because it dealt with the issue of pollution, and we thought it would get our non-science students interested, but we discovered that it was a much more valuable text, because it raised all sorts of issues about the validity and purpose of learning.

Then, we did Italo Calvino's *Cosmicomics* (1968), which takes scientific discoveries and puts a fictional character into the scene who says, "Oh yes, of course I was there when the big bang occurred and this was what it was like." So, it is a ludicrous piece but nevertheless teaches the students at the same time as they're being amused by the scientific issues. The final text was *The Dancing Wu Li Masters* (Zukav, 1979). What was interesting to me and what I think I was seeing happen with this astronomy professor was the realization that the humanities and arts and sciences, particularly physics, are not so far apart.

Common Instructional Goals

Another venue for bridging activities is a common goal, such as better writing or critical thinking, that is reflective of the trivium. One respondent explained how at his university a workshop on critical thinking allowed professors from different disciplines to begin to communicate about the curriculum.

In the critical thinking workshop, minor differences arose in how people defined critical thinking and what processes are involved, but they found out that although they come from different conceptual frameworks, ultimately they are driving for the same result in the student learner and the faculty. When scientists talk to humanities, social science, and fine arts people, they find that some of the methodologies and ideas that are taught within a scientific framework are quite ap-

> plicable to the humanities and vice versa. So, they find that they can learn from each other not only in terms of information but also methods of getting that information to students. We have found, contrary to popular opinion, some of the more creative teaching is occurring in mathematics and science.

Another respondent talked about trying to get people from various disciplines to look at the culture they have created around that discipline and to learn from other disciplines. In this instance, a common instructional problem brings professors together.

> This happens with our faculty development brown bags. The last time, there were people from atmospheric sciences, pharmacy, and history who were sharing ideas about how they deal with the pack-up syndrome in the last five minutes of class. They all recognized that they have the very same problem, but on the face of it, they would have thought there was nothing similar across their disciplines. To get off the content focus and on to the student focus is the essence of what we are trying to do.

These approaches to bridging disciplinary boundaries or communicating across them, rather than being full-blown solutions, are appetite whetters. They illuminate a variety of entry points where the learning environment can be improved—in a general approach, as in interdisciplinary studies or general education, or attached to common competency development, as in writing and critical thinking abilities, or in dealing with instructional problems, as in cross-disciplinary course design workshops or meetings. I will deal with these points of entry in greater detail in Chapters Four, Five, and Six.

Summary: The Effect of Disciplines on the Learning Climate

Disciplines are the central source of identity for faculty but differ in their state of epistemological and professional organization.

Disciplines form a political hierarchy based on claims of validity, utility, and longevity. The place of a discipline in the political hierarchy is reflected in an accompanying command of institutional policy and resources, which in turn affects the learning climate.

The degree of coherence or structure within a discipline and the principal methods of inquiry affect the quality of learning. In well-structured disciplines, the knowledge structures and modes of inquiry are more likely to be reinforced in the various courses in a program. Disciplinary control of curriculum is axiomatic and protected by academic freedom. One effect is to limit cross-disciplinary understanding and development.

Learning goals vary across disciplinary areas. The physical and life sciences emphasize the learning of facts and principles, while in the social sciences and humanities, communication skills and critical thinking are important. In return, students rate humanities instructors more positively than physical science instructors. Ways of bridging disciplinary boundaries include developing meeting places in interdisciplinary or general education programs, common student competencies, and instructional strategies.

3

Student Selection and Access

Of three major influences on postsecondary learning—the social context, the disciplines, and the students themselves—student characteristics may be the most important.

In this chapter, the second and third criteria for determining the mission of a university—the constituency being served and equity—are examined. To identify the institutional characteristics that enable students to learn, educational institutions must determine to what extent success is a matter of selection procedures, the fit of the student to the institution, student self-definition, procedures set in place to ensure that students are oriented to learning when they arrive, the curriculum and instruction offered at the institution, and the general learning milieu.

Approaches to the Student Body

Within an educational institution, students are a substantial constituency, and they have considerable influence on how the institution operates. The characteristics they bring to the learning situation affect what and how much they will learn, and so they themselves form an important part of the environment for learning. The issue of equity—equal educational opportunity or access—which has led to the development of diversified systems of postsecondary education, also affects the internal operations of an educational institution. As the student body becomes more heterogeneous, dealing with diversity has become an important task in most universities. The goals of this chapter are, therefore, to examine the student characteristics that are acknowledged to aid learning and to address ways of adapting the learning environment to diverse student groups.

The philosophical framework guiding educational practice in North America is one of practical utilitarianism. The general principle of utilitarianism is that people ought, in their acts, to produce the greatest possible amount of good for the greatest number of people (Bentham, 1948; Mill, 1863). In practical utilitarianism, this principle is applied to the development of society, as in the human capital argument that any population needs to ensure that all of its citizens are as productive as they can be. It also recognizes a basic tenet of North American political philosophy—that people should not be constrained by history or specific characteristics but should be free to develop to their fullest potential. For educational practice, this means that the population should be as well educated as it can be.

> There has been a changing perception about education, from considering it primarily a personal good to recognizing it as a social good; until five to eight years ago, education was seen by many people as an individual benefit. More recently, people are beginning to recognize that there is a national, social interest in the quality of our educational systems.

In educational institutions in the Occident, there have been two contrasting operating approaches to the student body. The first approach, which I shall label "attributional," has its roots in Calvinism and the Protestant ethic (Weber, 1958) and is based on the proposition that student abilities are inherent characteristics. In the strictest interpretation of this doctrine, students are predestined or preselected—they are either capable or not capable. In a more open interpretation of the attributional approach, the individual student is responsible for his or her development. The second approach, labeled "environmental," is that human abilities are the product of the interaction between an individual and his or her environment. These two approaches to the learner are analogous to nature and nurture explanations of human behavior and have multiple ramifications for an educational system.

In the attributional approach, an institution would be highly selective in its student body. This approach is apparent in the ranking of American universities; the most frequently used measurements of university quality are students' entering characteristics. Ratings of admissions competitiveness (Barron's Profiles of American Colleges, 1996) are based upon entering students' test scores, high school averages, ranks in class, and the proportion of applicants admitted (Volkwein, 1989). The effect of this approach is to focus attention on and to limit the responsibility of academic staff to determine on what basis students are selected for their programs, without having more explicit or detailed knowledge of the characteristics of incoming students that will affect their learning.

> I have overheard this conversation a lot over the last few years: Is the quality of students going up or down? There is a lot of mythology about how to measure it, primarily SAT (Scholastic Aptitude Test) scores. It is amazing how much faculty don't know about the students they teach and about the selection criteria.

For high school students and their parents, the best indicators of top-quality postsecondary institutions are the proportion of students admitted who were high achievers before college and high admission rates to graduate school (Litten and Hall, 1989). These indicators correlate significantly ($r = .40$) with rankings of institutional attractiveness. The explanation is simple: students' entering characteristics are the most consistently strong predictors for student success in a university, and ratings of American universities depend on student success. Measures of student ability have thus come to be used for institutional selectivity (Schmitz, 1993). The effect of this, according to one administrator, is to limit the attention paid to ensuring student development.

> We have been blessed in many ways, and it has kept us from having to deal with certain issues in many ways. We have an amazing undergraduate student population right now whose entering scores go up every year: most are in the 96th percentile coming out of high school; their SATs are an average of 1250, so we have always operated on the assumption, correct or not, that our students are highly motivated, that they are very bright, that they are totally capable of learning if they choose to do so. So, unlike many other universities in which the heterogeneous student body has forced you to come to grips with the student who might be underprepared or the student who might be rather unmotivated, I think we have avoided many of those issues on the argument that our students are so talented that they do not necessarily present those problems.

The attributional approach is cost-effective. In a highly selective institution, the students contribute to the reputation of the institution, which translates into greater support from parents and alumni, while the cost of aid to students in terms of student support services is minimal. This contrasts with the effects of the environmental approach, where attention to student development is a priority. In the environmental approach, a judicious use of academic advising in a campus community setting ensures that students develop to their fullest potential. The drawback of the environmental approach is that, carried to an extreme, it characterizes the student not only as customer but as patient (Muller, 1994). The university is then committed to becoming a therapeutic agent, which may require extended student services. In a number of universities and aided by government grants, this has led to an expansion of the cadre of student affairs professionals to meet the various needs of diverse populations. The environmental approach better supports the human capital argument and satisfies the larger political and economic agenda. A respondent made the argument in favor of this approach in the following manner:

> I am very much for access; I hope that we do not become more highly selective. Institutions are becoming more selective, but Peter Ewell has mentioned that twenty years ago, you heard that minority students needed to get into college and this was a social justice issue. Today it is not a social justice issue anymore, it is an issue of "everybody counts." It is an increasingly competitive environment; we need everybody, so it is stupid not to include people.

Another argument for greater access rests on research showing that in spite of the major effect of student selectivity on the learning environment, the most powerful learning effects are those that occur on campus. The amount of learning is related more to the learning experiences that occur than to student selectivity or institutional resources. One respondent based his stance on research findings that institutional selectivity in admissions is not a strong predictor of how much students learn.

> If you take into account the characteristics students bring to a campus and then try to associate selectivity with measures of student learning or gains on a variety of measures, selectivity has very little power as a predictor. In fact, most of the institutional characteristics that we use to define quality in this country—selectivity, the entering test scores of the freshman class, the educational expenditures per FTE (full time equivalent) student, the percentage of faculty who hold a terminal degree in their field, the size of the library, cost, student-faculty ratios—none of those are very powerful predictors of how much students learn, when precollege characteristics are controlled.
>
> GPA (grade point average) is the best predictor of subsequent GPA; it is not necessarily the best predictor of how much students are going to learn. Institutions who produce high-achieving students

> are generally the ones who admitted high-achieving students. I don't like to use the phrase "value-added," because it can be misleading, but if you identify those institutional characteristics that are associated with learning gains, the ones that are most powerful are the things that happen to students after they are on campus. It is not the characteristics of the campus itself, in terms of its resource advantage or selectivity or other traditional measures, that reflect institutional advantage more than institutional effectiveness.

This statement returns us to the general problem guiding this book—how to identify the institutional characteristics that enable students to learn. But a problem nested inside how students are selected into an institution and what the institution can promise them is whether it is inherent in the selection process and in the socioeconomics of the student body that a certain percentage of students will not succeed. A respondent gave this example to explain the problem.

> We have a highly selective research university and a not-so-selective comprehensive college, and the bottom 25 percent of students entering the selective institution are comparable in almost every way to the top 25 percent of students entering the comprehensive college. The bottom 25 percent at either institution have a high probability of not being there after the freshman year, and the top 25 percent are very likely to do very well at the institution. So, the challenge to the selective institution is whether it should narrow its field or whether it should do something for those people. It is obviously not targeting its curriculum and its experiences to this bottom 25 percent. Regardless of institution, we find that the bottom quartile has a very difficult time. In the comparison between the two groups, it is simply one of raw entering ability, high school GPA, SAT, as well as demographic background matching the range of instruction offered at a particular college or university.

To what extent is the problem of success—and therefore retention—a matter of student ability? Other factors affecting success include the validity of the selection criteria and procedures, how students define themselves in comparison with others in their cohort, the extent to which students are aware of the learning tasks ahead of them when they come to the university, and their interactions. Research evidence suggests that the harder it is to get into college, the more committed the entering student may be to staying there and completing the degree (Tinto, 1987). When the privilege of enrolling comes at a high cost both financially and in terms of academic effort and achievement, the perceived cost of leaving or failing to graduate is correspondingly high. Selectivity thus affects students' attitudes toward their learning experience.

In summary, questions of student selectivity and access represent a meeting point between attributional and environmental approaches to the student body, between individual merit, the needs of a learning community, and the needs of the larger society. Although the two approaches to the student body are bridged in the diversity of institutions that have entry requirements at varying levels of student preparation, this does not mitigate the need within institutions to examine policies and their underlying philosophies for dealing with student access, diversity, and responsibility. These questions are critical to understanding the environment for learning at several levels.

First, they juxtapose the global demand for productivity with the political agenda of equity and opportunity. Second, they determine the legitimacy of educational institutions in relation to their contract with their constituency and with the larger society. At a third level, in the daily operation of an institution, student characteristics have been shown to have more effect on the learning environment than any other factor (Astin and Panos, 1969; Schmitz, 1993). The net influence in differences in institutional characteristics on student knowledge acquisition is small relative to the difference in student entering characteristics. The challenge to post-secondary educational institutions may be to reverse this equation.

Measuring Student Quality

Analysis of the characteristics that enable students to learn begins with examination of the available measures of student quality. The primary use of criteria of quality for students has been for their selection into specific programs. In order to make decisions, selection or admissions criteria and student success rates are often compared by means of regression analysis. Results repeatedly show that prior academic grades have the greatest predictive value for subsequent student achievement (Astin and Henson, 1977). Pascarella and Terenzini (1991) point out, however, that entering grades may, in addition to measuring students' intellectual skills, indicate good personal work habits and attitudes. Recent research on student learning emphasizes the important role played by affective factors such as motivation and self-efficacy (King and Baxter Magolda, 1996; Pintrich, Brown, and Weinstein, 1994). Research on the comparative achievements of students admitted on the basis of characteristics such as maturity and motivation rather than grades (Pollock, Bowman, Gendreau, and Gendreau, 1975) or on the role played by other personal characteristics in determining academic success (Willingham, 1985) has also aided decision making.

Important characteristics to consider when measuring student quality are students' academic preparation, ability, educational and career goals, motivation, and their attitudes and views about post-secondary education. In a Delphi study designed to elicit important criteria and indicators of quality in universities from a broad sample of over 350 administrators, faculty, students, and community representatives, twenty-five criteria were identified by participants as the most important criteria for student quality (Nadeau, Donald, Konrad, and Tremblay, 1990). A criterion was defined as "a content area, a domain, an instance, an activity, a characteristic indicative of quality." A modified Delphi technique (Linstone and Turoff, 1975) was employed, because it is designed to obtain a group judgment or consensus on an ambiguous or difficult-to-measure issue or phenomenon. Participants in the study were first asked to provide criteria of quality they considered to be important for students in their own independent judgment, then in a later round they were asked to rate each criterion for its importance. The criteria were overall measures of student quality and could therefore be used at different points in a student's undergraduate career.

The most important criteria for student quality were a commitment to learning (a general or motivational factor), the ability to analyze, synthesize, and think critically, and general academic preparedness (Table 3.1). Next most important were basic communication skills, effective study skills and habits, a commitment to lifelong learning, secondary school preparation, intelligence, and independence in learning. Of these most important criteria, two dealt with preparation for studies, five with general skills and the ability to think, and two with motivation or commitment to learn.

Although student criteria are most frequently used for admissions purposes, they can also serve to gauge progress and student outcomes. In a validation study of over four hundred students' perceptions of the criteria of student quality, students verified the importance of the criteria but also considered most criteria to be more important at graduation than at entry or during studies (Donald and Denison, 1996b). Students appeared to have a talent development perspective in which the university is seen as a place where students develop their abilities (Astin, 1985). This perspective is closer to the environmental approach in contrast to the attributional approach to students. The students did, however, consider all of the criteria for students important at entry to university. The criteria for student quality can therefore be used to guide or test the selection process used in major university systems.

The criteria used for admission purposes tend to be limited; they are primarily indicators of general academic preparation as shown

Table 3.1. Mean Ratings of Importance of Criteria of University Student Quality

Criterion	Mean Rating[a]
General academic preparedness	4.4
Secondary school preparation	4.0
Preparedness for a specific program	3.0
Breadth of life experience	3.1
Basic communication skills	4.2
Basic mathematical competency	3.2
Competence in second language	2.8
Intelligence	4.0
Commitment to learning	4.6
Clarity of student's educational and career goals	3.8
Sense of responsibility	3.9
Openness and flexibility	3.8
Independence in learning	4.0
Ability to analyze, synthesize, and think critically	4.6
Ability to interact with others	3.9
Effective study skills and habits	4.2
Moral and ethical reasoning	3.7
Personal student development	3.4
Academic performance or achievement in courses	3.8
Completion of program requirements	3.9
Expertise at end of program	3.9
Self-confidence	3.9
Ability to get a job	3.3
Performance on the job	3.7
Commitment to lifelong learning	4.1

[a]Mean rating of 0 = no importance, 1 = very low importance, 2 = low importance, 3 = moderate importance, 4 = high importance, and 5 = very high importance.

in Table 3.2. For example, in California, the admission requirements include high school subject area requirements, with English and mathematics required for admission to universities in the University of California system and in the State University system, cumulative GPA, and SAT score (California Postsecondary Education Commission, 1988). Eligibility is based on meeting minimum requirements set for the two university systems. Secondary school leaving grades are often the major criterion for admission into university and, as could be expected, affect choice of university as well as choice of program (Watson and Gill, 1977). Entering secondary school average is the best predictor of college average four years later (Astin, 1993b). Summaries of relevant research show that high school grades correlate at about $r = .50$ with university performance (Bloom, 1976), while intelligence tests or standardized tests such as the SAT correlate significantly but somewhat lower (Pintrich, Cross, Kozma, and McKeachie, 1986).

Criteria provide a general sense of important factors, but to establish more specific measures of the criteria, in a second phase of the Delphi study, indicators for each criterion were gathered using the same rating scale (Nadeau, Donald, and Konrad, 1992). If used for admission purposes, to do justice to the indicators, the admissions procedures employed by an institution would have to go beyond attention to meeting requirements for general academic preparation as measured by transcripts, secondary school average, degrees and diplomas, types of courses taken, and performance on national examinations (Table 3.2). Indicators for one of the most important criteria for student quality—commitment to learning—are more difficult to measure. For example, effort beyond basic course requirements and evidence of independent study are behavioral indices useful at the time of admission, if students submit a portfolio or are interviewed. Such a procedure implies a more complex recruitment and admissions process but is consonant with attempts to match students to institutions. It also conveys the message

Table 3.2. Most Important Indicators of the Most Important Criteria for Student Quality

Criterion/Indicators	Mean Rating[a]
Commitment to learning	
Shows effort beyond basic course requirements	3.7
Evidence of independent study	3.7
Participation in more challenging courses or programs	3.4
Amount of time student dedicates to learning activities	3.2
Enrollment in educational institution	3.2
Ability to analyze, synthesize, think critically	
Considers all sides of an argument and makes an independent judgment	4.6
Can put things into context	4.4
Applies learning to real-life situations	4.4
Defines the essence of a problem	4.3
Conceives, plans, and executes goals and projects	4.2
General academic preparedness	
Transcripts	4.1
Secondary school average	3.7
Degrees, diplomas, certificates	3.7
Types of courses taken	3.7
Performance on national examinations	3.6

[a]Mean rating of 0 = no importance, 1 = very low importance, 2 = low importance, 3 = moderate importance, 4 = high importance, and 5 = very high importance.

that the educational institution is interested in students' attitudes to learning rather than just their grades, which may, in turn, orient students to learning rather than grade hunting. Colleges considered to be of high quality recruit and enroll students who not only have higher academic ability but also higher educational aspirations and level and clarity of career ambition (Pascarella and Terenzini, 1991). Since the recruitment process of an institution can be an important influence on the environment for learning, this is an area to be carefully reviewed for potential improvements.

The need for a more multifaceted admissions procedure is also reflected in the indicators for the ability to analyze, synthesize, and think critically. Since it is a pronounced aim of undergraduate studies to enable students to learn to think, this criterion might appropriately be used as a student outcome, but students considered it important at entry to the university as well (Donald and Denison, 1996b). The indicators for this criterion were also rated of higher importance than most other indicators. Some, such as considering all sides of an argument and making an independent judgment or defining the essence of a problem, can be measured in writing; others require more complex measures of performance.

Outcomes Expected by Society

The measures of student quality can also be used to fit practice to desired outcomes for students, especially since students perceive the criteria to be most important at the end of their undergraduate education. The outcomes expected by society and confirmed by research include knowledge and intellectual skills, values, and attitudes learned, and preparation for life after attending a university. These outcomes can be divided into two sets: what is learned or developed during a student's postsecondary educational experience and, summatively, what is expected upon graduation. Two respondents reflected upon the importance of more general and integrated learning outcomes.

> Employers want people who can work on teams, who know how to cooperate and deal with the ambiguities of working in groups, because one person cannot know it all, and you have to be able to work effectively with people. They want people who have integrity, can communicate orally and in writing, can do critical thinking, and have good analytical skills. So, I think we need to rethink undergraduate education in the sense of building in these cross-cutting skills, although I hate to call them skills; they are more than that, as opposed to just content.

> The notion of moving from learning bits and pieces of content to acquiring skills that will enable one to learn across a lifetime is important, because most jobs in the next century are going to involve the need to learn in an ongoing and continuing way.

The research on student outcomes has illuminated factors that are potential sources of influence on how, or the extent to which, knowledge and abilities are acquired. Involvement—the extent to which students invest physical and psychological energy in their educational experiences—has emerged as a major construct in ensuring positive outcomes (Astin, 1984, 1993b; Kuh, Schuh, Whitt, and Associates, 1991; Pace, 1988, 1990; Pascarella and Terenzini, 1991; Willis, 1993). In the Delphi study, several of the criteria of quality for students were related to involvement, for example, the ability to interact with others and openness and flexibility (Table 3.1). The finding that informal non-classroom interaction is related to gains in thinking abilities (Pascarella and Terenzini, 1991) confirms their importance.

The ability to analyze, synthesize, and think critically was one of the two most important criteria for students. If, as has been claimed, students lack analytical and critical tools, as well as historical and philosophical depth when they enter a university, an important function of the university is to teach them how to arrive at critically informed judgments in a variety of disciplines (Keohane, 1994). In the Delphi study, other criteria enabling students to learn were broader or foundational concepts; the two most important of them—effective study skills and habits and independence in learning—are often assumed rather than actively promoted in individual courses (Table 3.3). Alerting students to the importance of these skills and providing a means of developing them, whether through orientation programs or in courses or programs, appear critical to student success.

Of the criteria used to measure student outcomes summatively, the most frequently used is the retention or attrition rate, that is,

Table 3.3. Most Important Indicators of Criteria Enabling Students To Learn

Criterion/Indicators	Mean Rating[a]
Effective study skills and habits	
Demonstrates basic organizational skills	4.1
Adjusts learning strategies to demands of particular courses and learning tasks	4.1
Does advanced planning and preparation of essays, exams, and other assignments	3.9
Accesses academic resources such as the library	3.9
Observes deadlines	3.8
Independence in learning	
Knows how to use resources	4.4
Sets up own framework for learning, such as a study plan	4.2
Initiates and follows through on short- and long-term projects	4.2
Functions with little direction or support	4.2
Self-evaluates	4.1

[a]Mean rating of 0 = no importance, 1 = very low importance, 2 = low importance, 3 = moderate importance, 4 = high importance, and 5 = very high importance.

the proportion of entering students who persist through to graduation, which is often seen as reflecting the degree of fit and responsiveness of the educational milieu to the student (Noel, 1985; Tinto, 1982, 1985). In a study of what American college presidents considered to be appropriate measures of effectiveness in meeting their goals, retention was an important criterion for their success (American Council on Education, 1986). Other criteria that presidents agreed upon were job placement rates of graduates, ratings of the institution by graduates, long-term outcomes of graduates, and the quality of graduates' performance on the job. In the Delphi study, job placement and performance on the job were not named as criteria for administrators or programs but as criteria for students (Table 3.1). Students perceived them to be extremely important at graduation (Donald and Denison, 1996b).

One question these ascriptions raise is, Who is responsible for whether students graduate? Another is, What is the relationship of presidents to graduating students, say, in comparison with their programs? If presidents are responsible for student outcomes, what do presidents do to specifically affect them? Where does the onus for student outcomes lie? In addition, there is some confusion about what the larger constituency wants.

> All sorts of chairmen of boards tell us that they are looking for the well-rounded person, that they will supply the specialized training. That looks great on paper, but in real life it does not turn out that way, because hiring at the lower echelons is all done by job description, and job descriptions are done by ticking off, "Have you had this course, this course, and so on? Have you had typing?" So the upper echelon is talking about the well-rounded person who can articulate. They are not interested in how much you know but how well you can express yourself and organize your thoughts. Then down at the lower echelon, you have job descriptions and personnel people who are doing the hiring. It seems to me that higher education has got to reach out to the corporate world and say you can't have it both ways.

Another inherent problem in responding to societal requests for particular student outcomes is that there are few ways of knowing what the job needs are going to be in the future. Furthermore, employment needs may be dissonant with academic priorities.

> We have a conception of economic development that is dependent upon high technology rather than on training people who are going to move into good middle-class jobs. So, if you were to ask, "Where are the middle-class jobs going to be in terms of numbers in the next ten to twenty years?," they are not going to be in optical sciences. The growth areas are going to be in public service occupations like nursing, education, social services, and we construct those as being not productive in the United States, because they are not private. They are public, and we don't think very highly of public service. So it

> is really important to think about where the university is committing itself in terms of undergraduate education, because we are seeing a shift in American universities with more of a graduate emphasis on the sciences, and the social and behavioral sciences and humanities will become more service units. It will happen slowly but it is happening already.

In summary, academic leaders, students, and the general constituency have expectations of what students will be equipped with when they graduate from the university and enter the work force. Criteria are available but do not tend to be applied during students' undergraduate careers to guide their development. Greater use could be made of the most important criteria—a commitment to learning and the ability to analyze, synthesize, and think critically—as measures of students in recruitment and admissions procedures, or as gauges of progress. Effective study skills and independence in learning are important skills to develop and need to be enunciated early in a student's undergraduate life.

Dealing with Diversity

Diversity is a prominently enunciated goal in North American postsecondary education, but from the perspective of the institution it brings its own problems, particularly in students' preparedness for or fit to the institution. Ensuring access to underrepresented groups, the need for a skilled work force, and the intellectual enrichment resulting from the dialogue of multiple viewpoints are powerful arguments for promoting a diverse student population (Adams, 1992). The greater heterogeneity of the student population extends not only over cultural or ethnic background but also to stage of life and technological expertise.

> Students are becoming more diverse because of birth rates in the population, the openness of institutions, social mandates in this country to deliver education more equitably or independently of background or personal characteristics. In this country in the last twenty years,

> since 1965 and the Higher Education Act, a national policy decision was made to open public higher education to a far wider and more diverse population than had ever been the case in our history.

Attention to diversity is important in postsecondary educational institutions because of the continuing disparity in educational opportunity for different groups of students, when society is dependent upon an educated population. Educational establishments have been asked to change the general social fabric, to act as a community for those who may not have had a sufficiently supportive one to develop to their full potential—no small request. According to one respondent, recent legislation to support greater diversity in the postsecondary population should enable this to happen, but legislation effects change slowly.

> It will probably be twenty years before there is any noticeable difference. The first blacks were admitted to colleges and universities in 1835, and it wasn't until 1970 that there was anything resembling open admissions. We still have problems with the equitable distribution of educational opportunities to people of color. Maybe we have solved the access problem to the extent that people who graduate from high school can get into a college or university, but we have certainly not solved the equal access to benefits problem. Black students and low socioeconomic students are over-represented in our community colleges, where the opportunities to complete a bachelor's degree are 15 to 20 percent less than if they enter a four-year institution. We also know that students who enter and attend commuter institutions have fewer opportunities to benefit from a college education than those who attend a residential institution. So, equal access to the benefits of higher education is still a problem.

If academic preparedness and a commitment to learning are the most important criteria for students, how can diversity be supported while these benchmarks are maintained? One respondent who was asked what, in her view, were the most important issues for universities in the next century, commented on steps being taken to ensure diversity in her university.

> We are proactively trying to deal with the diversity of students that we are going to be encountering in the twenty-first century. I am on the Hispanic recruitment committee; we pay enormous attention to diversity—ethnic or cultural—more than level of preparation. For example, our Asian student body since 1988, when it was perhaps 3 to 4 percent, has grown to 17 percent. That may grow in the future. So for us, one issue will be cultural diversity.

Although university policy may promote greater ethnic diversity, at the same time there is a sense that universities, whether public or private, will have to put systems in place to support students from groups previously denied access and who therefore may not be prepared for the exigencies and tribulations of postsecondary learning. In the case of minority students or students from outside the traditional academic mainstream, this means acquiring a sense of their social norms and the attendant alienation, isolation, and injury they may experience when confronted with mainstream values and customs and a seemingly monolithic attitude (Marchesani and Adams, 1992). It also means examining the attitudes and behaviors of academic and administrative staff, transforming the curriculum where appropriate to one of inclusion, and expanding the repertoire of teaching methods to reach a broader range of students, as the following quotations suggest.

> How we assimilate diversity successfully into the institution is important in a state like this, where the representation of Native Americans is the lowest of all the different ethnic groups, and the retention is even lower, and yet we are a land grant institution that is supposed to serve our population.

> The chancellor feels it is very important to have a more racially and ethnically diverse population than in the past, so he has set aside a

> number of scholarships and support programs to try to attract highly qualified minority students. Merit-based scholarships also provide full support. Students do not have the same math and writing skills that they had a few years ago. The writing program has been revamped to try to handle that, and we are working on a program to assist students to improve their calculating skills.

In addition to the cultural diversity that ethnic and racial minority groups bring to the campus, diversity in age and competencies have increased over the last decade. These changes affect the educational process in the classroom and alter the role of faculty. Changes in the student population require adaptation in terms of university learning facilities and further education of faculty in educational technology and psychology.

> Our student body is becoming more diverse, not only in terms of ethnicity but in terms of age. We not only have multi-age groupings in the classroom, but we also have people who are at different stages in the educational process. Faculty at a university deal with cognitive aspects of learning, but they seldom . . . consider the affective aspects, so we have to look at how we as faculty . . . educate our students and . . . [whether] our education is relevant to the kinds of experiences they are going to encounter in society. Society is radically changing. For example, the kinds of students entering the university now are much more computer or multi-media oriented, and yet we have faculty who have no conception of the role of technology in the classroom and very few classrooms that are equipped [for] that. It is a problem of resources, as well as background.

To meet the university's commitment to diversity, a well-designed process for responding to the diverse student population was in place on one campus. A respondent described a benchmark program that had been developed to train graduate teaching assistants who would be dealing with undergraduates in small-group sessions or tutorials.

> One thing we do to promote the mission of the university is provide graduate teaching assistants with training in diversity-related issues, ranging from the idea of diversity within the student population to sexual harassment to the new laws on disabled folks. In order to provide quality training, we take graduate students who volunteer to go through a training program with us to become facilitators of diversity-related programs. It is voluntary, they are reimbursed, and they are provided with training materials. We find that we develop a very good cadre of skilled facilitators. More important, they are graduate teaching assistants, and there is a strong identification between what they do and the other TAs that they are communicating with, because there is common ground [for] talking about these issues.

Graduate student teaching assistants who have at least two or three years left in their studies are given priority in this program, so there is a self-regenerating group. In the sessions, the first purpose is to create awareness of the differences TAs will meet in the classroom environment by looking at how various cultures make decisions. In interactive sessions, the students are asked to reflect on how they developed their attitude toward differences. Difference is defined in a global way; students are asked to look at how learners are different and what implications differences in the classroom have for decisions about instructional methods, the environment, materials, and appropriate instructional strategies. Pedagogy and diversity are thus combined to provide a reflective look at the linkage between the two; the spectrum of differences examined includes learning styles, gender, class, ethnic background, and educational experience.

> There are all kinds of rationales for doing diversity sessions—for social change, for global economic reasons, as a humanitarian pursuit, or because we want to effectively teach, which is a different slant, but the most effective approach and one which probably provides the least resistance. We look at the differences between eighteen-year-olds and adults. For us, eighteen-year-olds are three months away from being high school seniors, but since the average age on this campus is just under twenty-seven, we look at how having forty- or

> fifty-year-olds in your class as well as eighteen-year-olds would affect how you approach the class. Adult learners have different characteristics from more traditionally aged learners. They are not as dualistic in their thinking; they have different kinds of expectations.
>
> We look at the history of the development of all of the "isms" in our society, whether racism, sexism, classism, heterosexism, or any of the isms we look at when we're looking at difference. We try to get students who are going to be teaching to reflect on how the attitudes we bring with us into that environment are going to affect what we do as teachers. We also discuss the area of ability. I ask the students, "Whom do you teach to? Do you teach to the brightest and best, the group in the middle, the students most at risk?" That is a challenging question, and there are diversity issues inherent in that question relative to ability and background and culture. We need to be much more responsive to what is a reflection of the character of society now.

This program is significant as a benchmark practice, because it targets the future professoriate, which means it will have a ripple effect. It places diversity in the center of the institutional context, the educational mission, and it deals with the entire spectrum of diversity issues.

Preparing Students To Learn

Questions of selection and access are brought together in a consideration of what students need to learn and how to prepare them to learn. Student selection and access to a program are based finally on the learning goals in a program and its coordination with students' incoming abilities. Respondents in the four universities spoke at some length about what is known of students and what is important for students to learn. A sense of intellectual challenge is apparent in the experts' views of the learning that should occur.

> What is it we expect our students to be able to do intellectually, and how do we define their education? and, How do we best go about facilitating that education or fostering that kind of development?

The challenge of defining an education for students is an intellectual issue but also a motivational and administrative issue. It is motivational, because in order to learn, students have to be able to set goals. It is administrative, because the way in which universities are operated provides the perspective students will adopt toward their learning. The next respondent explains the relationship between the administrative practice of measuring learning in terms of course credits and student goals.

> We should be trying to figure out what the learner of tomorrow needs that we can offer, because my own personal experience in the classroom shows me that we have trained a generation of very bright people to take tests, and we haven't yet connected with their ability to think. They have learned the lessons we have taught them, and that is very unfortunate, because we have taught them the wrong lesson. The faculty believe . . . that they teach well and that they spend a lot of time at it and that it's important to them, so it isn't a lack of effort we're talking about here. It is a sense of direction, and it is most obvious in a large-scale beginning lecture, but it is also visible in junior- and senior-level courses where the numbers are smaller but the orientation of the students is not where you would want it to be, which is on mastering the material, but is instead on figuring out what it is going to take to get a good grade. These people are smart enough to get a good grade, so you tell them what the hoop is and they can jump through it, whatever it is, including thinking.

To set the stage for learning, an examination of what the respondents have said about selection practices and diversity leads to the following practices. First, universities can be clear about their admissions policy and what they expect of students once they arrive on campus. The criteria of student quality can be used to deliver this message, particularly since students agree with their importance. Second, it is possible to use the criteria and indicators to explain students' responsibilities and tasks in some detail, as well as what help is available to accomplish them. Third, attempting to educate a diverse population necessitates a structure to explain what the learning tasks are in postsecondary education. Providing this kind of general instruction at the beginning of a student's undergraduate career may alleviate many problems of adaptation to a new environment.

Summary: The Effect of Student Selection and Access on the Learning Climate

To ensure that students in postsecondary institutions develop to their fullest potential, an important step is to identify the student characteristics that enable them to learn and develop. Academic leaders and students agree that the most important criteria for student quality are a commitment to learning, the ability to analyze, synthesize and think critically, and general academic preparedness. Student characteristics have more effect on the learning environment than any other factor, but the most powerful learning effects are related more to the learning experiences that occur than to student selectivity or institutional resources.

To identify the characteristics that enable students to learn, educational institutions must determine the fit of the student to the institution, then set procedures in place to ensure that students are oriented to learning when they arrive, and that the curriculum and instruction and the general learning milieu fit student needs. Since productivity and equity are related societal goals, meeting the learning needs of diverse populations is a priority. Practices developed for meeting these needs include providing support programs and training to take learner heterogeneity into account.

Administrative strategies that help students adapt to the new environment in turn set the stage for improving students' motivation to learn—the subject of the following chapter.

4

Fostering Students' Motivation for Learning

Postsecondary learning is qualitatively different from learning at earlier levels of education. Therefore, students need, first, to be open to new ways of learning in order to develop intellectually and, second, to be willing to invest personally in the learning process.

The study discussed in Chapter Three on criteria of excellence for postsecondary students showed that one of the most important criteria was a commitment to learning. An agreement or pledge to learn on the part of students is important, because students' attitudes and values serve as conditions or limitations on what and how they will learn. Changes over time in students' goals from intellectual to vocational signal the need to better understand students' goals and how they affect learning.

In this chapter, I begin by investigating theories of student motivation and the effect of motivation on learning. Helping students to see the intrinsic value of learning and to adopt an orientation to their studies that will enable them to become independent, lifelong learners is an essential strategy. A variety of methods at both the institutional and classroom level have been developed to assist students to become responsible, self-regulated learners. The goals of this chapter are, then, to examine how theories of motivation can be applied, to portray methods for fostering motivation, and to show how the methods might be adopted within universities. Here is the basic problem from the faculty's perspective.

> This is a university, and probably most people's conception in the university is that they don't have a great deal of responsibility for motivating students: students ought to be self-motivated. That is part of the "raise the entrance requirements" syndrome; you don't change fundamentally the way you deal with students. There are exceptions to that, but I think that is a fair thing to say generally. The faculty at this place will complain as faculty have always complained about unmotivated students, students who are unprepared. The assumption is that students should come here with certain skills and certain commitments. The concern is that those are declining, which is another way of saying, "We are being increasingly confronted with students who do not look like us, and we get upset by it."

Commitment to Learning

Professors have a built-in expectation that students will arrive with the skills and attitudes that will enable them to learn. It is for the most part how professors remember themselves as students, which leads to uneasiness when they find that most students do not have the same scholarly attitudes and competencies. But the majority of students enter a university from an educational setting in which the responsibility for learning has been primarily that of their teachers, who have expressed considerable concern for them and their learning (White and others, 1995). In the university, there is a shift in the balance of responsibility for learning from teacher to student, and students find professors, especially in large introductory courses, distant and indifferent rather than concerned. In addition to a diminished support system in the university, students may be experiencing life with a capital L for the first time.

> A great deal of education is wasted on the age group that we are trying to deal with. A lot of these kids are learning to break away from their parents, learning to drink, learning about sex, and that is one of

> the chief motivating factors in a lot of eighteen-year-olds. Students' value systems are in a whirl; they are not too sure what they believe.

In response to this situation, the professor just quoted suggested that students should be allowed to take real-life work breaks in order to sort themselves out. Although allowing students to come to their own decision about the importance of learning may be tempting, especially since efforts to influence students' attitudes toward learning may be difficult, frustrating, and cost-intensive, the human capital argument suggests that as a society, we cannot afford to leave students to their own devices. Furthermore, the outcomes of a college education include not only knowledge and skills but attitudes and values, which suggests some responsibility for their development during studies (Ewell, 1987). The importance of attitudinal components lies in their general, long-term effect on behavior. Although students' attitudes and values have emerged as pivotal constructs in explaining student outcomes in the higher education research literature, within the university the focus is on cognitive development. Broader psychosocial and attitudinal issues tend to be relegated to the academic periphery and are dealt with, for the most part, in student affairs offices. The crux of the problem from the point of view of faculty members is expressed in the following way:

> Responsibility for learning is that of the students, and the responsibility for presenting up-to-date, current information in a learnable fashion is the responsibility of the faculty. It is a mutual responsibility to see that learning takes place. I don't think it is possible for a faculty member to ensure that somebody learns if learning is not one of the goals of the student.

The problem for postsecondary educators is that cognitive development in the form of higher-order learning, because of its complexity and level of difficulty, may present an insurmountable challenge to students lacking motivation or a commitment to learning. One critical aspect of postsecondary learning is that it is qualitatively different from learning at earlier levels of education. It requires approaches or strategies that students may not yet have acquired. This means that students need to be ready and willing to invest personally in learning and to be open to and aware of the changes that must take place in their way of thinking in order to develop intellectually. According to faculty reports, student self-reports, and college records, the single most important factor accounting for success in college after entering grades and SAT scores is productivity or perseverance at the task of college work (Willingham, 1985). Perseverance is a behavioral expression of commitment or motivation to learn.

To what extent *are* students committed to learning? Perry (1970), in his studies of the intellectual development of Harvard students, found that by their senior year 75 percent had reached a level of commitment in which they were able to evaluate issues and explain beliefs from an informed, examined perspective. At this highest level of development, students have begun to clarify their values and are able to make and live their commitments. However, subsequent studies revealed few students at the level of commitment (Pascarella and Terenzini, 1991). Baxter Magolda (1992) found that students progressed slowly during the undergraduate years in acceptance of their role as independent learners.

In a study done to test the validity of the Perry schema, more than two-thirds of college students agreed with items representing commitment such as "knowledge is being able to defend a position with solid argumentation, even though others might disagree" (69 percent agreement) or "learning is challenging when we must look at all the ideas and from these decide where we stand" (71 percent agreement) (Bateman and Donald, 1987). Our study of university students' perceptions of criteria of quality for students showed that they consider a commitment to learning the most important criterion at entry and during studies (Donald and Denison,

1996b). These studies suggest two things: students may have the language if not the behavior of commitment to learning, and variations in degree of commitment can be expected among students.

Students have been typed according to their expectations, interests, behaviors, and reported abilities (Astin, 1993a). For example, "scholars" rated themselves as having high academic ability; they expected to succeed, spent more time studying, and reported improvement in their problem-solving skills and critical thinking ability. At the other end of the typology, "uncommitted" students failed to complete assignments on time, were bored in class, and were more likely to report feeling overwhelmed by all that they had to do. Having only a percentage of committed students in a class means that professors, no matter how devoted to their discipline and to their students' learning, are limited in the kind of learning goals they can achieve with their students. If students are not committed—or passionate, to use one professor's language—they cannot become independent learners. The following quotation also suggests that it is not enough for students to be accepting of what is offered in courses; in order to progress, they must be challenged to go beyond responding to basic requirements.

> Responsibility for learning is what is most important to me. I have a population in this department of 350 students. Of the half that I know personally, there are maybe ten who are passionate, and you cannot do much without passion. I don't know how you teach passion, but I know that one way you will never get to be passionate about something is by never being pushed to be better than what you're expected to be. Because they have been doing what they're told once a week for so many years, that's all students know how to do. If you don't tell them what to do, they freak out.

The level of devotion or passion for learning displayed by today's students appears to be a far cry from that of Chaucer's clerk of Oxenford who had a great desire for learning. If idealism is at its height among students at the postsecondary school level, what has happened to these students' goals?

Changes in Student Goals

Research suggests that in the last twenty years, students' commitment to learning has been subsumed under the desire for material prosperity, and student choices of college and life goals have become increasingly vocational. A goal is defined as an end toward which effort is directed. It encapsulates directed energy, or motivation, and hence is often used interchangeably with the term "motive." As of 1977, financial well-being became a more important goal for American postsecondary students than developing a meaningful philosophy of life (Astin, Green, and Korn, 1987; Stark, Shaw, and Lowther, 1989). Students are increasingly preoccupied with career concerns and are less interested in broader intellectual issues (Williams and Schiralli, 1991). Fewer students in postsecondary programs actually define themselves as students (Donald, 1997).

The importance of the change in student goals lies in the fact that student goals mediate between what instructors intend students to learn and what students actually learn. For example, if students are in school in order to get a good job rather than to understand, they are more likely to take only enough time to acquire the superficial vocabulary necessary to pass a test rather than developing a sense of the discipline, a theoretical framework that will remain in long-term memory and provide them with a means of organizing and retrieving their knowledge. In other words, if students entering college do not see the relationship between understanding their field and gaining credentials in it, they will not be in a position to actively control and organize their learning. More specifically, if students' goals do not match the intellectual demands of their courses, they may not find their course work rewarding. From the perspective of the course, the percentage of students whose commitment to learning matches the intellectual exigencies of the course may not be great enough to provide a sufficiently dynamic environment for learning. Worse still in such a situation, the rewards for learning may then remain unnoticed by a majority of students.

> What are the incentives for students to be responsible for learning? I don't think there are very many; students don't find much immediate payoff in their academic tasks, except for that subgroup that is intellectually oriented. In a fourfold typology of vocational, intellectual, social, and achievement orientations, it would be interesting to see how that would affect grade point average. We certainly have some students who are turned on by learning and are very excited, and others who are achievement-oriented and in danger of cheating and shortcutting, because the grade is what they need. It is an instrumental motivation toward getting into graduate school and making contacts for their job, which is very close to the vocational or career orientation.

Students who have not established clear goals or who change their goals after they enter college are one step further away from becoming actively responsible for their learning. Studies suggest that although three-quarters of students entering college have decided on a major or a career, most change their plans during their undergraduate years (Gordon, 1984). Chickering (1984) has pointed out the importance of helping students set goals in order to create a supportive learning environment. But that is just the first step toward having students commit themselves to the intellectual challenge and lifelong learning necessary in the knowledge era.

In a study of students' goals, students were categorized as having either an exploratory orientation toward their education, where they explored ideas for their intrinsic interest, or a preparatory orientation, where they pursued education because it was instrumental in achieving career goals (Morstain, 1973). Faculty can also be categorized as having either an exploratory or a preparatory orientation, and they influence their students' orientation (Stark, 1975;

Stark and Morstain, 1978). Applied fields such as business, medicine, or engineering tend to have a larger proportion of students with a career orientation, while others, particularly in the humanities, support an intellectual orientation (Katchedourian and Boli, 1985). Stark, Shaw, and Lowther (1989) point out that goal specification is badly needed if we are to understand student outcomes and student learning in postsecondary education.

The Relationship Between Motivation and Learning

To examine the effect of goals on learning, we turn to a more specific level of analysis: what motivates students and the relation of motivation to learning.

Research on the effects of motivation on learning has focused on intrinsic goal motivation and strategies for improving learning (Pintrich, Cross, Kozma, and McKeachie, 1986; Pintrich, Marx, and Boyle, 1993). Intrinsic motivation is defined as motivation in which the satisfaction or incentive conditions are obtained within the activity itself (English and English, 1958). Pintrich applies this concept to students' doing a task for challenge or mastery reasons (Harter, 1981; Pintrich, 1987). For example, in the Motivated Strategies for Learning Questionnaire (MSLQ), which was designed to gauge student motivation, intrinsic goal orientation is measured by items such as, "I prefer course work that is challenging so that I can learn new things" (Pintrich, 1987). Intrinsic goal orientation is thus close to the exploratory orientation suggested by Morstain (1973). Important for understanding the relationship between motivation and learning, in studies using the MSLQ, students who were more intrinsically oriented were found to use more cognitive strategies and to perform at higher levels on examinations, papers, and final grades (Pintrich, 1987).

Often, studies compare the effect of motivation across disciplines. In one study, natural science students were found to have both higher intrinsic goal motivation and more metacognitive strategies than students in the social sciences or in English literature (Garcia and Pintrich, 1992). To add to the complexity of the problem, while the degree of intrinsic goal motivation was a significant predictor of critical thinking for both natural and social science students, it was not for those in English literature. Within courses as well, groups of students with different goals display different levels or kinds of motivation, as a physics professor explained:

> I just taught a general physics course last semester, which is the course that our pre-medical students take and also that all other people looking for a first course in science take. The course had three hundred students in it. There were two audiences in it, one of them, roughly half, in pre-med who were interested in passing the MCAT, so they were here to master that material so that they could get a good grade, and they didn't want me to talk about Newton's philosophy. They wanted to know how to do those problems, exactly how to do a problem with a lens here and an object there and an image there, because "that's what is going to be on the MCAT, and if you don't teach me that, then you're not doing anything for me." The other group wanted to hear about Newton's philosophy, and the big picture, and how these ideas of physics fit into making the world a saner place to think about and be in: "How do I organize my own personal universe. How do you help me to do that?" So if they had never solved a problem, they would have been happy.

One group of students in the course sought to extend their understanding of the context of physics, while another group was extrinsically oriented; they were in the class in order to get somewhere else. Extrinsic goal motivation is defined as behavior that is controlled through the possibility of reward or punishment external to whatever satisfactions reside in the task itself (English and English, 1958). It is measured in the MSLQ by items such as, "If I can, I want to get better grades in this class than most of the other students." Extrinsic goal motivation has some elements in common with a preparatory orientation. Asked if either of the two groups in the physics course was going to come out with a better understanding of the basic physics concept of "force," the professor replied:

> No, the physics majors will eventually, but that's because we're going to give it to them again, the very same material but at a different level. At the next level, they learn a few mathematical tools, slightly more sophisticated, but they learn a whole other way of looking at the same thing. And then they get it again, and it's in the third pass that they are going to understand the concept of force. It's structured that way. You first have to cope with the concept itself and make it yours in the sense of being able to apply it to your problems, . . . then you have to learn some sophistication so that you can say that same thing but with more mechanical rigor, and now you're ready to understand the concept of force. This is in graduate school or senior year.

The intrinsic learning reward in this example is not readily obtained and requires considerable perseverance on the part of students. This quotation exemplifies the qualitative difference in postsecondary learning and, specifically, the problem that exists in teaching concepts that are too complex to be immediately grasped and must therefore be studied over a lengthy period of time—years rather than weeks. Students must have sufficient intrinsic motivation to continue to build upon their initial understanding of the concepts. The inherent complexity and difficulty of a fair proportion of ideas that students will encounter in their postsecondary studies may pose a substantial barrier for a large proportion of students.

Research in several countries has suggested that students' overlying approach or orientation to learning affects the quality of learning (Biggs, 1988, 1993; Biggs and Collis, 1982; Entwistle and Tait, 1990; Meyer, Parsons, and Dunne, 1990; Ramsden, 1992). The term "orientation" in this research indicates a combination of an approach to studying, style of learning, and motivation that is relatively stable across different educational tasks (Ramsden, 1992). Four student study orientations: meaning (deep); reproducing (surface); achieving (competitive and grade-oriented); and nonacademic (negative attitudes and disorganized study methods) have been found in factor analyses of postsecondary students (Entwistle and Ramsden, 1983). In the Study Process Questionnaire (Biggs, 1988), developed to measure deep, surface, and achieving motivation and strategies, a sample item describing deep motivation is, "I feel that almost any topic can be interesting once I get into it." Surface motivation is exemplified by the item, "I believe that teachers should not expect students to spend significant amounts of time studying material everyone knows won't be examined."

Students with a deep approach to learning, that is, those who conceptualize learning as a search for meaning that requires analysis and synthesis or critical thinking, would be expected to learn more, but the primary measure of learning—course grade—may reflect both meaning and achieving orientations. Students with a reproducing or surface approach, or those who are not academically oriented, would not be expected to learn as effectively.

The student orientation research suggests that some students are flexible and may adopt one approach in one course or subject and another in a different course, according to their goals and what they perceive the instructor's expectations or evaluation plans to be (Entwistle and Tait, 1990; Ramsden, 1992). The learning context interacts with students' orientations to affect their perception of the learning task and the approach they take to it. For example, students may prefer a meaning approach, but when overloaded with course content or evaluated on their knowledge of facts, they may adopt a reproductive or achieving approach. Sometimes, the ethos or institutional custom leads to a surface approach in both teaching and learning, even when students are capable of rigorous work. In the words of one respondent:

> We have very capable students who are pretty traditional. They expect to be passive most of the time in most of their courses. There is an implicit deal struck that it is a course where the learning style is going to be surface, where the assessment is pretty much surface, and the numbers are large. Faculty present the information, and students can learn the information even if it is not presented very well; good students can learn in spite of not having very good teaching.

The most positive finding of the student orientation research is that students who adopt a meaning approach to learning experience greater satisfaction in their learning, higher-quality outcomes, and better grades (Ramsden, 1992). The relationship of student orientation to motivation could be expected to be close, since high intrinsic motivation would be characterized by a meaning approach to learning, as reported by Entwistle and Tait (1990), Fransson (1977), and Ramsden (1992). Extrinsic goal motivation, on the other hand, is closely related to an achieving orientation.

Differences in orientation and in the time spent studying have been found across disciplines. In a comparative study of students' orientations in introductory majors courses in physics and English, although students in both courses displayed a meaning or deep approach to learning, students in the physics course had a stronger achieving orientation than those in the English course (Donald, 1996). Students also displayed high levels of intrinsic goal motivation, but physics students displayed higher intrinsic goal motivation than English students and also tended to display higher extrinsic goal motivation. The time spent studying matched their levels of academic motivation. The English students spent fewer hours per week (eleven to fifteen hours) on average than physics students (sixteen to twenty hours) studying or doing homework, and appreciably more hours socializing and partying. The physics students averaged six to ten hours a week socializing, while English students spent as much time socializing (eleven to fifteen hours) as they did studying, suggesting dual—academic and social—goals.

Self-Regulated Learning

How goals, motivation, and orientation affect achievement in courses is explained by their role in student self-management or self-regulation. For example, the amount of time students spend studying depends upon their motivation and directly affects academic success. The time spent studying could also be seen as a response to task demand (difficulty, perceived challenge, and importance) that leads to a regulation of behavior. In the comparative studies of physics and English majors, the physics students recorded both greater intrinsic motivation and time spent studying. Self-regulated learners monitor and attempt to control their behavior, motivation and affect, and cognition (Pintrich, 1995). Learning is goal-directed; the goal provides the standard by which students monitor and judge their performance and then make appropriate adjustments.

Students' expectations of success, their goal-setting, and their self-efficacy, or perception of their ability to achieve goals, are based on past performance (McKeachie, Pintrich, Lin, and Smith, 1986). The term "situated motivation" has been used to describe the phenomenon of students' motivation to learn being affected by their history of success and the relative incentives provided in different learning situations (Paris and Turner, 1994). Situated motivation is then the engine of self-regulated learning. According to Paris and Turner, academic tasks that motivate learning have four characteristics. First, choice—the freedom to choose among alternative courses of action—promotes interest, and students who perceive their tasks to be interesting and worthwhile report more self-regulation and persistence (Pintrich and DeGroot, 1990). Choice leads to commitment, deep involvement, and strategic thinking with tasks. Second, challenge, in the form of moderately difficult tasks, is motivating (Clifford, 1991). Third, control or autonomy has a positive relationship to interest and intrinsic motivation. Finally, collaboration is motivational through peer comments and ideas that introduce elements of surprise and encourage further exploration, models, benchmarks, or standards for one's own learning. Collaboration also promotes persistence, because there is an obligation to peers in the group. A respondent described a collaborative learning program that has been used to aid less well-prepared students.

> In a study of collaborative and cooperative learning, Vincent Tinto found that even in the context of remediation, those structures were very effective at integrating students into the regular academic curriculum and were particularly effective in persistence, at keeping those students in school. A lot of universities in the States are considering notions of supplemental instruction, where a student who has done well in an introductory course is hired by the academic assistance program and given a cohort of eight or nine students who are going to take that course next semester, and goes through the course with those students, essentially sits in the class and is there as a resource, facilitator, tutor for those students. So it is not independent of a course, but the students have a resource that helps them get through.

In this quotation, student guides enhance the learning situation by collaborating with new learners and maintaining an optimum challenge level. This method has also been used at Stanford University, where in an introductory course, successful second-year students tutor and assess the learning of a small group of students in residence to ensure that they understand the basic concepts, so that the professor can introduce higher-order learning in class (Donald, 1987b). Learning is thus promoted by student choice, challenge, control of learning strategies, and collaboration.

Students who are self-regulating learners, according to their scores on the MSLQ, display high cognitive and metacognitive activity and, as could be expected, value and are interested in the course work. The principal finding from studies using the MSLQ is that for students to be successful learners in a course, they must articulate their own goals in the course, attribute success in the course to their own ability or self-efficacy, and use learning strategies that will enable them to reach their goals (Pintrich and DeGroot, 1990). The studies suggest that preparing students to be self-regulated learners includes, first, providing a sense of the content area and ensuring that students have the prerequisite skills or abilities to actively investigate the field of study. Second, preparation provides an understanding of how the course fits into students' learning plans and what strategies for learning will be needed to reach their learning goals. This returns the onus to the faculty member. As one respondent encapsulated the situation:

> Motivation depends upon faculty members' attitudes. I spend most of my time convincing people that students are great, highly motivated, and there is nobody in the world who does not want to learn. One of the strongest motivators we have is the need to learn. There is no such thing as an uninteresting topic, but there are some uninteresting methods of presentation and situations and some ways that students may appear to be unmotivated to perform a certain kind of task. My view of the world is that is why a faculty member gets paid so much, because we're good at informing other people about how interesting and exciting our discipline is.

Ways To Foster Student Motivation for Learning

What approaches and programs will heighten student motivation for learning? Are some academic activities and campus experiences particularly helpful in increasing students' interest in learning? The campus or institution can play an important role in setting a context that aids learning.

Student advising and curriculum organization play important roles in motivating students. The academic leaders in this study couched their suggestions for fostering student motivation for learning within the constraints encountered in their institutions. At the broadest level, they called upon the university to redefine itself as a community. Respondents from two of the universities spoke of the importance of a learning community, similar to that advocated by Palmer (1993), in which faculty share their teaching experiences, metaphors, and insights.

> My favorite metaphor for the university in the twenty-first century is the learning community, which would redefine the roles of faculty, students, and administrators. It would be an organization that would have the characteristics of a community and that would be oriented toward learning, meaning more collegiality and less transmission going on, and a lot of tentativeness and probably less certainty. Rather than, "We know all this and now you are supposed to know all this, and then our job is done," beyond multiplistic thinking toward commitment, tentative in the sense of lacking certainty. However, I think that there is a faculty culture, and a student culture, and an administrative culture, and they are really very different and very separate, so that making one community out of those cultures may be pretty farfetched, institution-wide.

The changes suggested in this quotation reflect the concept of relatedness among learners, a more democratic approach to learning, and an openness to experience and to others that might appear to be a lost ideal. It is much closer to the band of scholars that formed the early disciplines, but most evidently it is collaborative. The reference to different cultures within the university provokes the question of whether the values and goals of students, faculty, and administrators are substantially different, whether they should be, and whether a common meeting ground can be found. Another reason to reexamine the culture of the university and to attempt to apply the metaphor of the learning community is the finding that student learning occurs at a much more general level than in the individual course. The results of studies on student learning in and out of class were discussed by a respondent who had participated in them.

> One thing that has become clear to us is that student learning should not be studied in isolation, as it occurs in or outside the classroom, in the context of a particular kind of institution or a particular program, because everything is so interconnected. In a study of out-of-class experiences of students in the first transition semester, the researchers found that they could not talk to students without having them talk about what was happening in the classes and how that was affecting what was happening outside of class.
>
> In focus group interviews, students were articulate in describing the need to have somebody who was committed to their success. It could have been a parent who was working at two jobs to help pay for their school or a peer support group, either from a collaborative learning experience or a freshman seminar in which there were students who were committed to each other's success. Students talked about actively getting on each other's case about going to class and calling at home if they were not showing up for study. In some cases, it was a faculty member. Students were not interested in having standards compromised or in having their way made easy, but they were very interested in having a faculty member who was a resource. In some cases, the resource person was located in a learning assistance center program or a supplemental instruction program.

Several respondents suggested that students and their learning experiences should be made the focal point in university organization and policies and practices. This would mean closer coordination between academic and student life. For instance, the organizational distinction between academic affairs and student affairs works against how students learn, and against the web of connected experiences. Student affairs professionals have begun to reexamine their roles and mission in reports such as, *An American Imperative: Higher Expectations for Higher Education* (Wingspread Group, 1993) in which they call for reemphasizing student learning and personal development as the primary concerns of higher education. One respondent recommended that faculty be much more attuned to the personal and developmental issues of students and that student affairs people be more attuned to the kind of intellectual experiences that are happening and less concerned with students' social life. In an attempt to develop a coherent philosophy that would guide practice at one of the universities in this study, a student compact was developed and then expanded to include all members of the community.

Creating an Agreement for a Learning Community

In response to a request by the chancellor, a task force composed of students, faculty, administrators, and staff created a compact—what others in the university variously described as an honor code, a defined set of rules, or a statement of academic integrity. The compact stated that the students, faculty, staff, and administrators of the university would support scholarly learning as the central mission of the university, promote a culturally and socially diverse climate that supports the development of each member of the community, uphold the highest ideals of personal and academic honesty, and maintain a safe and healthy environment for each member of the community. It further pledged all members of the community to work together to reach these goals. As an administrator at the university explained:

> We said there are four things that we want to see everyone committed to. If you are joining this university, whether you're a student, a faculty member or a staff member, you are going to be committed to promoting learning.
>
> Second, if you don't learn to respect yourself and others in a self-world dynamic, where diversity is focused on, where there are different perspectives brought by the cultures, then you are not only not mining the opportunities and potential of your own community, but you are not disposing yourself in the most intelligent way to contribute to a community beyond that. We think you can participate in an educational community.

> Third, you must be prepared to acknowledge your own strengths and limitations, your own successes and failures, in the classroom and out, with . . . all work being your own, . . . and abstinence from cheating or falsification. You cannot have . . . an academic community apart from a commitment to integrity.
>
> Finally, we are going to have to accept certain levels of concern for health and welfare, and that includes safety.

The general reaction on campus to the compact was that it was having a substantial, positive effect on individual and community behavior. It is introduced in convocations at the beginning of the year and appears to play the role of a constitution guiding university life.

Advising

Student advising is a point of integration between students' cognitive and affective development. In the early history of universities, it was the responsibility of professors and tutors who lived in close proximity with students in residential colleges (Kuh, 1992). Increasing specialization in academic disciplines and concomitant changes in the professorial role, however, led faculty members to shift their focus from student development to teaching and scholarly interests, particularly in large research universities. This in turn led to the development of a profession of student advising and to student affairs offices that were designated to respond to questions about student welfare. In spite of the fact that they frequently report to a dean who has an academic appointment, their major objective has been student life rather than student learning. In 1987, however, the National Association of Student Personnel Administrators affirmed that student affairs exists to enhance and support the academic mission of the institution, as well as to encourage independent thought and interdependent behavior on the part of students. As noted earlier, student affairs professionals have recently called for a reemphasis on student learning as a primary concern of higher education.

Most advising is still done, however, by faculty members; 98 percent of all instructional faculty serve as academic advisers to students, according to the American College Testing Program (Ryan, 1995). Professional development and training for faculty advisers focuses first on a conceptual understanding of student development, so that advisers have an understanding of why students' goals change and how students' backgrounds affect their choices. Second, an attempt is made to ground institutional and curricular information needs in the professor's personal philosophy of higher education, so that the relationships between courses and potential directions in higher education can be articulated to students. Third, professors need communication and interactive skills to model being a member of an academic community. Publications and a summer institute on academic advising sponsored by the National Academic Advising Association (NACADA) and the American College Testing Program are available to aid in the development of these skills (Gordon, 1995).

Academic advising, according to one respondent, is intended at his university to promote a close relationship between faculty, staff, and students. Advising goals are to help students get the courses they need, encourage them to explore, and provide support and encouragement right through to the time they are ready to enter the job market. But the responsibilities of students are also important in the advising equation. Students are told that they are responsible for scheduling, preparing for and keeping advising appointments, seeking out contacts and information, knowing the basic requirements of their individual degree programs, and making their own decisions based on the best information and advice available and on their own judgment. Advisers are responsible for developing a thorough knowledge of the institution, including academic requirements, program options, and general university resources. The university is pledged to provide the information and to help faculty and staff develop effective advising skills, to evaluate its system of academic advising, to make improvements where necessary, and to recognize advising through the institutional reward system. In order to do this, every school and college has developed a substantial faculty and student manual for academic advising. A respondent described the attention paid to advising and communicating with students to help them be self-regulating at this university:

> An information kiosk system provides easy access to academic advising assignments, the individual student's past and present records, financial aid information, outstanding bills like parking tickets, and internal transfer procedures that are continually refreshed. The libraries are on-line through the information kiosk, so students can see if particular books are available. If they need tutoring, they can set up an appointment through e-mail. The kiosks are located in every school and college, the student union buildings, and residence halls.

In this example, technology has been employed to provide students with ready advising and access to their records and tutors as needed. The system also lets students know that they are responsible for making contact and for planning their undergraduate route. The involvement of faculty in advising is supported by workshops that promote advising skills.

> Faculty members have two days of training on interviewing skills, listening, questioning, providing referrals, policies, curriculum, inter-university transfer, and new degree audit tools. Tenure review in the future will require evaluation of a faculty member's effectiveness in both undergraduate and graduate advising.

Advising has become sufficiently important that it is scheduled to be examined in tenure dossiers in this university. Although in research universities in general, this kind of service activity may continue to be delegated to professional staff, advising is central in locating students in the learning community. The university has instituted computerized procedures that respond to many of the student welfare needs that would otherwise be expensive in terms of academics' and professionals' time. Thus, an administrative step has been taken to integrate students into the learning community, with a reasonable cost to faculty (two days training in addition to what academics would be expected to provide in office hours), and a potential for developing students' skills as independent or self-regulating learners.

Curriculum and Instruction

Research established in Chapter Two that learning goals vary across disciplines, that students report progress matching disciplinary expectations, and that they rate their learning experiences accordingly. Students also have different kinds of motivation—deep, surface, or achieving, intrinsic or extrinsic—in different courses. There are, however, instructional strategies that can be used across disciplines to foster motivation. Improvements to the curriculum are based on the realization that the closer to the learning situation the change in practice, the more likely the effect of the change.

A study of influences from before college and during the first year on students' intellectual orientations in college showed that students' attitudes can be affected by the instructional methods used (Terenzini, Springer, Pascarella, and Nora, 1995). Students' interest in academic learning and the intrinsic value of learning were measured by their response to items about enjoying the challenge of learning complicated new material, and their learning in a course being more important than the grade they receive. Although factors such as parents' education, highest degree planned, and mathematics and reading scores had a larger effect than in-college factors on students' interest in academic learning and the intrinsic value of learning, class-related experiences had a significant relationship to students' attitudes.

Attitudes were affected by learning experiences such as participating in class discussions, trying to see how different ideas and facts fit together, working on a paper or project that required integrating ideas from various sources, trying to explain material to another student, and doing additional reading on topics introduced and discussed in class. Ways of improving instruction by focusing on learning is the subject of the next chapter. The following examples show, however, that there are numerous instructional activities that involve choice, challenge, control, and collaboration, and consequently improve students' attitudes toward learning.

> It's the kinds of instruction students get, the kinds of relations they have with faculty, their interactions with peers, the value attached to learning on the campus, the opportunities that students have to become actively involved in what they learn, and in learning to work with a faculty member on a research project. Those are the things that make the most difference. That makes a good deal of sense; those are the things that are closest to student learning, to how students learn.

Programs that make more of a difference in students' learning are those that pay more attention to students, according to this respondent. This statement may appear axiomatic or even tautological, but the rationale underlying it is complex. The respondent continues by stating the limitations of what learning in a specific discipline can contribute to general learning gains in thinking.

> We know, for example, that discipline or academic major is not a very powerful predictor of learning achievement, learning gains, or cognitive skills. In terms of more generalized intellectual skills like critical thinking or analytical reasoning, there are not strong relationships between particular disciplines and greater gains in those kinds of learning activities. Mathematicians will do better in math reasoning but will

> be approximately the same in more generalized skills such as critical thinking ability as students coming from other disciplines. What that suggests to me is that the source of influence may be more contextual, within the program, rather than discipline-based, that it is less a matter of being in one discipline or another than being in a department that engages in learning-efficient or learning-effective activities, that creates a learning-effective environment, where students and faculty interact fairly frequently, where there is a mentor-mentee relationship in the upper-division years of their program, where the course work or the methods of instruction involve the students in projects, where they are required to do something more than sit still and take notes and then regurgitate it back afterward, where there is a climate in which faculty and students share an interest in learning and the activity of learning. I don't think any discipline has a corner on the market for those kinds of activities. A department that engages in those kinds of things is likely to produce greater learning gains in some generalized measure than the department that does not, regardless of the discipline.

Ways of inducing better learning include giving students opportunities for more small-group learning experiences, involving them in research at the undergraduate level, providing clinical supervisions, and long-term group learning experiences. In the next quotation, a respondent describes the small-group, intensive learning experiences engaged in at her university.

> A series of junior-year tutorials are teacher-selected, that is, the teacher can select any topic and declare that he or she is going to run a junior tutorial on that topic, and the tutorial must hold between five and eight students, no more, no less. The impetus was to provide students, particularly in large departments that might have large classes, the opportunity to be in a very small class with a professor. There has also been a push to involve undergraduates in science

more in ongoing research, and more of the faculty in the sciences have become involved in that effort.

Courses where small groups of students interact with a professor give students the opportunity for contact with professors in their area of expertise, the occasion and the necessity for student expression, and major responsibility for learning. This combination is highly motivating; since it combines the choice, challenge, control, and collaboration of situated motivation, it should promote self-regulated learning. The next example combines these factors with long-term learning in teams that simulate work experience in several ways.

We are looking at clinical courses, highly scientific courses, one-on-one supervision of students who are working in clinical settings, so teaching often involves small groups or one-on-one instruction in addition to large lectures on theory. Students are mainly working in small groups, doing collaborative learning between designers and directors toward creative products, which is a totally different learning experience than one has in other kinds of classes. In some cases, they are with the same group of students for three years total in the same classes with the same professor, so we have talked about trying to videotape the three-year sequence of change and growth that is documented there. Some of the professors will have taught intensively, intimately students for three years, every week.

Another example of long-term group learning occurs in a program of general education. General education was seen in Chapter Two as a way of bridging disciplinary boundaries. It is also a way of providing situated motivation and promoting broader abilities such as thinking and communication skills.

We have an interesting partnership with a university where they are remaking their general education curriculum. There are three pieces to their general education curriculum. The first is a year-long course in discovery, because their first goal is lifelong learning. Since they decided that discovery and inquiry were primary general education goals, they asked, "Why not start on that first, and let's do it in such a manner that will facilitate students' movement from their work environment to college?" Because they have a lot of commuting students, an approach that relates their home or high school environment to academic and social interaction in the academic environment is particularly salient.

The second piece is to look at course clusters they might design that would accomplish broad, general educational goals. If they want students to understand people of different cultures, as a general education goal they should have a course cluster that incorporates understanding one culture then another culture and some way of being transcultural. You have to have some depth as well as some transitional skills to accomplish that goal. Also, different people acquire the skills in that package in different ways, so they work collaboratively both in teaching and assessment to accomplish those things in each cluster planned.

The third piece of the curriculum involves converting the curriculum into a resource that is turned back into the local community through service learning. Students would go out to the environmental center each year as part of their course, gather data on water quality, come back and make recommendations. They would have a base of all students who had preceded them in looking at water quality or proposing a new area for investigation, but staying with that problem and therefore turning the university into a resource base with an environmental center to understand some of the dynamics that occur as development occurs around the area that is enclaved for the maintenance of the ecosystem.

The program displays academic and social integration, collaborative learning experiences, and faculty working collectively rather than individually. Intensive programs may, however, have hidden costs of other kinds. For example:

> I know that my students could perform better and might be quite willing to accept higher expectations if I gave them more tasks to perform, to practice, and gave them more feedback, more cycles. Where am I going to find the time to do that? What goes on in class is just a tiny part of it. Reacting to student work, constructing the tasks takes imagination and energy, and then reviewing performance and giving them enough constructive feedback so that they learn. But they won't learn from feedback; they'll only learn if they do the task again or a version of it again and get some more constructive feedback, cycle after cycle. That is very time-consuming.

Planning, evaluation, and intensive experiential programs engender high costs in time for faculty and for students. The effect, however, appears to be worth the effort. The common thread running through these examples of fostering student motivation is the process of inquiry. To situate learning, according to one respondent, inquiry has to be centered on the questions that arise in a field of study and the most appropriate methods for answering those questions.

> Fields of study are constituted by questions; you pursue an inquiry from a perspective; you utilize those methods that are more directly inclined to yield data that might be relevant to the question. We ought to be able to start from any course being offered by a department or unit and see that as a microcosm of the field of study that is formed around certain basic questions, which can then be related to any subquestion that is driving a piece of research. You ought to be able to move from the microcosm to the macrocosm through whatever world you inhabit, and you ought to be able to run it both ways. I think the notion of a field of study does that. I used to show a film that

> focuses on a lake in Canada of a young man and his dad fishing. There are no words, simply music. It focuses on the boat, then the two people, then the dad, then a mosquito on his hand, then inside the mosquito, then the molecular structure, imaging a variety of activity. Then it moves back the other way at a more advanced rate up from the mosquito to the boat, and it keeps on going to the planet and the graphic imaging of the cosmos. Then I say, "That's reality. We're going to cut it in the following way." I talk about how our class is going to take a slice out of that, but that is reality, from a spectrum of course work, associated with our university. The students are impressed with the kind of feelings they have about what the university deals with. That is what I want them to feel, but not only in my course, when they come to university.

Summary: Fostering Students' Motivation for Learning

The fact that postsecondary learning is qualitatively different from learning at earlier levels of education means students must invest personally in learning and be open to the changes that must take place in order to develop intellectually. Having only a percentage of committed students in a class limits professors, no matter how devoted to their discipline and to their students' learning, in the kind of learning goals they can achieve. If students are not committed to learning, they cannot become independent learners. If students do not see the relationship between understanding their field and gaining credentials in it, they will not be in a position to actively control and organize their learning.

Students who are more intrinsically oriented to learning use more cognitive strategies and perform at higher levels. Those who adopt a meaning approach to learning experience greater satisfaction in their learning, higher-quality outcomes and better grades. Academic tasks that motivate learning have four characteristics: choice, challenge, control or autonomy; and collaboration. At the institutional level, the most important way to foster student motivation for learning is to create a learning community, where students and their learning experiences are the focal point. Other steps include ensuring an advising system that works, rewarding faculty for effective advising, and rewarding programs in which students and faculty interact more frequently. At the program level, ways of inducing better learning include giving students opportunities for more small-group learning experiences, involving them in research at the undergraduate level, providing clinical supervisions, and collaborative learning over an extended period.

Benchmark Practices: Institutional Level

1. Create a learning community, where others are committed to learning success; make students and their learning experiences the focal point in university organization and policies and practices.
2. Ensure an advising system that works; provide a framework for faculty and reward them for effective advising.
3. Reward programs for paying more attention to students, so that students and faculty interact more frequently, where mentor relationships are established.
4. Consider work-study programs that allow students to integrate their learning.
5. Recognize time costs for planning, evaluation, and intensive experiential programs.

Benchmark Practices: Program Level

1. Provide students at entry to their studies with insight about their disciplines and about the nature of learning at the university.
2. Help students to set academic goals.

3. Help students to articulate their goals in a course and attribute success to their own self-efficacy.
4. Aid students in becoming self-regulated; tell them up-front what is at stake.
5. Foster the process of inquiry, in class and across disciplines.
6. Make students aware that the learning task requires thinking on their part; show them how to do that in the context of the course.
7. Give students a sense of the number of hours of studying required to succeed.
8. Provide small-group learning experiences—tutorials, undergraduate research, collaborative learning over an extended period.
9. Give students choice, challenge, control, and collaboration in their learning tasks.
10. Provide students with learning tasks that improve their attitudes to learning: participation in class discussion, projects, explaining material to another student.

5

Improving Instruction by Focusing on Learning

The design of effective instruction begins with determining the kind of learning desired. Supporting that learning means increasing general institutional knowledge about the optimum context for learning and about learning goals.

In an analysis of the place of teaching in the research university, Rhodes (1994) states that few universities have come to grips with what their graduates should know and what skills they should possess. He argues that the cognitive process of learning and the act of teaching need to be studied with the same creativity and professional intensity that we now devote to research. In order for this to happen, the development of intellectual independence (Baird, 1988; Barzun, 1993) must be highlighted as a general institutional priority.

Research in previous chapters shows that disciplines determine the parameters of knowledge, the theoretical or conceptual structures and the mode of inquiry that guide learning, and also that different disciplines espouse different learning goals. Second, a panel of experts in postsecondary education and a large sample of students identified higher-order thinking, that is, the ability to analyze, synthesize, and think critically, as the most important criterion, along with commitment to learning, for students. Research on students' orientations to learning supports this finding and suggests that students who seek meaning or deep understanding experience greater satisfaction in their learning and have higher-quality outcomes. Tying these findings together is the concept of *intellectual development as the pivotal learning* goal. The goals of this chapter are to examine the context for improving instruction by focusing on student intellectual development, instructional methods and strategies that aid this development, and the management of postsecondary learning.

The higher education literature suggests that students' conceptions of learning are mediated by how well professors communicate their expectations to students, foster higher-order learning in their classes, and evaluate it (Pintrich, 1987, 1988; Ramsden, 1992). Research on the learning task has shown that professors expect students to achieve higher-order learning outcomes in their courses (Donald, 1992a). In a series of studies on the development of thinking processes in postsecondary education, professors in different disciplines applied a working model of higher-order thinking processes to their courses to establish which thinking operations they focused on and developed in their courses. Although the professors came from representative disciplines in the physical and social sciences and the humanities, they had in common the use of these higher-order processes in their teaching, and they expected students to improve in their ability to use them as a result of the course. Promoting higher-order learning then begins with understanding how professors can communicate to students that they should be analyzing, synthesizing, and evaluating, as well as how students can be helped to evolve intellectually.

Providing a Context for Improving Instruction

One problem in fostering higher-order learning and intellectual development in universities is that the institutional environment often sends a different message. A respondent who is responsible for the learning environment in his university explained the problem in the following way:

> As institutions, we have to do a better job on being clear about what learning is. There is a whole lot that is going on in the institution that

people are referring to as learning that is really not. Are students learning when they cram for exams and take objective exams, and then go on to the next course where the instructor assumes that they have learned prerequisite material and makes a reference to the material and the students do not know what she is talking about? That is a function of a system that is memorization-based. Grades undermine the focus on learning, because a lot of people become expert in the discipline, not necessarily having had one course about how people learn or cognitively process information or any other aspect of teaching. A lot of what we call teaching here is simply transmitting information, and the responsibility for the learner to receive the transmission is placed totally on the student. When we were working on a new building, we had professors who wanted the podium farther from the students, which symbolically represents this issue: Is the professor's job to transmit information, or is it to facilitate the learning of all those in that environment? We need to get into the nitty-gritty of what all that means.

To change attitudes about learning, entrenched ideas about teaching and learning have to be examined. The cognitive dissonance created by showing that what professors want students to learn is incompatible with the instructional and evaluation methods they are currently using is a first step to improving instruction.

I have served on committees such as the instructional computing advisory committee to try to promote faculty use of instructional technology. In many places, instruction is by straight lectures, a lot of passivity relative to engaging the students in the process. A lot of factors contribute to that: the size of the classes, the culture of teaching with a lecture method history. Students also are resistant to new methods, because they have been acculturated to be passive so that they want their instructors to do everything, and the effort required is totally different in active methods. The way we could approach faculty on that is with the question, "What do you want your outcome to

> be relative to your learner? How would you describe the learner that you want to produce?" What they describe is inconsistent with the method they are using to teach the curriculum. I think they are starting to realize that more.

Changing professors', administrators', and students' perspectives on the pattern and constituent elements of the teaching and learning task may be difficult. Professors often perceive that they lack control over the learning climate and need to be empowered to deal with their students' learning problems. One approach is to bring teachers and students closer together so that instructors have a greater sense of who their students are.

> In the last thirty to forty years, the distance between teacher and learner has gotten greater and greater, and if you want to improve teaching and learning, you have to put students and teachers closer and closer together. The teacher can then make a much better assessment of what kinds of strategies and approaches are successful with particular students and vary his or her actions accordingly. All of my experience tells me that to the degree that faculty get to know their students as persons, they find teaching more satisfying. It's not just that students learn more and like it better if they know their teachers, but that teachers like teaching better if they know their students. That makes for expensive instruction, but it gets results. The inexpensive instruction we so often expediently practice today is a greater waste (indeed, I believe more costly), because it produces so little meaningful result. Its main product may be alienation.

Respondents across universities were grappling with definitions of learning and the responsibility of the institution and faculty for that learning. A variety of approaches, if not solutions, were proffered. Some respondents focused on supporting intellectual development. Others talked about responding to particular needs or using new technologies. One professor recognized the complexity of the learning situation today and the need to create opportunities for students to meet the challenge.

> We are approaching a time when being a jack-of-all-trades is probably more appropriate than being a master of one. Being a master of one and jack of many others is the way I would like to see my students leaving this place after four years. You have to have an appreciation for many more aspects of what you do and the ramifications of what you do than we had to have twenty-five years ago. So, one of the higher or larger challenges of higher education is to create the environment and the opportunities for students to explore a wider range of educational activity or involvement.

Instructional improvement then must focus on understanding how professors can foster higher-order learning and create a supportive learning environment in their classes. Aiding students in their approach to learning as an intellectual pursuit through optimal instructional methods begins with examining what learning goals we want students to have. As one respondent noted:

> I think that cognitive psychology has advanced on a steeper curve than we would ever have imagined. It should be possible to transform the conceptions of human cognition that we currently have into extremely effective understandings for subject matter specialists whose job it is to make their field comprehensible to students. I wish we could do better in the transformation of what we know. If we were to sit down and think about it, in two years we might.

Insights into student intellectual development, instructional methods and strategies, and the management of postsecondary learning have burgeoned in the last decade. To conceptualize instruction in ways that will support intellectual development, an important first step is focusing on the learner and specifying the learning outcomes the teacher wants to achieve.

Clarifying Learning Goals

Research on student learning has shown that students enter the classroom with misconceptions about the subject matter (Brown, 1983, 1984; Vaughan, 1977) and that students have varying perceptions of causality, stability, and controllability that affect their judgment (Russell, 1982), as well as varying standards about what constitutes knowledge (Ryan, 1984). Although 90 percent of faculty members report that they are solely responsible for setting the goals and content of their courses (Bergquist, Gould, and Greenberg, 1981), teachers often do not know what students actually learn in a course. Professors have been shown to overestimate their students' learning in a course by approximately 15 percent (Fox and LeCount, 1991).

Recognition of the nature of university learning comes late to many students. In ethnographic research on the academic life of students, participant-observers in introductory courses found that students' lack of academic confidence and learning goals and their limited preparation impeded the efficiency and effectiveness of student learning (Donald, 1992b). To illustrate, in an introductory psychology course, students tended to ask questions that exhibited their concern with making sure their understanding of the basic facts was correct rather than making new connections with the material. In small-group tutorials with teaching assistants, the students tended to take notes and occasionally ask for clarification. They did not use this time to analyze and synthesize the material; they were still trying to encode the basic course content. Students asked more questions when the subject matter was less scientific and more human interest oriented. The tutorial leaders contributed to this trend, as their eliciting of student responses and participation seemed to hinge on the content material of the chapters—the more scientific, the more the tutorial leaders lectured rather than analyzed.

The series of ethnographic studies on the academic life of students resulted in evidence that many entering university students do not conceptualize learning in a way that will aid them in developing higher-order thinking and reasoning abilities (Donald, 1992b; 1994). These studies suggest that rather than searching for meaning, many students conceptualize learning as adding to their store of factual knowledge. This finding is consistent with research on students' intellectual development during the college years (Baxter Magolda, 1992; Kitchener and King, 1990; Perry, 1970, 1981). Baxter Magolda describes four ways of knowing, beginning with absolute knowing, in which students receive and master knowledge, and proceeding to transitional knowing, in which students understand knowledge. Later in college, students reach a point of independent knowing, where they embrace and subordinate others' ideas, then a point of contextual knowing, when they integrate their own and others' ideas.

Of crucial importance for understanding how to improve instruction is what students expect of teachers because of their own conceptions of learning. Just under 70 percent of the 101 first-year students interviewed by Baxter Magolda approached learning in terms of absolute knowing, where learning methods focus on acquiring and remembering information, and evaluation is perceived as an opportunity to reproduce for the instructor what has been acquired. In this situation, students view the professor's role as one of communicating knowledge. The remainder of first-year students displayed a pattern of transitional knowing, in which students' investment in learning is dependent on how useful it will be in the future. Students then expect the professor to focus on understanding and the application of knowledge.

By the time the students had graduated four years later, the majority (57 percent) approached learning as independent knowing, with 5 percent having reached contextual knowing, and with none still conceptualizing learning as absolute knowing. Students at a point of independent knowing view knowledge as uncertain and expect instructors to provide a context in which to explore knowledge. Students who are contextual knowers recognize that some knowledge claims are better than others in a particular context, and they expect their instructors to foster learning environments that promote application of knowledge, evaluative discussion of perspectives, and critique.

The learning and instructional problem these findings reveal is that only when students develop a pattern of independent knowing can thinking for themselves become part of their role as learners, and only when they adopt a pattern of contextual knowing can their role as learners include thinking through problems. In their first year, according to the Baxter Magolda study, no students were operating in a pattern that included thinking for themselves in their role as learners; in their senior year, only 16 percent were thinking for themselves, and an additional 2 percent were thinking through problems. The task for instructors is then to take into account students' level of intellectual evolution, while at the same time promoting evolution toward independent and contextual knowing.

Strategies for Supporting Intellectual Development

At whatever level of intellectual development, students' preferences for teaching strategies are for active, connected, and challenging learning, described as making the classroom active, getting students involved, connecting learning to real life, and creating opportunities for mutual responsibility (Baxter Magolda, 1992). The first challenge for teachers is to develop flexibility of approach to the variety of learners in a class.

> Our students vary greatly in how they best learn. An exercise that advances the learning of student A bores student B, and so you need to present material in a variety of ways if you are going to challenge and involve all the students—A through Z—at a university. The mark of truly gifted teachers is that they have widened the natural range of skills first brought to bear on teaching a topic, widened the range of whom they can teach, and expanded the settings in which they

> can effectively work. The truly excellent teacher can teach nearly everybody—from novice to sophisticate—in a wide variety of settings, across the full range of his or her expertise. We must eschew thinking that one style of teaching fits all. We must be a great deal more flexible and personal in how we approach our students.

Advocates of active learning techniques base their recommendations on the powerful impact that these methods have on students' learning (Bonwell and Eison, 1991; Silberman, 1996). Strategies promoting active learning are comparable to lectures in promoting the mastery of course material but superior in promoting thinking skills and writing (McKeachie, Pintrich, Lin, and Smith, 1986). These methods also have been shown to better serve the needs of a significant number of students who do not learn well from lectures. Silberman prefaces his book on active learning with the observation that you can tell students what they need to know very fast, but they will forget what you tell them even faster. Methods of active learning range from team-building strategies and on-the-spot learning assessment strategies to modified lectures, class discussions, peer teaching, and independent learning. Bonwell and Eison point out that faculty members must begin the process of introducing active learning methods but that faculty developers and academic administrators are needed to support these initiatives, because they engender risk and may require different physical resources.

Throughout the interviews, it became clear that getting the message to students is essential if they are to become independent learners. In a series of examples taken from an economics course, the professor describes the process by which he attempts to help first-year students evolve, first from absolute knowing to transitional knowing.

> I spend a lot of time framing for students what I want to do. I want them to understand why I am doing what I do so that they can see there's a point to it, and it will take them someplace. In my first class,

> I go through who is responsible for what. I make the distinction between understanding things and learning. Understanding is like seeing the thread of the logic. I explain to them that I don't want them to learn lots of pieces of information and memorize all the definitions and graphs. I want them to deal with it as an integrated story that makes sense and says something interesting. Using a hammer and tool kit analogy, I say to them, "If you take shop class, you are going to learn how to hammer beautifully, but if you are just hammering nails, you won't have a lot to show for it at the end of the day. I want you to build a beautiful cabinet, to saw and hammer and know which one to use when. I want you to know all the tools, when to use them, and how to use them in concert."

In the first example, the professor has stated that the learning goal is not merely to memorize but to understand. He also provides students with a guiding analogy that compares the outcome of what he wants—synthesis, in the form of a cabinet, with what he does not want—rote learning, or hammering nails. The second example from this course describes a strategy for helping students evolve to independent knowing. In the example, the professor focuses on a strategy that he models for the students to aid them in becoming critical thinkers.

> In one of the very first lessons, I discuss two kinds of assumptions—maintained assumptions and those that are to be relaxed. The ones that we relax allow us to build in the complexity, because you can assume away a lot of complexity by saying there is no one else in the world. Then when you relax that assumption, you have to ask how we coordinate all of our choices. One of the things I point out is that every time you relax an assumption, you have to build a whole new vocabulary to develop these new ideas that you are allowing to impinge on your analysis. I tell them that this is all to help them think; we are going to relax some assumptions and see what the implications are. If the assumptions are not strong or don't seem realistic,

> there is a fundamental flaw in the foundation. At the end of the course, I return to those maintained assumptions, and I talk about the one I do my research on, assuming that people's objective in life is to maximize their utility, which eliminates questions of ethics. I talk about the limits of the model, because I want them to reflect on its weaknesses as well as its strengths.

The professor then provides an analogy for contextual knowing, inviting students to look at the big picture, to locate the subject in comparison to other social sciences. He lets students know how complex the learning task is but provides a concrete analogy that students can use to guide their learning.

> Comparing economics to other social sciences, I describe the social sciences as a tool kit, in which economics is the hammer. Then I say, "If you're a carpenter, you can't build anything without a hammer, but you can't build anything with just a hammer. Social understanding requires a hammer and a saw and plane and a level. For example, when you get to the concept of market power and social creation of power, that is a social process, so you have to understand sociology. Political manipulation affects markets."

The approach to students' intellectual development is consolidated when the professor explains to students that they must practice, apply, and synthesize in order to truly learn.

> I want them to understand how to use all these pieces and how to integrate them, . . . but to learn it means you have to . . . practice. I tell the class that they may understand when they leave the class, but they won't have learned it, because it's not part of their permanent repertoire; they can't pull it up when I ask them later to explain something. Learning it means you take what you understand, and you practice with it enough to make it part of your own.

> There are two things that I offer them for practice; one is "homework" every week. The other thing is the study guide that goes with the text book. The most common conversation I have with students who do not do well on the midterm . . . is about how to work through the guide.
>
> In terms of assessment, constantly in class I want to make sure that they understand, because if I lose them someplace I am not doing my job. There has to be constant self-assessment so that if at any point they do not understand, they can stop me. I also try to create a very safe atmosphere for asking questions. The first day of class, I tell them that one of my key objectives is to make them feel safe enough that at least once, every one of them will raise their hand to ask a question. I have a pretty good percentage who do.

The professor has now conceptualized and communicated to students how they should analyze and synthesize course material, how much work it will take, what strategies they should utilize in order to understand the course material, and how the students should assess their own thinking and understanding.

Introducing Students to the University

Programs designed for first-year students can focus attention on learning, may save many students from a negative learning experience, and can lead to a sense of renewal on the part of professors. First-year seminars have been used primarily to orient students to the university and provide them with challenge and support as they adapt to a more independent learning situation. Orientation programs for first-year students that develop study skills and learning strategies have been found to have a significant positive influence on social integration and subsequent commitment to the institution (Pascarella, Terenzini, and Wolfle, 1986). Developing specific courses and programs that meet particular learning needs, often oriented to the most heterogeneous group of students—those in their first year—is becoming standard practice.

> It makes sense to let students make the transition to a new environment by taking courses in their area of interest rather than bringing students into courses where they have no natural motivation and they have not done particularly well. Let them gain some success, make the transition, adapt to the environment, learn some things about how to learn that they may not have learned in the past. We now have a group that is looking at the freshman experience. Students who are identified as being at risk are in a course specifically identified for them called "Language, Learning, and Culture," which addresses those kinds of things and facilitates retention.

First-Year Seminars

These seminars and learning-to-learn courses are increasing retention rates in colleges and universities across North America. Although they take many forms, from small-group academic experiences to study skills workshops, they involve students, give them personal feedback, and provide them with a clearer sense of what postsecondary education is. In a survey of first-year seminar programs in American higher education undertaken in 1991, over seven hundred institutions replied that they either offer a special course for first-year students or were planning one for the next year (Barefoot, 1995).

The most common first-year seminars are college survival or student success courses. Content includes an introduction to campus resources, time management, study skills, career planning, and student development issues. Another format for first-year seminars, more likely to be found at research universities, is the academic seminar—sometimes interdisciplinary or theme-oriented, or part of a required general education core. These often include academic skills components such as critical thinking and expository writing. The seminars are most frequently designed as elective courses and can be taken within the student's field of concentration with normal credit given. One course objective is that explicit attention be paid to the development of thinking processes. Often, seminars are organized around central themes, with topics chosen for in-depth coverage or seen through an interdisciplinary lens.

Most first-year seminars limit enrollment to 25 students or less. The great majority (88 percent) carry academic credit toward graduation, although credit may vary from one to three credits (Barefoot, 1995). Usually, courses are taught or co-taught by faculty, but over half are taught or co-taught by student affairs professionals and one-quarter are taught or co-taught by upper-level undergraduate students or graduate students. Thus, the entire campus may be involved with the introduction of students to the learning community; campus support from students, faculty, staff, and administration for first-year programs is usually high. More often than not, however, first-year seminar instruction is not linked to academic advising. The phenomenon of first-year seminars is relatively recent—60 percent have begun since 1986—but the effect of the seminars in increasing retention, student satisfaction, and graduation rates appears to be sizable.

Gateway Programs

Making links with first-year students may require another level of organization within the university, at the professorial level. One example is a program that brings together professors who are responsible for the basic introductory courses around campus. The professors meet on a regular basis to discuss problems and perspectives on first-year students. One unpredicted outcome of the program was the effect on professors' attitudes and identities.

> There is a conversation among them about the early education of undergraduate students apart from their departmental hierarchies. That group has become more and more articulate about concerns that cut across departmental orientations. There is a developmental psychology that makes decisions and concerns about people at different junctures of their lives, freshmen, for example, very key. Freshmen in the college of engineering have a lot more in common with freshmen in the natural sciences or communications than they have with seniors in engineering. So, there are certain issues that ought to be

> addressed and certain ambiances that have to be encouraged. In the Gateway Program, faculty for the first time were involved in issues that were not exclusively informed by their participation in their discipline. This begins to create a sense of "team" on an individual campus. If anything is going to happen to change the ambiance on an American research university campus, it is to get them to say, "I do have a home here in addition to that home on the national and international scene in my society or my subfield."

The professors became spokespersons for students at large and were able to transfer their knowledge of the campus as a whole into their departments. This in turn alleviated departmental isolation. Another strategy for rendering learning central to campus life involves making residences part of the learning environment.

Faculty Fellows

Faculty on some campuses have elected to provide students with insight into the academic experience by moving offices and courses into residences, providing personal, readily accessible contact, and enlarging the learning experience to include co-curricular activities with mentors. One program was begun when the dean of students gave four senior faculty members offices in a residence hall, as well as their own department office. The objective of the program was to add an academic dimension to the living environment.

> We had office hours. I, for example, had posters of art work all over my office walls, and I taught a section of humanities in the lounge of the residence hall. That has expanded so that we now have fourteen Faculty Fellows, and we are in several of the residence halls and in the athletic department. We have a woman in a fraternity house and a man in a sorority house. We have a Faculty Fellow in the off-campus student center, we are now adding one to the Afro-American Cultural Center and one to the Hispanic Cultural Center, and by next fall Asian and Native American centers will have been added.

> What the Faculty Fellow is there for is to be available to undergraduates. Sometimes, they just want a totally private ear that they can talk to. I think the Faculty Fellow program has developed into what I like to think of as an agent for change on campus, in that, because we come from lots of different departments, and because we have developed a kind of collegial community among ourselves, we see the university from a slightly different perspective than most people do from within the departments, and most of us have agreed to do this because we like people and we tend to identify the problems in terms of the human dimension that the student and the faculty experience.

Here too, the effect of the program has been to produce a cross-disciplinary learning community among professors who are then able to provide special insight into student life on campus. The professors may design special activities that bring students into the learning community in a variety of ways.

> We have one Faculty Fellow from communications who takes his students out for runs. He has a mile run every year, and he gives them tee-shirts. We have a small operations budget, but we will buy tickets at a group rate to the local professional theater or the opera or the symphony and sell them to the students for even less than that, so for three dollars, a student can go to the opera, and the Faculty Fellows will go with them.
>
> Perhaps because we have been doing it longer, or by word of mouth, some students will bring their friends, and ask some of us to help them decide what they are going to do with their lives. Or they will come in and say, "I just got a letter from my mother, and my father has run off with his secretary, and I don't have any place to go for Thanksgiving, and what can I do? I don't even know who to ask if there's a place to stay on campus, and besides, this means I don't have any money for school. Shall I drop out?" When a student doesn't know where else to go, we have a tendency to get a lot of

> those. There is a student service center, and a counseling center, a health center, and the dean of students' office, but we are a front line, somebody that they have learned through the grapevine or through our advertisement simply is available. "Now that I'm willing to admit I have a drug problem, where do I go?" Sometimes it is just an informational kind of thing.

This example describes the role professors can play in creating a learning community that cares about students and provides them with a nonobtrusive but easily accessible source of guidance in their personal, as well as their intellectual, development.

Making Courses Relevant to Particular Groups of Students

The human capital argument, to ensure members of a society are as productive as they can be, prompts a learning community to attend to the learning needs of diverse groups. In the classroom, this means ensuring that examples are gender- and ethnic-inclusive or representative. One respondent provided the following explanation of how he responds to this instructional challenge in an economics course:

> A lot of the examples I use in class are minority- or women-oriented. In the textbook I wrote, every generic person is a "she" except for nurses, who are "he's." That helps me when I get to the point in the course when I talk about social expectations and how social processes develop expectations. If you make laws that say things are all equal, does that mean that everyone is going to have an equal position? Then we talk about how social expectations also have a powerful effect on people's choices, on who you are and what role you should play in society.
>
> I also use newspaper articles, mostly obituaries, about women who have made various choices in their lives—one a woman who

> went to law school in 1917 and who struggled through all the discrimination to make a career for herself, and then one of jazz musician Billy Tipton in the fifties, who died in the eighties. Then they found out that she was a woman. Comparing the way those two women made their choices is fascinating, and brings a lot of consciousness-raising to the class, but also from the point of view of economics has a lot to say about discount rates—Billy Tipton had a much higher discount rate, or she wasn't interested in taking the system on, and they took different kinds of risks. I think it's important to mix and match one's images.

The professor has taken a series of steps to confront possible prejudices and to provide real-life accounts of their economic effects. This approach is particularly important in disciplines where in the past, the climate for minorities has been chilly.

New Media and Technologies

The exploration of new media and new technologies for teaching and learning requires development time, as well as a change in attitude. Although computers and multimedia instructional technology have been available on campuses for some time, the percentage of faculty using them remains low (Albright and Graf, 1992).

The opportunity to incorporate instructional technology into courses needs to be highlighted and pedagogical links forged between learning outcomes and technology. One strategy is to start small. Several respondents in this study had begun to explore the use of e-mail in their teaching. Two of them talked about how e-mail can be used to improve learning.

> We are slowly moving into different ways of teaching, at least we are aware of them. On my desk right now is a manuscript that will eventually be turned into a brochure in an effort to offer to the undergraduates some way of communicating with the professor and with

> themselves other than the discussion group section. The great drawback of the discussion environment is that it tends to be dominated by very vocal people who are not necessarily the best informed, and puts at a great disadvantage people who cannot frame answers very rapidly and therefore tend to clam up. The proposed program will allow the discussion section to go on through e-mail. This will alert faculty that it is possible to go on conducting the teaching process outside of the lecture hall or the discussion section.

> Some of the work going on in communication studies is in computer-mediated instruction, where the students are learning how to use many of the computer modes and then are interacting with their professors on e-mail as opposed to office hours. We're seeing a great deal of experimentation in those areas.

Professors noted that students are often ahead of faculty in many ways, in terms of knowing how to use the media, understanding what it can do, and its potential. An administrator suggested that in-service preparation for faculty for media and technological changes in instructional strategies was essential to let them know the different kinds of media that are available and how to use them and incorporate them. There are also limitations in the extent to which courses can fit the new demands for computer technology. One professor who was using computer tutorials recognized the need to respond specifically to students' questions in order to motivate them and because the kinds of questions that students pose are infinite.

> There are a lot of things that are well designed, like the computer tutorial I do for my students, like an iterative feedback loop learning process, where you work through something, try it yourself on a screen, and then have immediate feedback. I don't think there is any substitute for a good teacher, who can respond immediately to, "I don't understand this. This is what I think I hear you saying. Is that right?"—the divergent response. "How do I deal with this particular

> statement on the question?" Maybe someday they will be able to design a computer that can think divergently about questions and how to respond to a question in a way that encourages the next question, that teaches everybody else around the question and that keeps things in focus. It's beyond the limit of our imagination to wonder what students are going to come up with; there is no way to anticipate, so how could you build it into the computer? One of the best responses you can give a student is, "I hadn't thought about it that way, that's very interesting." Computers can't capture that moment the way a thoughtful human being can. I think computers can be incredibly good as adjunct.

Respondents were also employing situated cognition and apprenticeship techniques in their programs. The theory of situated cognition states that students learn at a higher level if they are given problems or learning goals in a particular context so that they develop thinking abilities that can then be applied elsewhere (Brown, Collins, and Duguid, 1989). The concretization of the learning goal enables students to develop models and frameworks that allow them to operate at higher levels of understanding, in essence to become contextualized knowers by beginning within a context and then expanding from it. One respondent explained how media have been used to provide contexts for situated cognition. The learning situation then generalizes to occupying students' larger life space.

> We have a number of internship programs, student teaching programs across the schools, so that students are in the field doing a variety of things. In the television film department, people are doing a combination of production and theory working in studios. The school has a large, co-curricular set of activities. We will mount forty-three shows a year in the theater, eight main stage and the rest a variety of student-directed or professionally directed. We do a variety of films and videos each year, and many of the student activities are in

television and film production so that much of their hands-on learning will be reinforced in their co-curricular activities.

Many of our students get a chance to practice and to work with many different ideas and media. They are learning as much outside as inside the classroom in many circumstances. They are in the theater until three in the morning rehearsing or painting scenery. In that sense, our experience across disciplines is tied to the co-curricular opportunities that are driven by the curriculum. When we talk about learning, we can't just talk about classroom learning.

The most advanced exploration of new media and technologies for teaching and learning I found in the interviews incorporated a computer network into classroom design. In the design of the building, the main computer network (one of three) is a fiber optic backbone with fiber optics to the desktop. A professor who was involved with the design of the building talked about its now being a pit stop on the international information highway.

We have three especially designed electronic classrooms that allow teachers and students to tap into the local area network and into the Internet. We can bring in full motion video from the antenna farm at the School of Public Communication and distribute pictures and sound throughout the building on computers. It is a way for us to bring the world to our students in real-time using concrete examples.

An instructor can call up the Internet on the screen in the electronic classrooms. There are computer connections at the desktops; my teaching notes could be downloaded into student laptops for each day's class. We can store for seventy-two hours a dozen or so television transmissions. This allows me, while preparing for a class, to call up on my terminal the last seventy-two hours of television coverage on a topic, clip out parts that I want for my lecture, set it in the context I want, send it back down to the server, and when I walk down to the classroom, call it up as I lecture.

Active student learning is promoted by the capacity built into the system for students to use the information sources to explore and then build their own videotape reports on topics of their choice. The student is, in effect, invited to construct his or her own project using the multimedia facilities and broad-based information system. The professor explained:

> The more meaningful changes, however, will be in how students use all this, not how the faculty uses it. We consciously built into the building easy access to all the technology and network capabilities. We have what I call, quite flippantly, "multimedia romper rooms," where students have access to all this technology and learning capacity. For instance, if students at the time of the Persian Gulf War had wanted to understand how differently that war was portrayed around the world—how the Saudis and the Jordanians and the French viewed the war—they could have sat at the computers and seen it all. As an exercise then, they could produce a videotape that might be shown as a project or report. The point is that these new capabilities allow students to actively learn at their own pace for their own purpose. Moreover, around computers people tend to talk to each other a great deal more, and so you are trying to create not only a structure that allows for self-paced and self-directed learning but also builds a source of intellectual community.

Computer-assisted instruction and multimedia learning in this example provide students with challenge, choice, control, and the opportunity to collaborate. The development of courses that employ such methods requires support and a considerable amount of time. Resources, opportunities, and in-service preparation are needed to explore new technologies.

Summary: Instructional Practices That Focus on Learning

The first step in the design of effective instruction is to delineate the kind of learning desired. Because there is little general institutional knowledge about the optimum context for learning and about learning goals, several steps have to be taken to change attitudes about learning. Entrenched ideas about teaching and learning have to be examined, instructors need to have a more accurate sense of who their students are, and the complexity of learning must be recognized. Research on student intellectual development, instructional methods and strategies, and the management of postsecondary learning provide ways of conceptualizing instruction by focusing on the learner.

Entering university students do not tend to conceptualize learning in a way that will help them develop higher-order thinking and reasoning abilities; they lack academic confidence, which impedes the efficiency and effectiveness of their learning. Flexibility of approach to the variety of learners in a class is critical. To help students become independent, self-regulated learners, one instructional strategy consists of providing them with a guiding analogy for learning, then modeling the strategies they should utilize in order to understand and to assess their thinking. First-year seminars and programs that bring together professors who are responsible for introductory courses or groups of students have been used to elucidate appropriate learning goals and how students can meet them. Courses and programs can be tailored to meet particular learning needs. The new media allow students to learn in a framework of situated cognition, where they develop their understanding of a model within a context and then expand from it to other contexts. Advanced computerized classroom design and adjunct facilities allow students to construct their own learning project using multimedia facilities and a broad-based information system. In-service preparation for faculty for media and technological changes in instructional strategies is essential.

Benchmark Practices: Institutional Level

1. Involve the entire community in the process of improving instruction—administrators, faculty, staff, and students.
2. Examine entrenched ideas about learning and teaching, and

attempt to change attitudes to embrace a philosophy of intellectual development through active learning.

3. Develop specific courses and programs to introduce students to the university, for example, first-year seminars.
4. Establish gateway programs so that professors teaching first-year students have a reference group across disciplines.
5. Engage professors as Faculty Fellows as a front line for students.
6. Make courses relevant to particular groups of students by ensuring that examples are gender- and ethnic-inclusive or representative.
7. Provide development time, resources, and in-service preparation for faculty to explore new media and technologies.

Benchmark Practices: Program Level

1. Focus on the learner, and specify learning outcomes to guide students.
2. Begin by asking what students should be able to do intellectually, then decide how to best go about facilitating or fostering that kind of development.
3. Create an environment and opportunities for students to explore a wider range of active learning strategies.
4. Clarify learning goals at the beginning of the course and throughout it so that students conceptualize learning in terms of developing higher-order thinking and reasoning abilities.
5. Take into account students' level of intellectual evolution, then promote that evolution so that students become contextual knowers, integrating their own and others' ideas.
6. Use evaluation methods that promote the development of higher-order thinking.
7. Ensure that there is student feedback on their learning experiences so that instruction can be improved.

6

Providing Institutional Support for the Improvement of Teaching

To improve teaching practices, academic administrators have greatest confidence in recognizing teaching in career decisions, teaching award programs, and the evaluation of instruction.

In previous chapters, a number of benchmark practices for improving the learning environment have been recommended at the institutional level and at the program level. The implementation of these practices requires the expertise and initiative of academic administrators. In this chapter, the center of attention is more specifically the steps that academic leaders can take to support faculty and departments in the improvement of teaching and the institutional planning and organization required to do so. In their analysis of programs and practices that improve undergraduate education, Eble and McKeachie (1985) pointed out that administrative support is critical to the success of such programs. To determine the role of administrators in the support of improved teaching, a needs assessment was undertaken to establish deans' and department heads' views on the teaching improvement practices with the greatest potential for success in improving the quality of instruction in their faculties or departments (Donald, Flanagan, and Denison, 1993).

Needs Assessment for the Improvement of Teaching

In this study, since deans of faculties had primary responsibility for teaching, budget, and personnel decisions, we solicited their views of the potential of various teaching improvement practices to improve the quality of teaching. In decentralized faculties, that is, faculties composed of departments with considerable autonomy, department chairs' views were also requested. A questionnaire was developed consisting of forty-two teaching improvement practices in employment policy and practices, potential leadership roles for deans, department heads, and senior administration, specific practices such as orientation sessions for new faculty or for teaching assistants, educational events, teaching resources, grants and leaves, programs and committees, and formative and summative evaluation of instruction. The deans and department heads were asked to rate each practice to indicate their degree of confidence in the potential of the practice to improve the quality of teaching in their faculty or department.

The academic administrators had greatest confidence in the recognition of teaching effectiveness and its evaluation as a significant and integral aspect of all career decisions, consistent with research on the effect of rewards on teaching (Table 6.1). Most of the teaching improvement practices that received ratings of high confidence (in the top third and shown in the table) pertained to establishing and maintaining an institutional environment conducive to instructional improvement. These included employment policies, leadership by academic administrators, teaching award programs, and the evaluation of instruction. Deans and department heads gave high ratings to praising and rewarding good teaching, and to fostering teaching as an important aspect of academic responsibility. In spite of surcharged schedules and responsibility for budgets, programs, and personnel, the deans and department heads gave themselves major responsibility for fostering effective instruction.

They also assigned high ratings to a variety of preparatory or in-house practices, for example, an orientation program on teaching for teaching assistants, workshops on teaching methods for targeted groups, and follow-up on course evaluations to address specific teaching needs. The results of the study suggested a strong degree of consensus among deans and department heads about practices

Table 6.1. Teaching Improvement Practices in Which Deans and Department Heads Expressed Greatest Confidence

Teaching Improvement Practice	Deans (n = 11)	Department heads (n = 58)
Recognition of teaching effectiveness and its evaluation as a significant and integral aspect of all career decisions (for example, tenure and promotion)	8.4[a]	8.6
Department follow-up on course evaluations to address specific teaching needs	8.4	7.6
Workshops on teaching methods for targeted groups (for example, new faculty, graduate teaching assistants)	8.3	7.0
Good teaching praised and rewarded by deans and department heads	7.9	7.4
Teaching fostered as an important aspect of academic responsibility by deans and department heads	7.7	7.9
Consultation regarding course materials (outlines, readings, evaluation procedures) with faculty peers	7.6	5.9
Orientation program on teaching for teaching assistants	7.4	7.1
Mentoring programs that include activities such as peer consultation and faculty support systems for new professors	7.3	5.7
End-of-term formal student ratings of teaching for administrative purposes	7.3	7.2
Courses on university teaching provided for teaching assistants	7.2	6.5
Orientation session on teaching for new faculty	7.2	6.7
Teaching improvement activities given high visibility by senior administration in order to illustrate their importance	7.2	6.6
In addition to promotion and tenure decisions, regular review of faculty members conducted with regard to their teaching effectiveness	7.2	6.6
Hiring practices require a demonstration of teaching	7.1	6.6
Temporary workload reductions for the purpose of developing new courses or making major course revisions	7.1	6.6
Climate of trust that supports classroom observation created by deans and department heads	7.0	5.8

[a]Mean rating on a 10-point scale, ranging from 1 = least confident to 10 = most confident.

that create an institutional environment conducive to the improvement of teaching. If department heads were somewhat more modest in their ratings of most improvement practices, it could be that they recognized their immediate responsibility for putting the practices into place and the potential costs and impediments. Although the needs in individual faculties varied somewhat, the overall effect of the study was to establish directions for the institution as a whole. In this chapter, we therefore look at three of the practices the academic administrators considered most important—recognizing effective teaching and providing teaching improvement awards, increasing the dialogue on teaching, and preparing teaching assistants. The evaluation of instruction will be investigated in Chapters Seven and Eight.

Recognizing Effective Teaching

The most traditional method of honoring exemplary teaching is to make awards to individuals based on recommendations and teaching portfolios, but more recently group awards and teaching academies have been established to honor teaching (Svinicki and Menges, 1996). As of 1993, seven in ten institutions of higher education reported giving annual rewards to recognize outstanding teaching (El-Khawas, 1993). The kinds of awards included ceremonial recognition (69 percent), salary increases (45 percent), special funds (40 percent), and release time (26 percent). Where teaching is not honored by means of awards, the argument has been that it should be its own reward. This suggests that recognizing exemplary teaching is rewarding it extrinsically, thus confusing valuing and peer recognition with what is external to the academy. On the contrary, valuing and rewarding teaching is intrinsic to the academy's well-being. A variety of ways of recognizing teaching were described by the respondents.

One of the universities provides teaching improvement awards in the form of yearly grant competitions for faculty who want to redesign or design new courses through three different committees, one for departmental awards of $25,000 for three years, another for small ($3,000) awards, and a third for special awards for specific improvements in courses, for example, those that address diversity. One university sponsors teaching awards that recognize faculty from all disciplines who have contributed to teaching by sending them on a three-day retreat with colleagues from other universities to explore issues of teaching and learning. The result is a change in the campus ethos.

> The effect of the upper-level administration's . . . not only providing visible recognition but also dollars for . . . making improvements is . . . better balance in the research-teaching-service mission.

Of the more recently introduced kinds of recognition, group awards shift the focus of accountability from individual faculty to groups, especially departments (Edgerton, 1993). More to the point, they recognize the importance of department collaboration in teaching and curriculum planning for students' intellectual growth (Kahn, 1996). Another form of recognition is teaching academies—groups of faculty who are considered excellent or highly interested in teaching and who engage in advocacy, service, or advising on teaching matters in their institutions (Van Note Chism, Fraser, and Arnold, 1996). Members are nominated or selected based on their expertise and interest, and may, for example, attend opening convocations for first-year students, facilitate orientations for new faculty and teaching assistants, be mentors for graduate students, and sponsor talks by visiting scholars. One of the most positive effects of a teaching academy is similar to that of the gateway program for professors of introductory courses; it becomes a community of merit, offering opportunities for interdisciplinary contact, sharing of ideas, and leadership.

In a set of guidelines for exemplary programs, Svinicki and Menges (1996) point out that the structure of a program to honor teaching conveys important messages about an institution's teaching standards. Programs that honor faculty for their teaching may revitalize senior faculty, inspire junior faculty, and invigorate the scholarly life of the academy. Svinicki and Menges suggest that programs should be grounded in research-based teaching competencies and should recognize all significant facets of instructional activities conducted by the faculty. Assessment practices to select candidates should be reliable and valid, employing multiple data sources, multiple measures, and consistency over time. They register two cautions—to reward collaborative as well as individual achievements and to ensure that those who have been honored continue to contribute to the development of others as models and mentors. Other important criteria for programs are that they contribute to collegial responsibility for promoting exemplary teaching, encourage self-reflection about wise teaching practices, and are open to scrutiny and change in accordance with new conditions. First and foremost for teaching award programs, however, is that they are consistent with the institution's mission and values, and communicate those values to the community.

Increasing the Dialogue on Teaching

Because teaching is a complex art, and postsecondary learning is beginning to be recognized as equally complex, establishing opportunities for academic staff to engage in reflective practice on learning in their courses and in instructional problem solving is a crucial step for a learning community. For example, Dinham (1996) suggests that knowing the program context for teaching now requires detective work to understand students' prior course work and the nature of courses that will follow, yet this knowledge is essential for effective course planning. Dialogue is needed to establish course and program context. More personally, establishing a teaching style that matches a professor's proclivities to course content and students' learning styles is a lengthy process. Dinham recommends finding a good mentor to aid in understanding oneself as a teacher.

One of the most supportive approaches for improving teaching and learning is to create meeting places for conversations about the learning process. Sometimes, these take the form of weekly or biweekly discussion groups, or week-long workshops for professors to discuss their teaching ideas and concerns and to provide support for teaching changes they want to implement during the year. These sessions also allow small groups of professors to investigate particular approaches to curriculum and instructional techniques. One respondent explained why dialogue is so important:

> A growing dialogue on teaching and learning issues, an intellectual conversation, promotes the idea that considerations of teaching and learning are not just considerations of technique, although techniques are part of the conversation, but are much more extensive—questions of how human beings learn, what it is we want them to learn, epistemological questions about what constitutes learning in a given discipline or generally, what thereby constitutes an education, a particular curriculum.

A dialogue that arose at one university concerned the question of student responsibility. The next two quotations show how interactive sessions can be used to deal with sticky or stressful issues.

> We talk about it not being a unilateral process, that it's a multilateral process, and that students have to assume some responsibility if not a lot of responsibility for the learning that goes on. We try to model methodologies that will involve the student more in the learning process rather than be passive receptors of the learning process. So, in the workshops, seminars, and programs that we sponsor, we try to model the techniques that we feel will enhance student participation in the learning process. We feel it's hypocritical to go in and talk to faculty about involving the learner in the learning process and to lecture at them for two hours. Therefore, we try to create interactive experiences where faculty actually go through the process of using new methodologies so that they develop a certain comfort level, and they are more willing to take a risk of using them when they go back

> to the classroom. We find that the biggest thing to overcome with faculty is the fear factor. We finally get them to explore "What is the worst possible thing that is going to happen to you if you do this and it falls flat on its face." We find out that sometimes the fear is much greater in their minds than what actually the consequence will be. Once we begin to get beyond that, the faculty are more receptive to trying something in the classroom.

This quotation focuses on steps that can be taken to help professors try new teaching methods in a supportive environment. The next quote describes strategies for eliciting feedback from students about the teaching process.

> I have asked faculty members in sessions, "If you were to see a classroom of bored-looking students, how would you respond to that?" Most faculty say that they would not respond; they would just keep doing what they were doing. When I ask them why they would not respond, they reply that they don't know. I then ask them what would happen if they said to the students, "It appears to me that you are all looking bored. Tell me why"? and ask them what kind of answer they think they might get back. One professor said to me, "The students might say that you're a boring lecturer or that this is the most boring course I've ever taken." Then I said, "Beyond that, if we were to look at that as an information-gathering opportunity and you heard that, that is the entree to getting students to assume some responsibility for their learning by asking them, "What makes this boring? What are other ways we could deal with these concepts in a more interesting, energizing, dynamic way?" and have them be partners in the process of determining what that is.
>
> My perspective about it, but I'm a risk taker, is that if what I ask them and the possible response to that is short of physical harm to me, I will try it, and try to get them to move at least an incremental step in that direction. A faculty member told me once, "I was using this technique at the end of the lecture where they would write a

> question on a card and hand it in to me. They were doing this at the beginning of the semester, and now I'm not getting many of those. Why do you think that is?" I replied, "Have you asked the class why that is?" He had not thought of that. There is a minimum dialogue with the students, who are the very best ones for helping you to know what will work.

Course Design

Dialogue is also used as part of the creative process in course development. A faculty developer describes how he works with professors to optimize the course design process.

> When we start a project here, we say, "Let's forget about evolving what exists. If you had the best possible world, what would it look like, and then see how close we can come." It is a very exciting process. As a result, we turn out courses and programs that often look significantly different. There are all these roadblocks that are quite often as much imagined as real. We try to get out of that restrictive mental set right from the beginning. One of the advantages of being outside the discipline is that we can ask the tough questions and not be a content threat to faculty. That is a key role of the developer. I and others on our staff have worked on courses where by the time we were done, the faculty realized that there was no relationship between their major goals and the way they were presently assessing students: the two were often mutually exclusive, and it was a much more sophisticated type of goal that they had.

Because the course design team starts by considering the ideal learning outcomes, these become the criteria for success and guide the design process.

Workshops and Seminars

Faculty development workshops and seminars often instigate dialogue. Over the years, they have had a wide range of objectives, from learning a common vocabulary for discussing teaching, mastering specific communication skills, developing course objectives, or analyzing teaching values (Levinson-Rose and Menges, 1981). Usually structured to respond to a particular need, our respondents had designed them to focus on special topics ranging from critical thinking skills to how to deal with cheating in the classroom, the use of multimedia, or integrating diversity-related issues into teaching.

> We did a workshop last year, for example, that dealt with the new copyright laws, and that was very well attended. We offered a two-part seminar and workshop on critical thinking in which we brought in faculty and people who are knowledgeable on campus about critical thinking theory.

In this workshop, on-campus experts acted as resources of knowledge and experience, a strategy that empowers faculty across disciplines.

> We brought in psychologists, cognitive theorists, people from education and the medical school, so we presented a multidisciplinary panel. They each presented a very brief five-to-ten-minute overview of their field and what it says about critical thinking, and then the audience, which was standing-room only, were allowed to raise issues and ask questions. We videotaped it, and it is part of our videotape library of people on campus or who have come in to speak on our campus on topics ranging from humanities to the university in the twenty-first century.

In a more formalized version of dialogue, a prestigious series on teaching, supported and endorsed by the president's office, has been designed to feature outstanding scholars from other universities who address teaching and learning issues of broad concern. The addresses are infrequent, once or twice a year, and are videotaped so that they can be used at later dates. This focuses campus attention on instructional improvement and provides a legacy of ideas for improvement.

Preparing Teaching Assistants

Teaching assistants (TAs), usually graduate students, are accountable for between one-quarter to one-third of undergraduate instruction in many institutions (Nyquist, Abbott, Wulff, and Sprague, 1991). TAs may have varied functions, roles, or duties depending on the department or course. Some students grade papers or are laboratory assistants, while others teach tutorial sections or lead discussion groups. Programs for teaching assistants are as diverse as the needs on individual campuses. However, some instructional duties can be generalized across departments and campuses and require knowledge about course planning, teaching strategies in large and small groups, and the evaluation of learning and teaching. Microteaching is often used to provide practice and the opportunity for self-critique of presentation and discussion leading skills (Centra, 1993; Levinson-Rose and Menges, 1981). These skills may be developed in courses, orientations, or programs.

The importance of TA programs becomes evident when one considers the large numbers of students who participate in them. In some instances, the programs have served a wider purpose of building a learning community and giving graduate students a more integrated role in it. The developmental process that led to the program at one university was the result of a need to improve teaching and learning at the undergraduate level but focused in the beginning on graduate students' needs. According to a senior administrator,

> You try to say, "We are going to have to modify the activity of our undergraduate classrooms, to get our faculty to demand more of students, but in order to do that we are going to have to approach something other than the faculty." We started with Graduate Studies

to create a teaching assistant program. There were a number of reasons. Personally, there is no more alienating, lonely, difficult experience than making a transition into graduate studies; it's what you really want to do, but when you do it, the very things that impressed you about professors and wanting to take responsibility for a field of study seem unattainable. When you get into seminars, you realize how little you know, how poorly prepared you are. Professors seem, even though you have the intimacy of the experience, further away. It's very difficult. The only thing that can make it absolutely worse is to be put in an undergraduate classroom at the same time, unprepared, unable to respond to real live human beings who are asking you questions about the field, in a way that you would like to respond.

In 1987, the student newspapers were running editorial after editorial attacking the TAs, and I figured that what they were saying about TAs could be said about half the professional teaching corps. We had no sense of community or preparation at the graduate level. Now, if you are ultimately going to change the academic climate, you have to change behavior in the classroom. But you just don't go to the faculty and say, "You're going to have to change your ways." You have to build a sense of community where people care about the stewardship of fields of study. We wanted to get some people to focus on the well-being of graduate students. The reason that we started there was that there was not a lot invested in the care and feeding of graduate students. You now see the mentoring relationship in departments for graduate students, and once the mentoring juices begin to flow, they nurture the future of our fields of study in the people who are committed to the fields of study and hence sustain and maintain the quality of the field.

The entire campus became involved in the preparation of the graduate students as teaching assistants. The rationale is clear: teaching and learning are central to the university community, so everyone needs to be a member of it. Graduate students are often focused on their research, knowing that the research thesis is the ultimate goal of their studies. In this university, their campus life was expanded to include a broader sense of scholarship as part of their experience. A starting place for TA training is an orientation session.

Orientations

Orientations are now often required as university policy, and they may take place at various times in the calendar year but usually at the beginning of the semester. They require considerable planning and evaluation of the effects in order to meet a variety of needs. Orientations of several days to a week are most common, although some are longer and begin in the summer. At one of the larger public universities,

> TA orientation takes place each fall, spring, and summer over a week-end, with the largest program in the fall when six hundred to eight hundred TAs go through the two-day board of regents' required orientation.

The variety of TA needs can be responded to by building in a broad range of activities. In this program, they are further differentiated into levels to accommodate the amount of experience TAs have had. General sessions are supplemented by more focused department sessions.

> We have tried to design it to be very interactive; we have breakout sessions so that the TAs can choose from twenty to twenty-five sessions at any given time. We have spent three years trying to figure out exactly what would be the most beneficial for TAs. This time, we are going to do something different: we are going to have tracks for inexperienced and more experienced TAs, because that is one of the complaints we have had in the past. One-third have had a fair amount of experience; two-thirds have very little, so we have sessions like "The First Day in the Classroom" that are very popular. We have personal and professional development topics.

The organization put in place to deliver TA orientation can be extensive and requires coordination across departments.

> We have a registration session and try to cap each section at twenty-five, because we want to provide as much opportunity for interaction in the sessions as we can. Friday afternoon includes a sign-up session of about an hour. We have well-developed materials that support the process, and we set up the senior ballroom in the student union with tables all along the perimeter. Everything is ordered by number, and people are instructed in the morning to go through the breakout matrix and use a little form to select what they want, then circulate around the ballroom signing up on the sign-up sheets on the table. On Friday afternoon, particular departments on campus, for example, English composition (which has one hundred TAs), math, and chemistry have their own sessions, which are coordinated with the overall orientation. We have required sessions on diversity exploration, a two-hour interactive-reflective workshop with twenty students per section, and we have training processes for that. We spend a lot of time in the summer preparing and producing a teaching resource book.

An additional step in the organization of TA activities is conducting tests for oral communication. Establishing a climate of acceptance or openness to different styles of communication in the university is the other side of the coin.

> We do a great deal of work with our TAs, and they have to go through a "Speak" test; they cannot be in the classroom if they do not get a fairly high score, although they can grade papers. We monitor that closely, and the complaints are pretty low, but we still have a few. But a lot of times it's freshmen from a rural area who have not been exposed to different accents; it is a big shock, but eventually they get used to it, and it's part of expanding your world: people from Georgia don't talk the same as people from Boston.

Preparing graduate students to deal with less sophisticated undergraduates and ensuring that they themselves meet standards for oral expression are basic requirements of universities with diverse student populations. Orientations are often the first step of a longer program. The one described next is the consummate TA program.

TA Program

This program begins with a summer orientation for some 850 teaching assistants, of whom 300 are new to university teaching. As part of the program, an English oral language course provides students with an intensive year of classroom and laboratory experience to improve their oral communication skills. The TA program, with its own administrator, works in partnership with sixty academic departments that appoint teaching assistants and associates to provide professional development seminars on major topics such as the teaching portfolio, evaluating teaching, and responding to student writing across the curriculum. There is also an outstanding TA awards program and a teaching consultation service.

> In an all-university, twelve-day summer orientation held in August, the general program, which is mandatory, consists of four days of large-group seminars led by faculty members on topics such as "Ideas for an Effective Presentation," "Diversity in the Classroom," and "Leading a Discussion." In small-group workshops led by twenty-four teaching fellows who are outstanding, experienced TAs, microteaching is used, and specialized teaching situations are discussed. The international program consists of five days and includes intensive language testing, practical assistance on housing and banking, and general sessions on topics such as American students and culture shock. An American family evening introduces each new international TA to a university-affiliated family for dinner and a relaxing evening. A three-day departmental component introduces TAs to department curricula and practices and provides initial orientation to assigned teaching duties.

An extended program provides graduate students with supervised long-term training to be college or university teachers when they complete their graduate degrees.

> In conjunction with individual academic departments, the TA program received external funding to develop three new initiatives. First, the "Faculty Teaching Mentors" seminars consist of an annual intensive summer workshop held at the university's conference center, where participants explore ways that graduate students in their disciplines or professional fields might be more fully prepared to join the professoriate. Four follow-up seminars advance the dialogue. Second, teaching associates are specially qualified graduate students with at least one, but usually two years of experience as a teaching assistant. They are assigned to more advanced teaching apprenticeships, which typically include holding primary responsibility for teaching an undergraduate class under the supervision of a faculty teaching mentor. A teaching certificate is given to students who have acted as a teaching associate, taken the professional development seminar, and created a portfolio of teaching accomplishments; the certificate attests to their ability to take on a teaching role after graduation. This program has become a recruiting advantage for graduate students, because the greater part of them see themselves as becoming teachers in the colleges and universities after graduation.

TA Training in One Department

An example of how the TA program operates in one department was given by the professor responsible for it.

> In biology, we have about twenty-two TAs who get a set of teaching notes, teaching resources, and so forth. We have regular meetings for new TAs. We also have a peer videotaping program; every TA is assigned to another, and they videotape each other and critique each other.

In the introductory course, we use an audio tutorial approach so the lab is open seven days a week; we have tapes to accompany the labs—a multi-method approach. The TAs instruct in the laboratory, teach the recitation or discussion sections, and I give lectures. In a recitation, students go over things, they have discussions of material that is on the tapes, and quizzes, preparation for exams; it is a class to highlight, review, reinforce. The lectures are designed to update things; I tell them about what happened last week. We have a set of objectives for the course, helpful hints, and class observations and critiques by students in a teaching methods course. Every Sunday, I do a "Bionews" bulletin to keep everybody up to date.

The teaching associates are more experienced TAs who may elect to get a university teaching certificate when they graduate. I set up the review system for that. We have a faculty mentor committee that makes policy and is also a steering committee that approves new associates and reviews portfolios. The teaching associates are assigned as personal mentors to new TAs. They may also teach several lectures in a course for a major professor who is their mentor, or they may teach enrichment sections to students in second semester who have demonstrated that they are good in first semester. The teaching associates develop the syllabus in conjunction with a faculty mentor in an area of expertise they are developing and then teach a course ancillary to the main course, so for example, they might teach a course on genetics or ecology.

You have to volunteer to be a teaching associate. The load is reasonable: they have two hours of recitations in two classes of twenty-five, about four hours of laboratory supervision each week, and they have to proctor exams. They feel the time pressure, but we handle it flexibly. We have an administrative assistant who is there all day long to help them out, and we provide them with all kinds of resources. They all have a set of overhead transparencies, video cameras, films, and a lab person to help them. We have an annual TA appreciation party at my house; we have a little family here; it is a very healthy

> relationship with the TAs. They are very dedicated, they like teaching, and they have very positive views about teaching.

Many of the steps taken to honor teaching, increase dialogue about it, and to prepare the future professoriate require extensive organization and expertise. Most often, these are supplied by faculty and instructional developers who are members of teaching and learning centers.

The Role of Teaching and Learning Centers

Three of the four universities in the study of the learning environment had dynamic teaching and learning centers. Teaching centers serve principally as resource centers, introducing new developments in postsecondary education to the university. Often, centers are expected to offer services and support to faculty in course planning, instructional methods, program development, and evaluation, all rated highly by administrators as teaching improvement practices. Centers serve as clearinghouses for projects and new initiatives—for example active learning and problem-based learning—and encourage and support department or faculty-based projects. Centers may produce newsletters, fund projects, or promote excellence in teaching. They also conduct research relevant to teaching and learning. To fulfill their multiple mandates, center members are professors or faculty developers and tend to function as consultants and researchers, offering orientations, formal courses, instructional groups, workshops and seminars, and group and individual consultations.

The centers in the universities were engaged in a variety of services and projects, including the training of teaching assistants and future professors. Some centers are responsible for providing evaluation and audiovisual services; some extend their mandate to classroom renovation and modernization, to ensure that classrooms meet instructional needs.

Assisting Professors To Analyze Their Teaching

The most widely used method of improving teaching is to work individually with professors to examine ongoing teaching, then help them make changes. To do this, microteaching is often used. Microteaching, which uses brief teaching sessions that are videotaped and then reviewed, began to be applied in universities in the seventies as a method for training teachers in presentation skills under less complex conditions than are usually found in conventional classrooms. In the process, feedback, diagnosis, and reflection with possible representation help professors develop a sense of how well their chosen instructional methods work. The process also allows them to try out alternative methods in a supportive climate. Research on microteaching has shown that participation in such sessions produces desired changes in behavior and higher subsequent ratings from students (Dunkin, 1992). In our week-long workshop on course design and teaching, microteaching is rated as one of the most productive and preferred methods of improving teaching.

A modification of the microteaching procedure is to videotape a class, at times supplementing this information by collecting student rating information on specific classroom behaviors. The information is then analyzed, and the professor, frequently with the help of a consultant, decides what steps should be taken to optimize instruction in the class. At one of the centers, a similar procedure had been implemented.

> The center helps individuals collect information about their teaching so that they can look at what they are doing, thoroughly, systematically, and thereby empower them to make decisions about what they are doing or might be doing, to help them gather the kind of information that would be helpful to say, "I don't want to keep on doing it in this way, I want to make some changes." We do that in a variety of ways, the most famous being the videotaping service. It is a standard process. We offer people the opportunity of having their classes

> videotaped, then we give them the videotape along with a viewing guide and an invitation to give us a call. The viewing guide incorporates a lot of things from the various experiences.

The role of the center in this instance is one of formative evaluation of teaching. Methods of evaluating teaching for purposes of improvement will be discussed in greater detail in Chapter Eight. In considering the institution of a center, however, assistance in course improvement to faculty members continues to be one of the most generally found objectives. Teaching centers frequently support dialogue on teaching and learning by providing conversation spaces. One center contains an open, computer-based library, quiet meeting rooms, and an atmosphere of welcome.

> A growing collection of articles, books, and videotapes is indexed in a computerized database in the two computers in the library, and faculty can come and look for particular things or, as is more frequently the case, we can search for things and circulate those items and get people to begin to read some of the literature on teaching and learning.
>
> A lot of activities come out of the focus in departments on teaching and learning issues, and the question that arises, quite naturally, is, "Has anyone written anything on this that would be helpful as we begin our deliberations?" We make recommendations on articles, chapters of books, things that come out of particular disciplines, from research on teaching and learning, and from scholars who teach, which in turn might be influenced both by their own experiences and their own exploration of the research on teaching and learning.
>
> One example is getting people to explore literature from one discipline to another, for a history professor to look at a piece that might have been generated by a physicist. To illustrate, a chapter from a textbook on how to teach physics is on fostering critical thinking skills, and it is quite provocative.

Orientation for New Faculty

A teaching improvement practice that meets with considerable approval from academic administrators (ranked eleventh out of forty-two by deans and department heads) is an orientation day for new faculty held at the beginning of the fall term. On the agenda are issues related to teaching, such as course preparation and course evaluation, and more general issues concerning academic policy, faculty benefits, and services. Newly appointed professors are introduced to the larger university environment; they can meet senior administrators and develop a sense of the university community.

We hold our orientation at the beginning of term in the Faculty Club and intersperse sessions on teaching and learning (in the morning) and research with general university policy and services (in the afternoon). Lunch is served at the Faculty Club to introduce new professors to the campus meeting place; campus tours are available, and the principal hosts a reception at the end of the day to which all deans are invited to meet the new faculty members. The intention is to begin dialogue about teaching and learning early. At one of the campuses in this study, new faculty were invited to a day-long workshop, with senior faculty invited at various times during the day to enrich the discussion.

> That was a major focus to begin to introduce very broadly the idea of workshops, of faculty getting together and actually talking about teaching and learning issues, and that there was something substantive to talk about, that it was not just simply a matter of "being full of your subject." As a result of that effort, we have begun to get an increasing number of departments and schools asking us to do departmental workshops, some of them a direct result of doing the new faculty orientation. The chairs of those departments inviting me to come to the department said, "You know, our new faculty member has urged me to do this because he or she was so impressed with the workshop that went on in September."

The Role of a Center in University Policy Making

Although the primary mandate of most centers is to provide service rather than to set policy, when they find areas where policy is lacking, center members may provide recommendations to decision-making bodies in the university or may institute them. For example:

> We get into issues involving curriculum, mentoring, and supervising of graduate teaching assistants in an advisory capacity. Because we are involved on a daily basis with these issues, we find where the policies are not in existence, and then we send recommendations to the appropriate administrator. We have an instruction and curriculum committee that operates out of the university senate, and we work with them. We also have a university teaching advisory committee made up of faculty that deals with a variety of questions and issues.

The teaching and learning centers in this study were involved with policy making at various levels. The director of one center had initiated studies that led to the development of the teaching assistant program, provision of assistance for course development, and changes in evaluation procedures in his university. Another had chaired the university committee that changed the ethos of his research university, persuading it to pay greater attention to teaching. The first item on the agenda during my term as director of the center at McGill University was to establish a representative university-wide committee on teaching and learning and to work with it to produce a statement on the university's commitment to effective teaching, so that it could be approved by senate and become university policy. In each of these examples, the director was a faculty member who was in a position to affect policy and practice in the university.

Resources Needed by a Teaching Center

It is increasingly acknowledged that centers for the improvement of teaching are cost-effective and in fact require a minuscule percentage of the teaching budget (Newman, 1988), usually far less than the infrastructure costs required to support the research office in a university. Teaching centers are small compared to university research centers on the whole, consisting of a director and a few faculty members, but they tend to have extended networks. Some centers are funded partly to provide service and to conduct research, with the remainder of funding provided for teaching in a higher education program. Centers depend on a combination of resources, including a hard money operating budget, a small capital budget, research funds, and often funds from a foundation. All of the centers in this study have external funding for research projects; one was developed with funds from the Kellogg Foundation. The director of one of the teaching and learning centers explained the size and complexity of funding for such a center.

> There are charge-backs from room rentals to outside groups, the rental of audiovisual equipment to off-campus groups, and test scoring and services that we charge departments for. The center has videotaping capabilities and either reproduces the videotapes or helps people in videotaping programs, and there are charges for that. Part of the money comes from the provost's office, but the main budget comes from the Vice Provost for Arts and Science and Undergraduate Education. The operations budget runs close to $200,000, not including the auxiliary budget or staff salaries and benefits.

Human resources are more scarce; ways of linking faculty to the centers are needed to support a teaching and learning dialogue. To accomplish this, another university instituted endowed teaching professorships, as the director of the center explained:

> Right now, we have six, and eventually we will have ten or fifteen fellows of the center, the first endowed, named professorships created by this university that solely recognize teaching excellence at the undergraduate level in the six undergraduate schools. The appointment

> is for three years and includes a special stipend, equivalent to an administrative stipend. Various schools and colleges have created additional teaching chairs so that there are now fifteen to sixteen such chairs around the university that recognize primarily or exclusively teaching excellence as a basis for appointment. They are all rotating chairs, for a period of three to five years.
>
> We carefully define how such teaching excellence will be measured. We don't want to take people away from teaching, but we don't want to put more burden on them. By very deliberate design, I am not involved in the selection of these professorships. That is done by a universitywide committee of faculty on which the senior fellow at the center sits. Some of the other professorships are located in the graduate or professional schools, for example, the medical school and the law school. We want to appoint them as fellows at the center as well, so that there will be a great deal of interaction.

The role of the senior fellow at the center is important for providing support and guidance to younger colleagues.

> I am a friendly viewer of other people's videotapes, of either their discussion sections or their lectures. There are units within the university that require all their TAs and their new faculty to videotape at least one of their performances during the first quarter that they are here and bring it over and let the center review it with them. This last fall quarter, I had six or seven of them come over. We try to encourage anybody, any young professor or instructor who feels that he or she is having trouble communicating. We offer them free videotaping, then they bring the tape over, and the individual and I sit and listen to it and talk about it.

Centers cannot accomplish all that needs to be done to improve the teaching and learning climate. They can serve as focal points, responsive to campus needs and, with sufficient critical mass, to accomplish many organizational and educational tasks, but there are other tasks that require administrative line decisions. An example from one of the campuses describes the enlightened role that administrators can play in rationalizing the teaching function.

Administrative Strategies That Support Student Learning

As a philosophy for improving teaching, an associate dean of a social science faculty described the changes being made in his faculty in order to promote learning. His strategies include decreasing class size but also recognizing the need for efficiency and effectiveness by reducing the number of low-enrollment courses and increasing the teaching load of professors who have elected to publish less. The message here is that focusing on teaching requires adaptation on the part of faculty and administration.

> As a teacher, I think of myself as a coach. Good teaching in a classroom is principally about motivating students and showing them efficient information-acquiring and information-organizing techniques; it involves, perhaps surprisingly, very little information transmission. You never play "the game" for your students; you show them how to block and tackle, to use an American football metaphor, and you then provide a supportive environment for them to go out and block and tackle on their own. If you look at most coaching, it is very labor-intensive; the student-teacher ratio is always small. With some quite clear and defensible exceptions, I seek to drive down the average class size as much as I can—but with the same size or slightly smaller size faculty.
>
> One way to achieve this result is to reduce modestly the number of graduate courses taught every semester and to reduce the number of courses taught to too few people, at both the undergraduate and graduate level. The casualties here are usually highly specialized courses on the periphery of both the graduate and undergraduate curriculum. And finally, to achieve this result, we all must teach a bit

> more and publish a bit less. This redistribution of efforts is encouraged in a number of ways. To give just one example, professors are advised to teach three instead of two courses per semester if they are not continuing to be productive publishing scholars, have the capacity to be good teachers, and desire to continue to be considered for salary increments. I also believe more generally that over the long run, American higher education cannot continue to raise prices without raising the standard teaching load for many faculty who currently enjoy a two-two, or even lighter, load.

Some of these decisions will not be happily received by professors who have vested interests in highly specialized courses, but in times of diminishing budgets and calls for accountability, guidelines for permissible course sizes are a way of ensuring a degree of fairness in the teaching load. Some universities have opted for a minimal class size of fifteen students. Where the number of students is smaller, however, professors can give courses as reading courses or seminars on an overload basis. In this situation, professors are not given official credit in terms of their teaching load (they still may have to teach four other courses, for example), but they are given credit overall in their contribution to teaching for merit purposes.

Summary: Providing Institutional Support for the Improvement of Teaching

Administrators who have major responsibility for fostering effective instruction expressed the greatest confidence in the effects of recognizing teaching in career decisions, teaching award programs, and the evaluation of instruction. Teaching can be honored in a variety of ways, through formal recognition, salary increases, development funds, release time, and by means of individual or group awards, grant competitions, or election to a teaching academy. Acknowledgment that teaching and learning are complex processes has meant that longer-term methods allowing for problem solving and reflection are being used and are proving more effective in dealing with instructional issues. These include discussion groups, week-long workshops, course design consultations, and mentoring. Programs for teaching assistants reflect their diverse needs for learning about course planning, teaching strategies, and evaluation procedures. Teaching centers engage in a variety of services and projects, serve as clearinghouses, and conduct research relevant to teaching and learning. Administrative strategies that support student learning include decreasing class size and providing guidelines for course size.

Benchmark Practices

1. Establish the needs of the campus by doing an in-depth survey of administrators who are responsible for effective teaching practice.
2. Honor teaching and provide opportunity for dialogue on it. Teaching improvement awards assist faculty in redesigning or designing new courses. A dialogue on teaching and learning supports improvements in course design and instruction. Model techniques, for example, for enhancing student participation or for using student feedback to enhance teaching and learning methods. Promote lateral thinking to optimize course design.
3. Establish an orientation for new faculty that leads to dialogue about teaching and learning. Work individually with professors to examine ongoing teaching, then provide assistance to make changes in it. Microteaching sessions or videotaping classes and providing consulting assistance are effective if not inexpensive procedures.
4. Establish teaching and learning centers; these can serve as resource centers and introduce new developments in postsecondary education to the university. To be effective, they require some physical resources but also high-level human resources. A collection of articles, books, and videotapes

enables people to explore literature from one discipline to another.

5. Institute faculty development workshops to provide a cross-disciplinary meeting place for a range of topics such as thinking skills, student responsibility, or the use of multimedia. On-campus experts can act as resources of knowledge and experience. Outstanding scholars from other universities can address teaching and learning issues of broad concern.
6. Establish a program for teacher assistant training that is responsive to the variety of needs across disciplines but that also attends to general issues such as the first day in the classroom.

7

Using Assessment to Define Tasks and Measure Learning

Assessment is the process of evaluating student learning and development to improve learning, instruction, and program effectiveness.

Recognition is growing in universities that the assessment process in courses and programs has a major effect on the way students approach learning. Renewed effort to define and measure learning outcomes in higher education is an effect of a more general public accountability movement. But there are multiple barriers to the institution of assessment procedures, even though assessment provides useful feedback for improving instruction and learning and for strengthening academic programs. In this chapter, I examine potential barriers to the use of assessment processes and strategies for overcoming them, the research available to aid in this endeavor, and specific procedures that have been used to improve courses and to assist students in becoming self-assessing.

The Origin of the Student Assessment Movement

A major impetus for student assessment in North America was the educational testing movement in the 1960s. At that time, computerized scoring capabilities became available, and watershed events such as the launching of Sputnik led to a general demand for better schools (Erwin, 1991). The development of standardized tests to measure abilities, aptitudes, and achievement at all educational levels meant that educational achievement could be compared on a continental basis from elementary to postgraduate school. Standardized tests developed to measure postsecondary student achievement were, however, criticized for their limited ability to test higher-order learning and for not providing sufficiently detailed information about what students knew and did not know (Banta, 1992). The tests failed to meet faculty requirements for knowledge about what their students were learning and failed equally in alerting institutions to successful and less successful program outcomes.

Demand for accountability in higher education began in the mid–1980s, heralded by the publication of a series of reviews of undergraduate education that marked increased interest by governments and the public for quality assurance in postsecondary institutions (Ewell, 1991). Over the last decade, funding agencies, governments, and the media have pressed for measures of institutional quality or student progress. By 1990, the great majority of American colleges and universities reported that they were engaged in some form of revision of their undergraduate programs, but little actual change was noted in curriculum or in student performance (Ratcliff, 1992). External pressure led to a less-than-enthusiastic response on the part of academics to provide proof of student progress (Banta, 1992). National indicators of the conditions of undergraduate education in the United States are, however, being developed by the National Science Foundation (Suter, 1994). The question then becomes, Who will do the assessment?

> The problem in the States is that either it is going to happen at the university and be under the aegis and control of the university involved, or it is going to happen at the state legislature level and will be mandated. Our states are so autonomous that there are some that are very forward-thinking and have a lot of insight and have work done, and then there are others that are in the Dark Ages.

Let us compare this quotation with that of an award-winning university teacher asked for her perspective on student assessment. For her, the idea of assessment at the institutional or state level raises questions of her competence in her discipline and provokes a sharp reaction to the impingement of outsiders in her area of expertise.

> Since I have been involved in the steering committee for the Teaching Center, I have discovered that my whole way of evaluating students and assigning grades from this is unsystematic. I don't know how open-minded my colleagues would be to anyone providing them with additional ideas on that score. It's the nature of professional teaching that if there is something they feel confident about, it is their ability to assess their students' achievement, and in many ways it's the part of teaching that remains completely unreflected upon. I am very clear in my courses about what the grades are and what you have to do to reach a certain grade.

This quotation raises several points. First, the language the professor uses to conceptualize student assessment—and that of most professors—is the assignment of grades. Second, she states that professors are most likely to be confident about their ability to assess student learning (who else has the expertise?), although they may not have spent very much time thinking about the process of evaluation. Third, she acknowledges that few professors would welcome advice on their assessment procedures. These statements alert us to the difficulties inherent in attempting to improve student assessment practices. Assessment requires both subject matter and evaluation process expertise, yet these two kinds of expertise are rarely found in the same person or even acknowledged. The professor moves one step closer to optimal assessment procedures by describing the time spent developing examination questions that reflect the course learning goals.

> People who have put a great deal of energy and thought into their teaching have spent a lot of time perfecting the kind of examination

> questions they prepare so that they feel that's in alignment with the goals they have established, and it allows them suitably to assess what skills and knowledge students have acquired. A colleague and I just taught a brand-new introductory course with 390 students in it, and we spent a lot of time fixing and polishing and changing the kind of questions we pose so that we felt it gave us what was in line with what we could expect students to have acquired and gave them the opportunity to show us that they had acquired something. But part of me bristles at the idea that people who work hard at this need outside help with it. It seems to me that is the core of teaching.

Universities may balk at the idea of instituting assessment procedures for another reason. As I noted in Chapter Three, universities are most frequently compared on the basis of student selectivity, that is, how much students already know when they arrive at the university. Assessment of student progress threatens to turn the equation around, so that selectivity would not be an advantage. Worse still, providing evidence that the best students have learned substantially more or better could prove an impossible task, as research on performance funding and on the effects of college has suggested (Banta, Rudolph, Van Dyke, and Fisher, 1996; Pascarella and Terenzini, 1991), and the process might put the institution at risk. A respondent elaborated:

> In the U.S. as a whole and in research universities in particular, if we are talking about assessment of the quality of learning, nobody wants to use a value-added approach, a strictly Astin "test them when they come in, and test them when they leave, and see how much we've taught them," because that is too dangerous. What we have written up and what we follow in our institution are very like what other institutions do. We don't stick to a strict value-added approach; we do multiple forms of assessment, most of which do not have too much in the way of teeth in them.

One implication of this statement is that since universities have relatively little control over the amount students learn while they are at a university, it would be unfair to be judged as institutions on this basis. Presumed lack of control over student learning and development leads many universities to respond less than willingly to requests to assess the amount of value added to a student from his or her college education. In spite of this sentiment, a variety of college assessment programs have been designed to measure student performance to establish to what extent student competencies have increased (Banta, 1992, 1996; Mentkowski and Strait, 1983). Where attempts have been made to measure changes in student learning, indices of the academic selectivity of the student body—most commonly students' entering average and standardized tests like the Scholastic Aptitude Test (SAT)—are used as a baseline for measuring gains and therefore predicting students' ability to benefit from college programs. Knowledge about where gains occur can be used to increase the efficiency of postsecondary education.

The importance of student assessment lies in its relation to the human capital argument, which places considerable onus on university effectiveness. That is, if it is the responsibility of the student to come to the university prepared to benefit from the experience, it is the responsibility of the university to effectively assist the student to develop. The underlying principle of the student assessment movement was that educational reform should be focused on ways to directly benefit student learning (Mentkowski and Chickering, 1987). The assessment process was envisioned to consist of identifying, collecting, analyzing, and using information to increase students' learning and development. The terms "learning" and "development" overlap—learning being defined as the acquisition of knowledge and skills or behaviors, and development more broadly defined as growth or progressive changes in the person. As considered in Chapters Three, Four, and Five, the range of learning and development extends in a continuum from the explicitly cognitive (learning calculus, for example) to more general changes in moral and ethical reasoning, or commitment to lifelong learning. The role of assessment is predominantly formative.

> My view is that when people talk about assessment, it helps clarify university tasks. It unavoidably requires somebody to define what it is the institution is about, what its goals are, and what is to be assessed. As I define assessment, it is a subset of evaluation, and it is specifically the study of institutional effects on student learning.

This quotation implies that it is the effect of the institution on student progress that is being measured, and that the focus should be on what steps the institution is taking to improve curriculum and instruction. Some assessment programs concentrate on reinvigorating the curriculum (Association of American Colleges, 1985). A pioneer in the assessment of student progress, Alverno College developed an abilities-based curriculum, with regular evaluation of the level of ability shown by the student (Mentkowski and Loacker, 1985). In keeping with research findings on the effects of college, developing analytic and communication skills are primary goals of the program. For example, consistent with the trivium, first- and senior-year differences in speaking and writing skills, controlled for aptitude, increase significantly and are due substantially more to college than to maturation (Pascarella and Terenzini, 1991; Steele, 1986).

At Alverno College (1989), expected student outcomes at increasing levels of ability for each year in a program have been published. To illustrate, for communication ability, students at the first level are expected to identify their own strengths and weaknesses in reading, writing, speaking, listening, and in using media, quantified data, and the computer. At the second level of communication ability, they are expected to show an analytic approach to effective communicating, by the third level to communicate effectively, and by the fourth (required for a bachelor's degree), they are expected to communicate effectively, making relationships out of explicit frameworks from at least three major areas of knowledge. Abilities are tested by a variety of methods, including an annual videotape of the student making an oral presentation.

Thus, major college outcomes can be delineated, made part of the curriculum, and assessed. Critical to the adaptation of such procedures in any postsecondary educational institution is the understanding and proactive support of administrators for the effort that must be put into the design and use of assessment procedures.

Barriers to Student Assessment

Broader student development goals may be difficult to measure, but in addition, the way in which postsecondary institutions operate throws up a further set of barriers. Higher education institutions tend to frame policies globally, while decisions about learning and student progress are assigned to programs and disciplines. But programs have comparatively few resources to examine these questions. Academic freedom may further limit an organized approach to curriculum and instruction, and students report learning relatively independently of the programs in which they are enrolled. Decentralization constrains feedback.

The principles enunciated by the assessment movement indicate that postsecondary institutions are responsible for the development of broad skills on the part of their students. Historically, American colleges and universities have included in their educational mission statements both the cognitive development of students and broader psychosocial and attitudinal dimensions that prepare students for membership in a democratic society (Pascarella and Terenzini, 1991). In the Delphi study reported in Chapter Three, personal student development was rated moderately important. Postsecondary institutions in North America have tended for the most part to interpret their mission more narrowly as one of providing opportunities for cognitive development, less frequently taking responsibility for the broader set of developmental changes that might be expected. When college and university programs that profess to aid student development are evaluated, the results are mixed or disappointing (Barnett, 1977; Bateman, 1990; Guthrie, 1992). Even if mission statements refer to student development, the way most institutions of higher education are organized may preclude effective practice.

This is due in part to the fact that experience in a large postsecondary institution is highly diverse and uncontrolled, and thus psychosocial development may not be directly affected even when intended. Moreover, psychosocial development is difficult to measure, because it is a broad construct; some in the academy may equate it with maturity, and assign responsibility for it to time. Given difficulties of measurement and the variability of the postsecondary educational experience, most developmental gains are not directly attributable to educational experience, although recent attempts to determine what learning gains are due to college have shown some success (Pascarella and Terenzini, 1991). On the whole, large postsecondary institutions have not been in a position administratively to assess general student development. The decentralization that has accompanied growth has made planning for and assessment of general abilities more difficult. Often, other procedures or demands supersede the assessment of learning outcomes.

> The assessment movement has had very little impact at this university. Since we are not accountable to public bodies, there is not the pressure from outside to assess student outcomes. We are accountable to the market place, so it is very important for parents and potential students to find the education credible, but those people have not pressed for assessment in the sense of student outcomes assessment. The place where there might be an impact is with accrediting associations, and there has been some upper-administration conversation looking toward that possibility. I have heard that this is probably coming, and we ought to start thinking about what we can say about the impact of our educational programs. There are some

> things in place like course evaluations and exit interviews for students, so some of those data are in the system, although it might not be acceptable psychometrically for the kinds of outcomes assessment some institutions are attempting to do. But it is fine for program planning and probably is of use in public relations.

Why have the general demand for accountability and the student assessment movement had relatively little effect on institutional policy and practice? Four barriers are discernible. First, higher education institutions tend to frame policies at a global level, leaving the specifics of learning to programs and disciplines. Programs consist of individual courses. Academic policy committees habitually limit their examination of proposed changes to academic programs to one-paragraph course descriptions in order to approve an individual course; course outcomes and the relationship of what is learned in the course to other courses in a program are not required to be specified and are not evaluated. The potential for lack of coherence among parts of a program is inherent in the defined procedures of the institution.

Second, programs have comparatively few resources—usually only the time of the professoriate, which is already stretched—to examine questions of learning and student progress. Even in ideal situations, where professors have the help of a core of teaching assistants, the planning required to examine for higher-order learning is substantial. The next quotation sheds light on the organization required and the workload exacted to do adequate and appropriate assessment of learning.

> The ultimate evaluation is the most baffling one of all, trying to figure out what the students really are learning. We try to evaluate it in terms of examinations and essays. In this particular course, because I had four graduate students and they had very light loads in terms of the number of students they were servicing, I insisted that every week during the quarter (for eight of the weeks), the students write something

> and turn it in. Sometimes, it was a short, one-page statement; other times it was a three- or four-page essay, but every student had to write something once a week. On the basis of that, you can get a sense of what it is they are learning from the lectures or the reading. It is very time-consuming, very demanding for the TAs, and you simply cannot do this in a big course where each TA is servicing not twenty-five students but close to eighty.
>
> Every student had to write something each week. I required the TAs to answer the same questions themselves, and then we exchanged papers among the five of us, and discussed their answers, so that each TA would have a kind of model in his or her head of what to expect the undergraduates to do. And because we had four different answers to the same question, there were very often four different approaches.
>
> They were almost all evaluation kinds of questions, fairly cosmic questions. For instance, we were reading Chaucer's "Canterbury Tales." I was using the "Canterbury Tales" as a way of analyzing the strengths and weaknesses of the medieval church. In the introduction, there are short descriptions of the knight, the priest, the monk, the friar, the prioress. One of the questions was to order the ecclesiastical officials in terms of which one, in the estimation of the undergraduate, represented the greatest threat to the old church and the successful operation or the ideal operation. In other words, it was a question about corruption and what constitutes corruption—venial corruption or more serious kinds of corruption. Would the corruption of the prioress as a noblewoman coming from the upper echelons of society have a greater impact on society than the corruption of the friar? That is the kind of question that I tended to ask them.

Here, the teaching assistants must first display mastery of the subject matter that will stand up to the scrutiny of their professor and peers, then spend as much as twenty-five hours per week using the model answers to provide feedback to their group of students on their essays. This is more than double the amount of time most graduate students are allowed to work on research projects as part of their graduate training.

The third barrier is that of academic freedom, which may limit curriculum involvement, if courses are considered to be within the province of the individual professor. Although the definition of academic freedom is commonly taken to be the freedom to teach or learn without interference, as noted in the second chapter, such freedom can be interpreted to mean "with limited requirement for curricular coherence across courses." At one university, an attempt is being made within the discipline to ensure that colleagues are aware of what other members of their program are teaching.

> In the name of academic freedom, we have avoided questions of common academic floors or minimums of expectation, and we have to confront that. We have tried to introduce the notion of a student-centered syllabus, which we hope to have reviewed by members of an academic unit. In other words, you have academic freedom, but your syllabus is going to be discussed and approved by your faculty colleagues and your chair, so that we're assured that young people are given a very significant challenge, and so that professors are assured that if they put a syllabus as a public document into consideration and show the department that they would like to do certain things with their students and that some support is going to be needed to achieve that level of participation, whether it be dollars or assistance, that is heard as part of the community's assessment of the proof. Until syllabi become more public documents, taken seriously at the unit level if not the college level, the notion that each individual course is a reflection of the field of study will not be engaged with the energy and imagination that will bring renewal to the fields and connect them to others.

This quotation suggests the limits of poststructuralism in the curriculum, that is, a program supposes a field, which in turn supposes some degree of coherence in the knowledge base. The suggestions in the quotation are also more in line with department teaching teams or curriculum alliances that share the responsibility for student progress. If awards can be made to groups of faculty or to departments to honor their teaching, then it should be feasible to develop an environment in which professors enjoy the support of their colleagues in assessing learning. British universities have external assessors as a rule; some form of external concordance or ratification ought to be possible on the North American continent.

A fourth problem in instituting a program of learning outcomes assessment is that students, although formally registered in programs, often function relatively independently of them at the undergraduate level, with the exception of a few honors or professional programs where there is a well-structured curriculum. Even when a program is tightly designed, graduates comment that a considerable percentage of their learning takes place outside the program or in extra-curricular activities (Donald and Denison, 1996a). The potential for fragmentation of learning and the limitations on the development and assessment of broad abilities, given the current operating procedures, are evident. In spite of this situation, universities are beginning to feel the need to attend to assessment issues, primarily because of legislative and peer pressure.

> My sense is that as some of the accreditation agencies begin to look at more of the assessment indices, we will slowly get on that bandwagon by virtue of being forced to do so, not by virtue of necessarily thinking that this is the best way to go or the most important way to go. In this state, the state schools are far ahead of us in terms of dealing with the issue because of legislative mandate. As a private institution, we have not had that kind of outside force pushing us. Our communication science and disorders department has all kinds of assessment tools in place, because they have had to do it for the accreditation or certification of their students, but neither our history department nor our theater department has done that, because it has not been required by any outside force, and there has not been any major internal mandate.

> As accreditation bodies are going to be forcing us to do more of that, you will see more of it on this campus, but I think it will be more externally driven than internally driven. Some of the internal drive will come as more people pay more attention to teaching, and I suspect that as the center remains here longer and more people talk about teaching, there will also be internal interest, but until recently, except for individual faculty members or programs that had to respond to outside accreditation or certification courses, there was not much attention in a systematic way to assessment. The state schools are far ahead, but many of the things that they are doing are low-level and undesirable kinds of assessment, but they are trying to do something to demonstrate to legislators that they are assessing. Most of the large associations are dealing with assessment and have put more effort into those kinds of assessment issues.

In summary, barriers at four different levels must be dealt with if assessment is going to be useful in the academy. For assessment to work, the university, represented by the central administration, must display more interest and support in the procedure and must recognize the cost of the work involved in delineating learning outcomes and in providing substantial feedback to students. Since professors are going to carry the burden of student assessment, they must be provided with assistance and recognition for doing so. Cooperative and collaborative teaching must be promoted to even faculty load, and students need to be made aware of and responsible for more challenging learning goals. The student assessment movement has raised a number of questions for postsecondary planners and policy makers. These questions, particularly the inherent difficulty of assessing learning when knowledge and skills are complex, fast-moving targets, are the basis for research on student assessment.

Research on the Assessment of Learning

By 1987, student assessment occupied a prominent place on the research agenda of the American Association for Higher Education and the American Educational Research Association Division of Postsecondary Education (Mentkowski and Chickering, 1987). The aims of the research agenda were to provide feedback to the student and the institution on strengths and areas to be improved, thus aiding student and program development. The agenda further recommended research on knowledge, skills and learning, psychosocial outcomes, and the assessment process. Research on the assessment of learning has been spearheaded by a longitudinal panel study at the National Center on Postsecondary Teaching, Learning, and Assessment (NCTLA) on how academic and nonacademic experiences influence student learning, attitudes, cognitive development, and persistence in college.

> As a National Center, we are feeling the need with regard to faculty to get people to wake up to the realization that this is something that is not going to go away, that this is not a management fad like strategic planning or TQM or management by objectives. Assessment is going to be here, but I view that as positive. Faculty may have no faith in the indicators, whether it is an exam or not, in part because faculty are so sloppy in their own thinking about student learning, and how you measure it, and what it is, and how you know if it occurs, and whether or not there is any way you can tie what is being learned to what is happening in the context of the curriculum, the classroom and the experience of the institution.

The NCTLA studies employ a variety of methods to assess learning, from the broadly based American College Test (ACT) assessment of academic aptitude to subject matter tests.

> The national study of student learning, the panel study, will be a good exemplar of the time and effort and money that it takes to evaluate learning in a comprehensive way. We are measuring learning in many different ways: we are using pieces of the ACT test, instruments that we have made ourselves, following a large cohort at multiple institu-

> tions. This is a carefully constructed student sample that will allow us to call it a national study of student learning, using a lot of innovative assessment techniques.

In the longitudinal panel study, researchers followed a sample of some five thousand students from more than twenty colleges and universities to investigate how academic and nonacademic experiences influence student learning, attitudes toward learning, cognitive development, and persistence in college. Academic experiences include the quality of teaching and classroom instruction, the level of student involvement in academic work, and the pattern of course work taken. A second goal of the project was to determine the extent to which academic and nonacademic experiences differ among students attending different kinds of colleges and universities (National Center on Postsecondary Teaching, Learning, and Assessment, 1993). According to a participating researcher:

> They are administering subject matter tests, subtests that are not course-specific but discipline-specific in scientific reasoning, attitudes about learning, motivation, and persistence. The idea is not to compare institutions, and the numbers are not large enough from any single institution to generalize to students in that institution, but add everything up and comparisons could be made among types of institutions or student characteristics or the effect of place of residence off or on campus.

One of the effects of this study has been to increase interest in specifying when and where change occurs, so that programs can be designed to fit learning to the needs of specific groups.

> The things that interest me are research problems not only on how students change and how much they change as a result of different institutional experiences but when those things occur. Most longitudinal research will look at change measured from beginning of the

> freshman year to the end of the freshman year, or start of the freshman year to end of the senior year. And we can say with some confidence that change has occurred, and we can also say that some of those changes are attributable to institutional experiences of certain specifiable kinds, but we don't know anything about when those changes occur, whether all the change occurs in the first year and a half or whether changes in certain areas are all linear. They may be quite episodic.
>
> We don't know to what extent the rates of change vary for different kinds of learning outcomes, and all of those have important implications for the way we design our instructional programs. If we can learn something about when these changes occur, maybe we can more finely tune the programs we offer. Right now, we offer programs as if everybody learns at the same rate and as a consequence of the same activities. We do it that way because of a production function: deliver the same sort of thing to as many people as possible. When we reviewed the literature, we found very little research on what we call "conditional effects," that is, how learning varies according to the characteristics of the students involved, whether that be race or ethnicity, gender, socioeconomic status, or academic ability.

In a project on the effect of differential course work patterns, learning improvement among graduating seniors from general education programs in a variety of selective and less selective postsecondary institutions was examined (Ratcliff, 1992). Little relationship was found between formal requirements and gains in learning, but different course work developed different abilities. For example, reading comprehension was increased by students' taking different courses in French, history, and math, among others (Jones, 1992). Analytical reasoning—defined as understanding a given structure of relationships, deduction of new information, and assessment of the conditions used to establish the structure—was aided particularly by specific courses in chemistry, economics, history, and psychology. Studies such as these can be used to help program planners construct curricular sequences that emulate the experiences of successful students.

Since the complexity of the assessment questions being asked and the data files required to answer them appeared to be massive, I asked how many institutional research systems in postsecondary institutions would have the capacity to use the assessment model and procedures that have been developed in these studies, and how many institutions would have the capacity to keep track of their programs or the effect their programs were having.

> The comprehensive, doctoral degree-granting universities generally do not have a problem. They may not be familiar with the steps and procedures, but having access to student records in a database in a computerized form that would allow them to do the kinds of things that we have been advocating is not a problem. Again, the model was designed for institutions that have a general education program that is largely distributional in nature rather than core. That describes about 85 percent of the four-year institutions. In the community college sector, there is a significant increase in the number of problems in utilizing it, mostly in relation to the quality of transcripts as an information source. In the private liberal arts colleges of four thousand and less, you run into the same kinds of problems, largely because they are in the beginning stages of computerizing records. There are six states at least that could do this on a statewide basis now.
>
> For institutions that have developed their own record-keeping systems, if you want to share information across institutions, there are political questions as well as the structure of data and where it is housed and what brand of computer and what format and how big the fields. There are a lot of issues that arise when you move from an institutional base to a state and provincial base, so six out of fifty is not bad, in my estimation. The record-keeping has been good; the utilization of the records to some end other than archiving is minimal. Most institutions I encounter invested heavily in computerizing their

> records but do not utilize them for anything other than the reports that they made in the registrar's office in the first place.

To accommodate wide-scale assessment procedures will evidently require greater communication across the institution, particularly with offices of institutional research. In the past, institutional research and planning offices' central duty has been to report on the number of students enrolled and courses given, and time to graduation. Program reviews focus on the status of the resources and products of the system. An assessment program would bring these evaluations together with an emphasis on learning. It would also require operationalizing the educational mission at the program level. The following examples describe how this might be accomplished.

Strategies for Implementing Student Assessment

A first step in implementing student assessment is to determine what competencies all students should have when they graduate and how and when students acquire them. Where learning assessment has been instituted, the most immediate effect is curricular reform. Assessment studies highlight where learning gains have been made and where they have not, and require institutions or programs to adapt to meet the learning requirements. The assessment of learning is being approached at one university in the following manner:

> In some of the schools and colleges where we are working on the curriculum, we're asking what competencies every student should have when they leave this place and how we get students to this point. Institutions avoid this issue with enthusiasm. Employers are telling us that graduates from universities and colleges around the country cannot write, cannot speak, cannot problem solve, cannot work in small groups, don't have computer literacy, and yet any group of faculty I've met with will tend to agree relatively soon about the competencies that are needed, which are the same. We are trying in

> some of our new professional courses to build them in right away. The Schools of Management and Human Development are prototypes on developing survival skills in the freshman course in the disciplinary context. We have to reeducate students on how to work, think, and study.

Different forms of organization into college- or program-based learning might be necessary to achieve these goals. Other methods that have been used to provide program coherence are capstone courses that require students to bring together the skills, or independent research projects, or comprehensive examinations to measure the extent to which independent learning, analysis, and synthesis have been developed. General learning criteria require more general assessment procedures. An example of this kind of procedure is the junior-year examination of writing ability.

> The junior-year examination is a two-hour period in which you read an essay and respond to one of three questions on it in an essay of your own. Every time I have participated in the grading of those, I am not at all sure I have seen the best writing that student is capable of doing, because it has a tendency to be rather superficial, but the examination is definitely a step in the right direction. It at least lets the students know they are going to be expected to do that at the junior year.

Such practices, although with limited authenticity, set an institutional standard. However, some programs may choose to interpret the meaning of the assessment within their own requirements, rendering the assessment toothless.

> We have a junior writing assessment, which everyone takes, but if I'm in engineering and I fail, that may mean that I have to take one course that has a lot of writing in it, and that is the way I fulfill the requirement. If I'm in sociology and I fail, maybe I don't have to do anything; each department has its own rules about how you deal with people

> who fail the writing proficiency exam, because they say you can't require the same things of engineers and physicists that you do of sociologists and English majors; we can't make these rules for all the departments, because the expertise is within the department or college and not at the university level. So, there is a writing proficiency exam, but to what extent is that a meaningful assessment process?

Coherence in assessment planning is essential. The planning process may begin with the recognition that program and curriculum work is needed in many areas to ensure that courses and examinations dovetail, that they are not redundant, and that learning outcomes are clearly stated and measurable. Student administrative records can be used to study the effect of course choice on the development of broad skills. For example, certain course work patterns were shown to develop quantitative abilities of college students with high verbal but low math skills (Ratcliff and Yaeger, 1994). Student evaluations of programs at graduation also provide data for program planning purposes. Several kinds of data can be collected.

> We collect data from lots of sources, faculty, staff about how things are going or how things went; we'll use some of the information collected in exams and quizzes, which become part of the general record of how students are progressing. We also often do follow-up studies where we look at retention, GPAs in subsequent semesters, in the fall and then at the end of the year, then into the sophomore year. We also ask students for their opinions. Generally, the retention to graduation rate is about 67 percent, which is a lot better than public institutions and not as good as more selective private institutions. When we track retention, we find that we lose between 10 and 15 percent of the entering cohort between the entering and sophomore year, then another 8 to 12 percent after the sophomore year; then it flattens out, and we lose another chunk after the fourth year. They don't finish up. The average time to degree is five years; we still have a number of students who change majors and then have to make up

> requirements. We look at those kinds of data in relation to the programs to see if there is any difference between students who have gone through the programs successfully. Second, we work with faculty members in assessing students, developing exams, quizzes, databases or banks of items, or getting them in a format so that they can be scanned and can be used in item analysis.

Most of these strategies operate at the institutional level, although input from faculty and students is present. At the level of individual students, to enable them to understand what their program of study could and should be, one useful strategy is to provide a contract or set of guidelines for students that goes beyond a general statement to describe the kinds of knowledge and skills that they should be developing in their programs. Including estimates of the range of time required to achieve the knowledge and skills in a program in the contract would provide students with guidance in how to plan their reading, writing, problem solving, or other skill development. In several of the examples that follow, goal clarification leads to more focused and yet open and independent learning.

Assessment in the Classroom

Classroom assessment techniques allow professors to enunciate teaching goals and the ways in which they can assess how well they are achieving their teaching and learning goals. As an initial strategy for employing assessment of student learning at one university, emphasis has been placed on aiding faculty to implement assessment in their classrooms. The process of developing and using classroom assessment techniques advocated by Angelo and Cross (1993) provides a common vocabulary and a starting point for discussion of teaching and learning goals among colleagues.

> The university in the last two years has been doing a lot of work on classroom assessment and has been running seminars for faculty for

> three years, with national key speakers. A certain amount of money has been allocated for faculty to improve techniques. There is a strong thrust for a student-centered university, with a lot of emphasis on what the students want and need and perceive as needs. The techniques have included the quick and easy classroom assessment techniques that Tom Angelo proposes. We have had brown bag lunches once a month, and seminars, and small grants of $500 to $1,000 for faculty members to implement assessment in their own areas.

The steps for an individual classroom assessment project include focusing on an assessable teaching goal or question, designing a classroom assessment project, and assessing and analyzing learning by means of student feedback. After experimenting with individual classroom assessment projects, comprehensive projects can then be developed to respond to larger course and program questions. At one university, after a seminar on classroom assessment techniques, the university took the idea one step further.

> Using the Angelo and Cross book on teaching techniques as a basis, we created one-page "Here's a technique you might want to try" sheets with an example. We had a group of graduate students work on that, and it became one of the products of our assessment program this year. In addition, we funded about a dozen individual classroom assessment projects. Sometimes individuals, other times teams of faculty come to us with an idea they would like to try out or an assessment question they would like to get an answer to. The committee has put anywhere from $700 to $3,000 to help them implement this idea and see what we can learn about classroom assessment. Next year, we're hoping to move toward departmental or program assessment, for example, a portfolio project where graduate students are developing prototype portfolios that will then be discussed by faculty and other graduate students in the department to develop a master model to be used in annual reviews of graduate students and also faculty.

Assessment of Prerequisite Skills

If students are to be assessed and given feedback on a regular basis on the knowledge, skills, and attitudes that they acquire while at a university, entry-level abilities and attitudes must be assessed to provide baseline data, and expected outcomes for various programs of study should be delineated and made available to students. For students to acquire the necessary knowledge and skills, requirements need to be clearly specified. The following example explains how assessment of students at entry to a course can aid the learning process.

> We did a pilot when we were working on the economics course on assumed math prerequisites. The professor stated what he thought students would know. When we tested a class, we found that 72 percent could not understand the profit and loss curve, 30 to 40 percent had problems with algebra, so we designed an independent learning module to help reduce the problem. A front-end diagnostic test, a one-to-two-hour module for remediation, and a posttest based on our data saved about 30 percent of the students who would have failed. We have just completed a study of first-year courses, and we are finding correlations between specific math skills that are assumed in the text and success in the program. Dealing with mathematics prerequisites becomes a generic, across-the-board thing, and I hope we will be doing a number of course-specific pilot units to address those problems. The problem in math is that while the mathematicians think sequentially, the courses using math do not use it in that sequential order, and a remedial course offered concurrently won't solve the problem. It has to be taught at the time the student needs the competence. In many cases, it is a matter of skills that students simply haven't used, a matter of review.

The professor of this course explained why meeting the math prerequisites is so important for success in the course and how the math test is carried out.

> The first level of assessment that can assure a level of learning is whether students have the prerequisite skills. In economics, the key prerequisite skill in the introductory economics course is geometry—graphs. The traditional style of a lot of teachers is to assume geometry. They might wonder whether students have it, but they start speaking it rather rapidly, and if students don't have it, that's their problem. The discipline is analytic and model-oriented, so math is a proxy for a larger conceptual framework. What I see in class is the echo of social expectations; students still have trouble with the graphs.
>
> We give a math skills pretest on the first Thursday class. Students get a feedback card that tells them that their skills are up to speed or they're not. If they're not, we have a remediation package on reserve in the library. Assessment and learning are inseparable; you cannot be learning unless you are constantly assessing what you already have. The main issue is the key role of ongoing self-assessment. I can give a brilliant lecture but teach nobody anything, because early on they got lost. So, there is formative, course-level assessment of whether they have the skills for the course.

The professor has introduced the idea of ongoing self-assessment on the part of students in this quotation. Self-assessment and classroom assessment are important strategies, because they tie the teaching and learning process together.

Student Self-Assessment

Student self-assessment is a strategy for developing skills of self-reflection, bringing students more fully into the educational process and helping them build active and meaningful relationships with the material they are studying (Kusniac and Finley, 1993). The concept refers to both a written product and the process that produces the writing, and requires self-representation on the part of students in the form of self-questioning or journal keeping. Kusniac and Finley describe it as consisting of an attitude of inquiry that requires the integration of learning from other courses, previous understanding, or experience, which in turn creates meaning and relevance in the learning situation. It is an important input to student self-regulation. It gives students greater voice and authority by challenging them to be articulate, providing an external audience, and validating their right to speak and have an opinion.

It is also self-directed, that is, students identify the questions that emerge for them and become conscious of themselves as learners, and they then connect more actively with the world outside themselves. The contexts may include entire courses or programs, or specific exercises for planning learning or reflecting upon it, as in journal-keeping or one-minute papers on what was learned in class in the last hour. Student self-assessment has the effect of personalizing students' learning and allowing them to take ownership of it, while creating a sense of community (Eaton and Pougiales, 1993). It thus appears to be a powerful strategy for integrating students into the learning community, inducing student development, and assessing student learning outcomes.

Assessment in a Biology Course

In a course consisting of large numbers of students, the process of clarifying the learning task and its assessment begins in the first lecture. In this course, although grades are used to set standards of excellence, the emphasis is on the experience of learning. Teaching assistants participate in the complex grading process, which is then used in course revision.

> For students, in the first lecture in helpful hints, we go over how the grades are given out and what is expected of students. Three major exams are given at night, so that there is no time limit—an hour exam, and they have two hours to write them, for 70 percent of the grade. They are multiple-choice so that we can grade it quickly and get what we need to know about students' grasp of the material. Thirty percent is on the recitations (or tutorial sections) in two in-class

essay quizzes, take-homes, lab reports, and participation. Quizzes are put in the resource book, and they are available as resource information for new TAs. At the end of the semester, the TAs add up the points and come to see me individually and go over every student and then discuss problem cases.

We also offer "benefit-of-the-doubt" credit. We have a distinguished lecture series, and the students put their names on the tickets and put them in a box and then get benefit-of-the-doubt credit. We do that with attendance, too. If a student is borderline, we will give him or her the benefit of the doubt if he or she has attended. In this course, the experience is more important than the information. I tell the students that I want them there to experience things and that they are paying a lot to be there, for the experience. We made a rule that it doesn't matter what your grade is, if you do not attend class and participate fully, you get an F. Students who get A's get a letter congratulating them, and people who get A's both semesters get a special wallet-sized certificate of excellence.

We have a formative assessment for the TAs three weeks into the semester. They have to hand out a form saying, "What am I doing right? What do you suggest for improvement? What do you think about the whole course?" I tell the TAs that I don't want to see it unless they want to show it to me; it is a personal classroom assessment. At the end, we have a major open-ended questionnaire for the students in which they write about all parts of the course, then we summarize that into things they are doing right and suggestions for improvement. Every TA gets an evaluation profile after the grades are given out. I encourage them to pick out a teaching trait that they would like to work on to improve.

We revise, but the nice part is that we have a base; we know what works; we know where the problems are going to be. The first semester is more structured, but the second semester we are more flexible. In the second semester, students do a cooperative project. We also do a pig dissection, and students have a personal interview on the structure and function of the pig. A plant project is done in teams, and students design an experiment, report on it, and get a group grade.

In the course, learning outcomes are clearly specified, TAs are supported in their work with small groups of students but are given major responsibility for their students' learning, and inducements for students to learn abound. Because it is an introductory science course, emphasis in assessment is on knowledge acquisition, but the course is designed to be experiential and cooperative.

Formative Assessment in an Economics Course

Another method of in-class assessment in large classes helps students to focus on the close relationship of assessment to learning through continual questioning.

> One of the major misunderstandings about assessment is that it is exogenous to the process of learning; that you teach and at some separate time, you assess. I think it has to be an integral part, constant, like "Are your wheels on the ground or are they spinning?" My own technique is to constantly ask questions, tell students to think about their answer, listen to the person who answers, listen to what I say to them, and listen to see if they're in tune. I say this many times, and I always wait awhile when I ask a question, even if a hand goes up immediately, so that they have time to think. Occasionally, I will ask them to jot down, particularly if it's a graphic answer, what they think it is going to look like. So, they are constantly testing themselves against the constant barrage of questions, even though they are not going to raise their hand. I tell them not to be passive, that it does not cost them a thing to think about, and no risk if they are not going to raise their hand. They have everything to gain in finding out if they really understand it right now, because if I go on and they don't understand, they will be lost. So there is a constant self-assessment.

In this example, students are continually called upon to self-assess, to assess their peers, and to monitor their understanding of abstract concepts.

Long-Distance Assessment

Technology can be used to facilitate contact and feedback when students are learning in the field. This is an important procedure, when students are attempting to integrate what they have previously learned and are miles from campus. Professional faculties with field placements or internships often suppose that assessment must come from the field supervisor and only at the end of the placement. The following assessment method is formative and intended to prevent problems:

> We have received a grant for using faxes to get frequent input from the retailing students who are out in the field, in New York City or Boston or Orlando in a nine-to-twelve-credit practicum; they have reports and a structured workload they are supposed to be carrying out. When they have difficulties, they have not always been timely in reporting them, sometimes because they are afraid it will reflect badly on them. They are told that they are supposed to be problem solving and using faculty as a secondary resource; they are employed by the retail stores that they are working for, as assistant buyers, for example.
>
> We decided that we needed weekly contact, so starting next fall, they are going to be faxing in very brief reports, which will be coded for confidentiality, on problems running from lack of adequate supervision to sexual harassment. We think that will be helpful in making the students aware that we are here to back them up immediately if they have problems. A TA will collect and sort the reports so that if there is an emergency, the faculty member can be alerted immediately. We also have questions about what they are learning, but we thought that some of the things that were interfering with learning were important for us to know, because students are not going to be learning if they are worried about problems with their supervisors.

Thus, a problem caused by a geographical and potential cultural gap in the learning environment led to an assessment procedure that ensures continued contact and self-reflection on the part of the student. Evidently, this procedure could be utilized in a variety of field placements, particularly those with Internet and e-mail access.

Curriculum Assessment

Assessment can also be used to develop a program by employing the first-hand knowledge of students about their learning experience. In this case, students studying to be dietitians who are in the field for 950 hours in their junior and senior years bring the function of assessment full circle—back to the optimal curriculum.

> The juniors complain that the theory courses are too intensive, that they cannot possibly learn all the detail; the seniors come back and say that they needed to know more than they were taught and suggest additions. Additional courses are not possible to add, because the program is already full. In this project, the senior students critique the junior lecture content, once they come back from their field work experience. The teachers share their exams and lecture notes, and the students critique what is most important, what can be left out, and what needs to be added.
>
> We used the entire senior class of fifteen students who turned in voluminous reports that are now being analyzed. We think that even if we don't leave much out, it will have the advantage of showing future students what the seniors felt was needed. We would like to extend that into the field to see what dietitians think should be included.

These examples from different fields and with very different learning goals show how assessment can be used to strengthen student learning, create a positive climate, avoid or deal with negative learning experiences, and improve courses and programs. The learning environment then becomes more challenging and more meaningful.

Summary: Using Assessment to Define Tasks and Measure Learning

Assessing student learning and development to improve learning, instruction, and program effectiveness has become increasingly important in response to demands for quality assurance in postsecondary institutions. Two classic institutional barriers to the implementation of assessment procedures are the lack of global policies about learning and student progress and the few resources assigned to assessment. Academic freedom and the fragmentation of learning may further impede assessment programs.

On the positive side of the ledger, research on the influence of academic and nonacademic experiences on student learning, attitudes, cognitive development, and persistence in college has suggested potential solutions. One finding is that improvement in analytical reasoning is aided by specific courses. Sources of data on learning outcomes include student administrative records of success in courses, student averages in subsequent semesters, student evaluations of programs at graduation, and faculty, staff, and student opinions. To accommodate wide-scale assessment procedures, greater communication within and across institutions is vital.

Classroom assessment techniques focus on teaching and learning goals and allow professors to reflect on how well they are achieving them. Student self-assessment is a powerful strategy for integrating students into the learning community, inducing student development, and assessing student learning outcomes. Assessment can be used to increase positive outcomes and reduce negative ones.

Benchmark Practices

1. Use assessment procedures to reinvigorate the curriculum; one way is to develop an abilities-based curriculum.
2. Examine the effect of individual courses or groups of courses on the development of specific types of cognitive abilities at

the institutional level using course grades and general outcome measures.

3. Assess entry-level abilities and attitudes to provide baseline data. Use assessment procedures early to ensure that students have the prerequisite skills.
4. Delineate the expected outcomes for programs of study, and make them available to students. Specify requirements clearly. Include estimates of the range of time needed to acquire the knowledge and skills in a program.
5. Incorporate ongoing self-assessment of teaching and learning. For example, weekly writing assignments that are subsequently discussed develop students' communication skills and the evaluation skills of teaching assistants.
6. Use classroom assessment techniques to focus on cooperative projects, student questioning, or curriculum development.
7. Assess overall student progress, and determine when changes occur by using follow-up studies of retention and achievement in subsequent semesters.

8

Faculty Responsibilities, Rewards, and Assessment

The criteria used by society to judge universities contrast with the criteria of import for faculty and administrators. Where society demands the solution of problems and the development of expertise, faculty and administrators' priorities are academic freedom and quality.

In this chapter, the focus returns to the interface between the university and society, but as it applies to faculty—what the constituency asks of faculty, what faculty goals are, and how faculty are evaluated and rewarded. In an early study by the American Council on Education on the goals of faculty and administrators in American universities, the top-ranked goals, in order of priority, were protecting academic freedom, maintaining prestige and quality in the university, ensuring the confidence and support of those who contribute financial and other resources, training students, and carrying on research (Gross and Grambsch, 1968). Quality is the second-highest priority, although academic freedom outranks it. These goals differ considerably from the roles enunciated for universities by society.

The Relationship Between Social and Faculty Imperatives

One of the respondents, when asked what the most important issues in postsecondary education were, replied that the first one for him was how higher education fits into and contributes to the society that bears and nurtures it. Given the varied demands placed on universities, and hence on faculty, stress levels appear to be reaching epidemic proportions.

> One of the issues in higher education today is that the general public expects institutions of higher education to fulfill all functions. That means that we expect faculty members at a small liberal arts college in the Midwest that has a lot of money to be exceptional undergraduate teachers and to maintain an extraordinary research program, and if a given faculty member does not want to do that, that is OK, but since it is such a good school, there are other people lined up in the queue who will take that position. We expect faculty members at unnamed midwestern liberal arts colleges to do U.C. Berkeley research and conversely, we expect undergraduates at research universities to have the same quality of undergraduate education they could expect to get at the liberal arts college. That is absurd. This is a systemic problem, to say that we have a wonderfully diverse higher education system in this country, and yet in many instances we expect every institution to be everything to everybody. The obvious ramifications for the individual professor are increased levels of stress to the point at which new faculty are terribly stressed.

At the same time, research that is undertaken in the universities often does not have the hoped-for impact, because the goals of academic researchers are influenced by the university career progression pattern and are therefore centered on academic outcomes rather than on the development of the community in which they are doing their research.

> The difference between social problem-oriented research and academic research is best characterized by an anecdote. I was asked to speak before an association for higher education, a group of college presidents and legislators. One legislator came up to me and said he was a graduate of the university, was very loyal to it, and would love

> to give more money to it for its operations, because he believes in higher education. He said, "There is terrible unemployment in the state, and the largest draw on the state treasury is the unemployment. I would love to give a grant to the sociology department to do research to identify what the problems are and how we might alleviate some of the misery in this state so that there wouldn't be such a draw on the public coffers and so that people would be in better shape. But I won't do that, because I have a fear that the money will go to the sociology department and they will pay some assistant professor who will publish three or four papers and present them at professional meetings, use that for promotion and tenure, and come back to me asking for more money for his salary because he has been advanced. And I am still without a solution to the social problem, which is the unemployment in the state."

The exigencies of the Cold War era, which still dominate thinking in some research universities, add to the dilemma in which faculty find themselves when responding to social imperatives. A respondent talked about the effects of that era:

> I believe that for a period of time at least, universities in the States got off the track and focused on research to the detriment of their stated mission. It is not hard to figure out what a university is for; it's chiseled in marble right over the door; it says, "Come in here, we'll teach you, we'll make society better, the world will be better than it was before." That is what we do here. It does not say, "Inside here are a bunch of people hiding from the world and writing articles and applying for research grants from the government." Primarily because of political realities in the United States and the world, in the fifties and sixties the mission changed, and administrators came to believe that they could keep the doors open by soliciting federal grants to enhance revenues for the institution. Over the more recent history, in the last twenty years or so, if you asked higher education administrators what the money from the state budget is meant to cover, they

> would probably say, "faculty salaries to do research." This is a breed of administrators that developed who were researchers and believed the Eisenhower myth of funding universities to develop the military-industrial complex to push us into the next century, build interstate highways, bombs, things like that. The embarrassment of Sputnik was the original impetus for all of this. Many state or public institutions in the United States have 40 to 50 percent coming from the taxpayers of the state. If you ask taxpayers or legislators what they are giving this money for, they don't say to create new knowledge or to do research—they say to teach our children.

Research, Teaching, and Service and Their Rewards

The goals habitually enunciated for faculty members are research, teaching, and service, yet maintaining a balance among these responsibilities has been a major issue in postsecondary education in North American universities since the late 1800s (Centra, 1993).

> There are so many different perceptions of what we are supposed to be that ultimately, the tensions that are created by that make those of us within the university sometimes our own worst enemies.
>
> The truism is that at a big research university, the faculty never quite know what hat they are wearing, whether it is a research hat or a teaching hat. It is perfectly true that in terms of promotion, research means more than teaching. The balance between the two was weighted fifteen or twenty years ago very heavily toward research. That balance clearly is being rectified. It is also clear that the administration and the various departments are trying to do something. We are aware of the issue of teaching, if only because academe recently has gotten very bad press on the subject of teaching.

Reasons for the unresolved conflict between knowledge production and dissemination are, first, that they *are* in some ways incompatible and, second, they have been rewarded differentially. The higher prestige accorded to research, the availability of interinstitutional metrics for judging it, the rarity of the skills required to do it well, and the fact that it is often more pleasurable to pursue one's own work at one's own pace rather than to translate it for the uninitiated, combine to give research undisputed primacy in the self-definition of the university (Keohane, 1994). In the ideal teaching environment, the goals of knowledge production and dissemination are symbiotic, with faculty research and student learning a cooperative endeavor. In reality, this is rarely the case.

Frequently, a professor is called upon to present fundamental concepts in the discipline to a multitude of undergraduates, some of whom are prepared and some of whom are not, to digest this material, while the professor's research lies in one or two corners of the curriculum at a distance too far to be grasped conceptually by the students. Time spent preparing for class is time taken away from research. Arguments (for example, Centra, 1993; Winkler, 1992) that research influences teaching by communicating the excitement of the domain, that it maintains the professor's interest in the subject matter, and that discussions with students may lead to productive research, are predicated on the immediate relationship of one's teaching assignment to one's area of research. The preference for teaching advanced seminars in one's area of specialization becomes readily understandable.

When faculty rewards are based on productivity (rather than, say, seniority, as was the pattern in many institutions in the first half of the century), with disproportionate rewards going to one area of responsibility, the conflict is heightened. Although faculty at research universities report spending an equal amount of time on research and teaching (twenty hours per week), they believe their research is much more important (Rees and Smith, 1991). Almost all faculty members (98 percent) consider good teaching to be an essential goal, but as few as 10 percent believe that their institutions reward good teaching (Higher Education Research

Institute, 1991). At the same time, most faculty (80 percent) acknowledge that research is the highest priority at their institutions. Faculty members also believe more specifically that their administrators favor research, while administrators say they weight teaching more heavily (Diamond, 1993; Gray, Froh, and Diamond, 1992). The rewards for research are evident—grants, prestige, honors, invitations to speak and to travel. The rewards for teaching are more subtle—good student ratings, a sense that students have learned something, a student who continues in the field. Corollary to the rewards is the problem of self-development versus the development of others. The professor has the dilemma of altruism or self-actualization, of responding to a younger audience or to colleagues in the world of scholarship.

> In the research universities, even the faculty in the sciences feel the system is out of whack on many campuses. If faculty work in the community or do interdisciplinary work or at a number of things that the universities say are very important, they do so at their own risk. For example, there are many outstanding professors who are innovative, who write excellent texts, win teaching awards, and are not being promoted to full professor by their department, because they have not published enough, although each is one of the department's major assets, nationally recognized and has won all kinds of awards. It is a story that one hears over and over again. To focus on teaching or community service is often done at the risk of promotion and merit pay increases.

Also underlying the debate between teaching and research are the expected difficulty of each kind of task, the announced role of the postsecondary institution, and hence the social contract between faculty members and the institution. In research universities, traditionally primacy has been given to research, based on the axiom that the production of knowledge is inherently more difficult than its dissemination. This is reflected in tales of salary negotiations. Lipset (1994) tells the story of a faculty member who reported that every important special salary increase or improvement in his situation was brought about by a salary offer from another school, occasioned by his research standing. This he took as the *real* instructions about how he should budget his time. Meanwhile, governments and parents assume that university operating funds are intended for teaching purposes. This has led some administrators to allocate rewards such as annual merit increases based on evaluation of teaching. An administrator elaborated:

> As an associate dean, I am in charge of the promotion and tenure process, the merit review process, and so forth, and I am very aware that in the last four years the emphasis on teaching has changed dramatically in the university. Five years ago, we did not send anything on teaching other than just a summary statement. Now, we must send an entire teaching portfolio over, and people pay attention to it; it is not just sent over and put on a back burner. The central administration has put their money where their mouth is. They are beginning to reward or not reward with a much higher emphasis on teaching than they did before.

Faculty rewards for service, which could be expected to respond most closely to the societal demand for the betterment of humankind, have tended recently to be given decreasing weight in promotion, tenure, and merit decisions. Another approach some universities have taken is to define service specifically as the act of graduating students from a program, who will then provide service to the community. Other indices used are participation in university committees and professional organizations, some distance from community involvement and development (Donald, 1984). Faculty report spending approximately 4 percent of their time in public service (Bowen and Schuster, 1986). In a research university where faculty devote twenty hours a week to research and twenty to teaching, there will be little time left for service. The result of multiple competing expectations is that faculty report early burnout. One respondent provided a dramatic example of what happens:

> From my experience, I am stretched so thin across all my responsibilities that I can almost not function anymore. I have nine Ph.D. students, I'm on a lot of committees, and this year I'm teaching six courses when I should only be teaching four, and I'm the director of undergraduate studies in my department, and so I feel as though my undergraduate teaching is no longer even adequate. So, it is an incredible irony that you might throw yourself into teaching when you're a junior person but oddly enough, when you're finally a senior person you are so encumbered with other responsibilities that almost perforce, your teaching suffers as a consequence. Here I am finally supposedly a local paragon of pedagogy, and I think that I no longer have the time to do what I should be doing, because after all, I'm also trying to write a second book so that I can get promoted.

The Effect of University Policies on Faculty Priorities

Although university policies commonly support excellence in teaching, research, and service, there are large variations by institution and by discipline in the importance given to each area and in the combination of duties that professors undertake. Of particular importance in improving the learning environment is a focus on teaching. While undergraduate teaching is considered to be rejuvenating and at times inspiring, in a study of over eight hundred professors at doctoral degree-granting institutions it was ranked twenty-fourth in terms of role preference and was liked only moderately (Bess, 1982). Instruction to graduate students was ranked most highly, followed closely by long-term theoretical research. In liberal arts colleges, attention to teaching might be expected to take precedence, but faculty members valued highly by their peers are those who rate highly in publication and scholarship (Blackburn, Knuessel, and Brown, 1988). One respondent elaborated on this situation:

> The president of a liberal arts college in Michigan was quoted as saying that when young faculty asked him for advice about what they should do in order to get promoted, in all honesty he had to advise them to do research. Small liberal arts colleges in their recruiting material brag about the faculty members they have who are getting published or are getting research grants. We know that the correlation between research productivity and instructional effectiveness (at least as measured by student ratings, which are known to be moderately related to objective measures of student learning) is about .15; less than 2 percent of the variance is shared between research and teaching. They are largely independent; the best thing you can say is that doing research probably does not hamper teaching, does not damage one's teaching ability, but you certainly cannot make the argument that the best teachers are also the best researchers.

To be promoted and given tenure in a university, a professor must devote as much time as possible working to attain the approval of specialists recognized as authorities in the field (Wilshire, 1990). Because recognition, promotion, and tenure have come to be based primarily on the indices of research, a career-oriented academic must put research at the forefront (Donald, 1984). Early promotion and tenure are based on research productivity, as is promotion to full professor. Another reason for the imbalance in prestige accorded research and teaching is that faculties, departments, and programs are rewarded differentially by the university based on research productivity; those that hold major research grants or have affiliated research centers have greater economic and political power. Clark (1987a) points out that the greatest paradox of academic work is that most professors teach most of the time, but teaching is not the activity most rewarded by the academic profession and not most valued by the system at large. Administrators continually praise teaching and reward research. According to Clark, the paradox has its own rationality: teaching maintains the system by appeasing essential clienteles and by paying operating costs. It also produces an intense commitment from many academics. But research appeases the disciplines and rewards members of a discipline for advancing knowledge and technique.

An administrator described the problems created by the promotion and tenure system at her university and suggested potential alternatives:

> We have an extremely formal promotion and tenure system. It is perhaps too narrowly focused on research as the thing that will get you rewarded and promoted. It's cumbersome; it takes a long time; you turn in your dossier in the fall and you don't find out until April. I think it's perceived as secret and not supportive of people. There is some sentiment that six years is not a long enough probationary period. There is some sentiment to have ten-year renewable contracts and to do away with tenure.
>
> Our guidelines already say that you have to be an excellent teacher. You cannot get promoted if you are not doing your job in the classroom, but you could be doing your job in the classroom and not get promoted. If the performance evaluations in fact were tied to a reward, monetary or promotion, something like the California step system for example, and they were also tied to the faculty members' objectives, where they were in their career—maybe they've been in research and they want to get back involved with freshmen in the classroom; maybe they have been teaching upper-division courses and they want to start some research in a completely different area (you cannot expect people to be happy and productive for forty years doing exactly the same thing, and that is what we're set up to do)—you would not have as much sentiment to have tenure. We need a lot of first-class training on how to do effective performance evaluations.

The reward structure for faculty often varies across departments and, in addition, demands on faculty are not consistent across disciplines or with the reward structure.

> On most campuses, what happens is quite varied across departments. If effectiveness is rewarded, if the reward structure fosters that

> kind of competitiveness, model programs will be spread across campus, but in a lot of campuses, that is not so. In large research universities, research productivity in various forms is more strongly related to compensation (not just salary) than is teaching. That relationship is found right across institutional types, including liberal arts colleges.

The effects of rewarding research more than teaching are widespread. One major effect has been that teaching undergraduates usually falls at the bottom of the priority list for most faculty (Kimball, 1988). The effects are felt across departments. Disciplines divide work in significantly different patterns; for example, scientists teach less and do more research, while in the humanities, professors teach more and do less research (Clark, 1987a). The sciences, as respondents noted in Chapter Two, then assume greater prestige than the humanities, with greater credibility, faster promotion, higher salaries, and more decision-making power in the university.

> It is not the concern for research that has led to an indifference and sometimes a hostility toward undergraduates on the American campus; it has been a consistent policy of reward that has reflected a perverted sense of prestige associated with prizes and appearance in certain kinds of journals or money, grants, and the like. Too many professors will tell me behind closed doors, by direct language or by inference, that they would like to have been more concerned for their undergraduate students, that they should have given more time or it would have been nicer to. They express guilt and concern for a life that has been highly segmented, compartmentalized to the detriment of people around them, and to pulling their weight in the department. Some people realize that they have siphoned off a larger amount of the unit's resources than maybe would have been for the best of the unit, but they say that is the way the game is played.

Assessment of Faculty

Faculty are the most thoroughly assessed constituent of postsecondary institutions; one could say they are given 360-degree feedback. They are assessed continually and in diverse ways—for promotion and tenure, for merit, on their teaching, for research grants. They are regularly monitored via annual reports and curriculum vitae. Relatively little of the monitoring has rewards attached to it, and the accountability process for faculty is not perceived by professors to be a productive way to spend their time. Can the assessment process for faculty be made more valuable?

In a cross-institutional study of the criteria used by academic leaders to assess overall performance of faculty across fifty-five Canadian universities, the most important criterion was research productivity, closely followed by teaching competence, being up-to-date in the subject matter, having an academic degree, having effective communication skills, and the ability to obtain research funds (Donald, 1991) (Table 8.1). All of these criteria were rated as highly important (3.5+ on a 5-point scale). Student-oriented criteria such as student-centered teaching, advising, and supervision were rated as moderately important, as were involvement in course development and service.

Results varied, however, depending upon whether the universities were larger or smaller (less than 6,600 students). Most larger universities (91 percent) considered research productivity of high importance, while 61 percent of the small universities did. The percentage was almost reversed for teaching competence, with 62 percent of the large universities considering it of high importance compared with 96 percent of the small universities. Student-centered teaching was of high importance for more small universities (68 percent) than for large (23 percent). Student advising, service within the institution, and service to the community were also more frequently considered important by the small universities than by their larger counterparts. Few of the universities attached high importance to innovative activities such as participating in professional development, being a change agent, using a multidisciplinary approach, or computer and technology literacy.

Given these circumstances, how do we create a learning community? How can attention to student learning be increased in large

Table 8.1. Criteria for Assessing Faculty Performance

Criterion	Mean Rating[a]
Research productivity	4.2
Teaching competence	4.1
Up-to-date in subject matter	4.0
Academic degree	4.0
Effective communication skills	3.7
Ability to obtain research funds	3.6
Student-centered teaching	3.2
Involvement in course and program development	3.0
Service within the institution	3.0
Service to the profession and the community	2.8
Student advising and mentoring	2.8
Supervision of graduate students	2.6
Change agent in academic role, innovator	2.5
Moral and ethical sensitivity	2.4
Experience outside the educational institution	2.2
Participation in continuing professional development	2.2
Appropriate personality characteristics	2.1
Multidisciplinary in approach	2.0
Computer and technology literacy	1.8

[a]Mean rating of 0 = no importance, 1 = very low importance, 2 = low importance, 3 = moderate importance, 4 = high importance, and 5 = very high importance.

and small universities? Changing an institution's organizational structure may require the same kind of dialogue suggested for the improvement of teaching.

> I think the structure at the university will be breaking down. There is nothing that says we have to have departments, schools, and colleges. My hope would be for more team teaching, collaborative learning, by changing the way the faculty look upon the courses. There are two visions of faculty. The public's vision is that we are lazy and arrogant—we come into work around 10 o'clock, and we check our mail; we go off to lunch with a friend, we go off and play golf at two

> in the afternoon. If that view is true, then what needs to happen is to fire those faculty, because they are not doing what we the public want them to do. I have probably interviewed as many faculty as anyone else in the country in the last ten years, and that is not true.
>
> The faculty I know, by and large, are terrifically hard working. They get up at five in the morning, they take work home with them, they work on weekends. They say that one of the major reasons they are faculty members is the freedom to chart what they want to do, and they are talking to me at 7:30 in the morning, because that is the only half-hour they have found. We may not like what they are doing; maybe they should spend more time with students than write an article or get a grant, but they are not lazy. That means the structure is wrong, in relation to faculty workload. People do respond to stimuli, and we need to change the reward structure.
>
> To change the structure is much harder. You begin with real substantive changes that bring the faculty together to talk about the nature of our program. I think that leaders can make a difference. In the U.S., leaders are primarily defined in roles: presidents, provosts, deans. We expect presidents to raise money; we do not expect any form of intellectual leadership from them, and we don't get it, but we can. That role is not circumscribed by fundraising. The board needs to realize that, and the faculty needs to make the board realize that. Because of the vast structural diversity in the United States, I don't think there is one answer.

Attempts to give greater status to teaching by linking it to other forms of scholarship may, however, turn the tide. In *Scholarship Reconsidered: Priorities of the Professoriate*, Boyer's (1990) redefinition of the tasks of faculty members as the scholarship of discovery, integration, application, and teaching has led to exploration of how knowledge is developed in different disciplines. The scholarship of integration, which is concerned with interpreting information, putting it in perspective, and illuminating it, often using an interdisciplinary approach, brings together research and teaching. This reconceptualization of faculty pursuits has induced learned societies and professional groups to examine the kinds of scholarship valued in their fields (Diamond and Adam, 1993).

A study to determine the relative importance of faculty roles in different disciplines suggested how disciplinary and university missions could be coordinated.

> The role of faculty is much broader than recognized in the reward system, and each field has its own terminology. The fields are telling us that there are many important things that in the past have not been rewarded and that what is recognized and rewarded must be decided in the context of the individual college or university. Our model tells us that you take the priorities of the institution, its mission statement; you move to the school or college, then you move down to the department, and as central administrators, you get out of micromanagement. The department is looked at as a whole, so it is a matter of a combination of different individual strengths. The approach the disciplines are taking is that each department should pick from the list of competencies those which are appropriate for their mission. The department makes the match between the discipline and the mission statement of the university.
>
> As we have been moving through the process, departments have been evolving promotion and tenure and merit pay guidelines that are based on the nature and practice of the department. We're saying that you need flexibility in weighting teaching, research, and service at the department level, because you need to recognize that it is the synergism of different talents that gives you a quality program.

This decentralized procedure places the onus on departments to juxtapose the university mission with what is important to them in their fields. The departments must, however, enunciate clearly what their mission is, how they will ensure that it is met, and how they will show that they have succeeded.

Assessment of Teaching

If, over the past decade, research has been the focus of university life, teaching has now become part of the performance review system, both in promotion and tenure decisions and in annual reviews. At one university, the attention took the form of a university-wide committee, changes in promotion and tenure regulations, and changes in annual performance reviews.

> Teaching is annually becoming a greater part of the system, although the faculty are still questioning the extent to which this change is more window-dressing than real. I am seeing some of our faculty becoming surprised at how real it is, as someone is turned down for tenure or promotion because of teaching, or someone gets an extra reward that is specified because they had such a wonderful year in the classroom. That kind of information is only beginning to filter through the faculty at this point and beginning to raise eyebrows. I think it is going to be another five years before we have stabilized in a position where teaching will have its defined place.

The importance of this change in attitude for improving the learning environment should not be underestimated. However, the judgment of effective teaching is complex; many factors and effects must be considered. The lengthy literature on faculty preferences and student ratings of teaching (Donald, 1984; Donald and Penny, 1977; Hildebrand, Wilson, and Dienst, 1971; Irby, 1978; McKeachie, Lin, and Mann, 1971; Seldin, 1980) suggests that for higher-order learning to occur, the effective teacher can be described in the following manner. The effective teacher provides students with a conceptual framework of the discipline, which in turn facilitates the retrieval and application of newly acquired knowledge, shows enthusiasm for the subject matter, gains student attention, and promotes a positive attitude toward learning and the particular course content. While modeling the thinking and the methods of inquiry associated with a field or discipline, the effective teacher encourages students to actively participate in the teaching and learning process.

Varying levels of importance have been ascribed by different constituents to the elements of effective teaching. Students often describe effective teaching in terms of warmth, using words such as enthusiasm, rapport, charisma, dynamism, or personality (Eble, 1986; Feldman, 1976; Kulik and McKeachie, 1975; Perry, 1985). Others have described effective teaching in terms of course presentation, the learning environment, and showing genuine interest in the student (Thomas, 1989, 1990). Academic leaders across universities rated being up-to-date in the subject matter and effective communication skills most important (Donald, 1991) (Table 8.2). Course organization and clarity have the highest correlations with student achievement; stimulating interest in the course and subject matter ranks fourth (Feldman, 1996). In our cross-institutional study of academic leaders' views, a mixture of intellectual and administrative functions was also considered important.

All of the indicators concerning interaction with students were rated highly important by more small universities than large as factors of effective teaching. The greatest difference was in the percentage considering student-centered teaching an important indicator, with over 80 percent of small universities but only about 33 percent of the large universities considering it important. This was 10 percent higher as a factor of effective teaching in both large and small universities than it was as a criterion for assessing overall faculty performance. Generally, criteria in the areas of instructional qualities, interaction with students, and management skills were rated more highly in small universities—all indicators leading to increased student involvement. This finding parallels the greater importance assigned in the study to teaching compared with research in smaller universities.

The Use of Student Ratings

Student ratings have been widely accepted as a source of information for evaluating faculty performance (Braskamp, Brandenberg, and Ory, 1984; Centra, 1993; Cohen, 1981; Donald, 1984; Ericksen, 1984; Feldman, 1989; Marsh, 1984; McKeachie, 1990). The

Table 8.2. Importance of Effective Teaching Factors

Factor	Mean Rating[a]
Up-to-date in subject matter	4.4
Effective communication skills	4.4
Defined grading procedure	4.3
Ability to stimulate ideas	4.2
Maintenance of class hours	4.2
Maintenance of office hours	4.0
Relationship with students	4.0
Rapport and interaction	4.0
Tolerance of other viewpoints	4.0
Provision of course outline	3.8
Student-centered teaching	3.6
Course and program development	3.3
Prompt in returning assignments	3.2
Knowledge about graduation requirements	2.5

[a]Mean rating of 0 = no importance, 1 = very low importance, 2 = low importance, 3 = moderate importance, 4 = high importance, and 5 = very high importance.

use of student rating questionnaires is sometimes stipulated by collective agreements, employment contracts, or tenure and promotion documents that require the inclusion of the results of evaluations in teaching dossiers. As a result of the interest in and concern about teaching, many universities have taken steps to establish policy, identify dimensions of effective instruction, and introduce methods to evaluate whether instructional goals are being met (Abrami, 1985; Donald, 1984, 1985; McKeachie, 1990; Perry, 1990).

Student ratings can provide information about areas where improvement is needed, as well as professors' particular strengths (Cranton and Smith, 1990; Kremer, 1990; Marsh, 1984; McKeachie and Lin, 1978; Penney, 1977). Motivated teachers can use feedback from student ratings for self-analysis and can take steps to improve their instruction (l'Hommedieu, Brinko, and Menges, 1990; Penney, 1977). The evaluation of teaching by students has helped department chairs make decisions about teaching and has proven to be more effective than other forms of evaluation.

> I happen to come from a department that has an internal culture that is oriented to teaching. We simply do not hire people who cannot teach. One of the things we are looking for when we hire new assistant professors is how well they can project themselves, how articulate they are, how well organized they are. Though again, the initial basis on which we bring them to us is always their doctoral dissertation, we have been known to turn down people simply on the grounds that they would not be able to live up to the high standards of the department as far as teaching is concerned. When I was the chair of my department, I would quite often, in trying to find some base for teaching evaluation, drop in on the members of my department just to listen to them perform because, again, in terms of promotion, this was a consideration. That was a system that never worked very well; it was always very awkward for the chair to drop in unannounced. You never knew whether the performance that particular day was a typical performance or an abnormally good or bad one. We have, since those days, developed what almost all major universities have now, which is the student evaluation. Like all other departments, we depend on that for helping us judge the quality of teaching.

In spite of twenty years of research on the evaluation of teaching in universities, reliable and valid methods for the evaluation of instruction are still being tested. Greater reliability has been reported for student evaluations of instruction than for peer evaluation (Kremer, 1990) or for evaluation rendered by alumni, colleagues, and classroom observers (Cohen, 1981; McKeachie, 1979). Although academic rank (instructor through professor) does not affect overall rating, the number of years of teaching does (Centra, 1979). Centra found that instructors in their first year of teaching generally received lower ratings; those with one or two years experience or more than twelve years' experience received higher ratings; and those in the three-to-twelve-year range were rated higher still. Teaching assistants received significantly lower scores. Since the variability within groups is considerable, the number of years of teaching alone is an insufficient index to determine who the best teachers are.

Although in the cross-institutional study, student rating questionnaires were often used alone, other methods included evaluation by a department chair, course outlines, peer evaluation, teaching awards, evaluation by the dean, and research and publication related to teaching (Donald, 1991). The two most powerful methods of getting feedback from students for improvement purposes—videotaping of classroom teaching and instructional diagnosis using a small group of students—tend to be less frequently used. They are resource-and time-intensive methods, but they have been found to be most effective in improving teaching (l'Hommedieu, Brinko, and Menges, 1990). As noted in Chapter Six, they are used by teaching centers.

One of the respondents focused on the need for meaningful formative evaluation of learning and teaching but bemoaned the fact that the reward system in the university works against teaching improvement efforts.

> I have student evaluations in an autopsy that will be performed on Thursday asking, "Was this a good class, was it interesting, too much or too little?" That may help me in the future, but I have interviewed enough faculty that I know this is a fake. It does not help me improve my teaching; it is an evaluation. We have scales of one to seven; if you get above five, you're OK. If you are a junior faculty member, don't get above six, because then the senior faculty members will say that you are working too hard on your teaching. Don't get below four, but if you fall between four and six, don't work on your teaching; you're doing OK. One of the questions I asked junior faculty members is, "If teaching is a bunch of activities, we all know that we can improve in some area; what is the area you would like to improve in?" They all have something different. They'll say, "I'm not good at creating discussion" or "I'm not good at creating tests." When I say, "How can we make it work for you to improve that aspect?," they say, "I don't have time for that. I'll do it after tenure."

This quotation marks the problem of oversimplified measures of quality and a reward system that works against teaching improvement. Incentives are needed to make specific changes in instructional methods.

The Administration of Student Ratings

The purpose of student rating forms is usually both for the improvement of teaching and for tenure and promotion. The time at which student rating forms are administered, most frequently in the last two weeks of the course, is an important factor in their subsequent usefulness. The practice of administering the rating forms in the last two weeks means that no improvements can be made to the course as it progresses. The optimal time in terms of making improvements and respecting the need for reliable data is in the middle third of the course, but in one-semester courses, this time period is also the time of midterm examinations, which may introduce bias into the results. Recommended practice then becomes the use of a brief questionnaire, which may be informally administered for improvement purposes in the middle third of the course, with the use of a form for general administrative purposes in the last two weeks of the course. To ensure that students understand why the questionnaires are being used and take them seriously, it is critical that forms be administered with the care necessary for any test administration. At one university, the university teaching center has designed a multifaceted procedure for the assessment of teaching.

> We provide two kinds of instruments. One is an instrument that is a fairly short form that will facilitate decisions for promotion and tenure, merit, and other types of administrative decisions. We're more concerned with promoting diagnostic evaluation instruments, something that is designed by the faculty to help them look at what they are doing in the classroom. We have made an agreement with the administration that the data that deal with diagnostics will be extrapolated and not be used in any kind of administrative decisions. That information is provided solely to the faculty for the faculty member's use. We are also trying to promote other ways of evaluation and to provide suggestions or materials that will help faculty accomplish that.

> For example, we are developing a teaching portfolio; we are working with some departments on peer evaluation techniques, on self-evaluation. We are trying to say to people that the instrument of faculty evaluation is only one way to measure teaching and should not be the sole way. We are also trying to educate administrators who use these instruments about the correct and incorrect way to use these instruments. That is an important step in assessment.

One problem that has arisen in response to the widespread use of student evaluations is a boomerang effect in student expectations of their responsibility for learning. Questionnaires that focus on the instructor's behaviors without examining students' may lead students to place the burden of responsibility on the professor's shoulders rather than approaching learning as a shared enterprise. If students are to assume greater responsibility for their learning and become self-regulating, they need to become self-monitoring in class. As one respondent pointed out,

> Everything in terms of course evaluation is typically oriented toward the professor's comportment and not the student's role, and the forms ought to have items where students report their own behaviors and the social structure of the course for which the teacher isn't really held accountable, because that would be informative and would sensitize students to their role. It is not all the responsibility of the professor. It is a counterpart to an honor code.

End-of-term Evaluation

For end-of-term evaluation at one university, a campuswide service is available to every department and to faculty individually. The service is one of the most sophisticated in operation and requires departments to consider the use of the questionnaires for decision-making purposes.

> If we contract with a department to provide department-wide service, we require a statement from the head of the department explaining what the departmental policy on the use of student ratings in per-

> sonnel decision-making processes is and who has access to the results. This is also a noninvasive way of getting feedback about how well department practice conforms to what we might describe as generally accepted standards for practice, at the common-sense level, using ratings. In providing the service, we are a change agent, because when departments do business with us, we provide materials that talk about issues in interpreting and applying ratings data to personnel decisions. We discuss with faculty in these materials issues of sampling, for example, no personnel decision should be made based on the results of a single administration of a teacher-course evaluation.

The forms are laser printed with the course identification and are certified response sheets, one printed for each enrolled student. This increases the perception of fairness. A packet label provides course information, type, and how many people are enrolled. Student monitors sign a statement saying that they personally handed out, collected, and returned the materials, after counting the blank sheets and the used sheets that they put into the packet. The respondent continued:

> If you are in a department that has contracted to do business with us, you receive your report of results first individually. You have two weeks, which is a fail-safe in case packets have been switched, then all the reports go to the department heads. If the long report was used, faculty members get a descriptive diagnostic report that shows the items and the scale, with the frequency and the percentage of the response, deviation from the mean, and the 95 percent confidence interval. The goal is to encourage them to interpret this in a qualitative manner. "Look at this and ask yourself, What percentage of my students say what? If half your students say that you do each of these things more than half the time, then you know that you are generally speaking doing things that contribute to student achievement." Some of these things are more important in some content areas than in others. If students say you are doing some of these things half the time or less, those are areas where you need be concerned.

> The questionnaire has four parts: the instructor's scale, course design (including outside assignments), the overall organization of the course, and student demographics. It is hard to convince people that the course items, like course text, which instructors often do not get to choose, are not value-laden but are there for information purposes. It is important to be able to gauge the effort that your students expend. I explicitly tell department heads and faculty that course design items are not to be used for personnel decisions.

The four parts of the questionnaire provide feedback to the instructor, the department, the program, and the university. Course design questions can be used for program improvement, while student demographic questions establish student preparation and motivation, as well as gender, program, and year of study. More of the factors that affect teaching and learning in a course are recognized in this format, and the results can be used more broadly to establish the relative effect of different factors on learning in the course.

Formative Evaluation of Teaching

For formative evaluation, a confidential questionnaire that focuses on specific behaviors of the professor is used.

> The midterm evaluation is a walk-in service available to faculty and teaching assistants, midsemester, confidential, for which we use a teaching behaviors inventory. When I speak with someone who has used this instrument in a consultation, we have a brief discussion about the difference between low-inference items and what their value might be compared with the end-of-semester evaluations, so they understand that it is a different kind of evaluation.

Low-inference items are behaviors that students can see in the classroom, for example, "stressing important points" (Murray, 1985). These have been linked to student learning achievement and have been used in training to improve teaching. An evaluation method used at another university gives students greater responsibility for the instructional process.

> In my teaching, there is a new moon once a month. In the Native American way, especially with the Sioux, there would always be a new moon meeting at which you look at the past and at the future. So when I teach, I have a new moon meeting once a month. My classes generally meet twice a week. In the class before the new moon, I pass around pieces of paper, two of which have circles on them. The people who get the circles are the new moon facilitators, and it is up to them to use the last fifteen minutes of class as they determine. They can ask me to leave the room or to stay; we can have a formal handout, or we can talk about something in particular. From that, I will change what is going on the next month.
>
> My point is not to justify what I am doing; my point is to change. I also hand out a midterm evaluation of me that is anonymous and send it off to the teaching center and then have a conversation with the director of teaching and learning. I think that is insufficient, because an anonymous evaluation is one form of assessment that is helpful; new moon meetings are helpful for any number of reasons, not the least of which is to involve students in the ownership of the class. They can't tell me fifteen weeks later that I talked too much.
>
> What I would like to see is to put names of teachers in a program in a hat and pass it around so that I would sit in your class, and you would sit in my class a minimum of two or three times during a semester. We would not evaluate it in the sense that I am going to write something up that goes into some file. We would make a pact that I am not going to go next door and say, "Boy, I saw ____ teaching, and is he terrible!" It would be an honest dialogue about one another's teaching. The faculty are very hesitant to do that. But the process says that teaching is important.

At a third university, one method involves all class members and allows students to think about what has gone on in the class and to become aware of others' opinions.

> A consulting faculty member would go to the class, usually in the last twenty minutes. The teacher would leave, and the consulting faculty

member would take over the class. The consulting faculty member would then either divide the class into relatively small groups of five to seven students or in small or large classes, would divide them into pairs, and would ask them to spend eight to ten minutes addressing these three questions: What's right about what's going on and what's wrong? and correspondingly, What suggestions do you have? and third, Are you learning anything, and what and why, from this experience? The groups are turned loose to discuss these matters with each other, with a note-taking form that asks those questions in a more formal manner. At the end of the eight to ten minutes, the consulting faculty member brings them back together to get reports from at least some of them in this fashion: ask the entire group to listen to the groups you pick and begin with a group with the first question, asking them, "What did you say, what did you consider?" Then you clarify, ask them follow-up questions, then verify by asking the rest of the class for any additions or any disagreements. Then ask another group to deal with the second question, and so on.

You really only get to three groups intensely in ten minutes, but you are able to give everyone the chance to say, "Our group reached a completely different conclusion." In the end, we collect the note-taking forms from all the groups, so thus within twenty minutes, we've talked to the students, we've had a chance to do some follow-up questions, and get, in my view, a surprisingly strong sense of the student responses to teaching in this class. Normally, this is done between a third and halfway through the course. The consulting professors are chosen by the departments who make the pairings.

I have found the activity enormously useful in getting some insight into the student responses. I have found that faculty will respond more favorably and more extensively to such feedback from students than to any other feedback. There is a tendency for faculty to be somewhat jaded about student evaluations, but in this process students are much more thoughtful than they might be operating on their own. In addition, it is an opportunity to find out the various viewpoints that exist and to realize that not all students agree with one another and for the students to realize that. It is quite revealing for many stu-

> dents when a group of students on one side of the room offers its suggestions for how the class should be conducted and suddenly discovers that other students would find that an abomination.

These methods of formative evaluation provide alternative and innovative ways of determining what needs to be changed in a course. More important, students become aware of others' perspectives and of their role and responsibility as learners.

Summary: Faculty Responsibilities, Rewards, and Assessment

Societal demands for the solution of problems and the development of expertise differ considerably from faculty and administrators' priorities, which are academic freedom and quality. A faculty reward system in which all professors are expected to excel in research, teaching, and service may lead to early burnout. Because recognition, promotion, and tenure are based primarily on research, and departments and programs are also rewarded within the university according to research productivity, an imbalance between research and teaching functions has developed. Disproportionate rewards to one area, usually research, affect quality in other areas. Faculty research and student learning are symbiotic when faculty teach in their area of research. Attention to the scholarship of integration, concerned with interpreting and putting information in perspective, may link research and teaching more closely.

Promotion and tenure criteria and annual reporting procedures that require evidence of effective teaching will lead to the improvement of teaching in the institution. End-of-term evaluations provide departments with information about generally accepted standards for practice and whether they are being met. Formative assessment for the improvement of teaching may take the form of midterm questionnaires, diagnostic instruments, class-directed or peer evaluation techniques.

Benchmark Practices

1. Focus on the scholarship of integration so that research and teaching are linked more closely. Help faculty teach in their area of research.
2. Match the department mission with promotion and tenure and merit criteria, so that faculty can set goals within the department framework that are meaningful to them.
3. Encourage the improvement of teaching by using promotion and tenure criteria and annual reporting mechanisms that require evidence of effective teaching.
4. Carefully attend to the administration of teaching evaluations. These provide departments with information about generally accepted standards for practice, whether they are being met, and factors that may affect teaching and learning in courses and programs. Administrators must show that the evaluations are useful.
5. Include items on teaching questionnaires that ensure students' understanding of their responsibilities as learners. Items may establish student preparation, motivation, and their role as self-regulating learners.
6. Use formative assessments of teaching to provide information about where improvement is needed. They may take the form of midterm questionnaires, diagnostic instruments, class-directed periodic evaluations, or peer evaluation techniques such as the use of a consulting faculty member who works with students in small groups.

9

Institutional Assessment to Improve Learning

The challenges facing postsecondary institutions in the twenty-first century include determining the future role of universities in the creation of new knowledge, mastering technology and using it appropriately, and establishing effective planning and monitoring processes.

The main themes in this chapter are institutional accountability and opportunities. Given the increasing pressures on universities, as discussed in the first chapter, what are the optimal strategies for improvement? External agencies' reviews can serve to make institutions aware of the need for effective planning and monitoring, but more important are internal administrative processes that are transparent, fair, and lead to a sense of community. The chapter begins, therefore, with a review of the effects of external evaluation, followed by an examination of forms of institutional evaluation, program reviews, and student and alumni surveys. The chapter concludes with a summary of strategies for program improvement.

The most significant external challenges to the university are to supply the best education possible and to compete successfully in the knowledge industry. Two respondents describe these challenges:

> This is an interesting, exciting time, with a lot of balls in the air. The excitement ought to be that it is a true opportunity to reform. That has been true of a lot of opportunities in higher education; the difference now is that schools that don't reform are going to go under. The private schools will go under real fast, and the public schools will

> be irrelevant in the sense that people just won't pay attention to them. If a private school cannot compete, it will go under. A state institution won't go under, but people will say, "I won't go to that school. I'll take my learning through the distance education program on the information highway. Why should I go to a watered-down place that doesn't focus on what's needed to be an educated person?" The information highway will have that kind of impact; it is part of the financial challenge. It wasn't part of the financial challenge when we had educational TV, because you could get by by saying it's a fad.
>
> The ultimate issue is a matter of defining the institution in ways that make sense in light of competing institutions or other institutions like research institutes and economic influences and technology.

The larger issue encompassing these challenges is the extent to which the university is a center for change. In *The Academic Ethic*, Shils (1983) described three views of the function of academics and academic institutions. The first is the discovery and transmission of truth, and the second is to educate students for those occupations which demand mastery of a coherent body of organized knowledge, a capacity to assess evidence, and readiness to look at situations afresh. The third view is to be centers of revolutionary change. Shils argues that universities have been the points of origin of profound changes, based on an intellectual foundation, in the world at large. This argument is supported by Pelikan (1992) in his reexamination of the university: he states that during a period of revolutionary social change such as the present, the university urgently needs to find new ways of protecting freedom of inquiry, particularly when scholars undertake, as they must, to construct and propose models of the good society as alternatives or improvements to the present.

Universities are sources of innovation and should be readily able to plan creatively. The list of relevant innovations introduced in universities in recent years is impressive (Sutton, 1994). These include new courses dealing with other cultures and international relationships, area research centers, and junior year abroad programs. Third World economic and social development has become a subject of scholarship, with growing attention to global issues such as climate change, energy dependence, and the implications of worldwide communications networks. Earlier in this book, a respondent noted that universities are places where difficult issues are dealt with. The question then becomes, Which issues will have priority? To respond to that question, one strategy is to reexamine the roles of the university.

Since most universities have multiple roles, their definition requires consideration of the relative emphasis placed on each. To return to the roles discussed in Chapter One—as a center for research, a guide for the betterment of humankind, critic of society, intellectual center of a learning society, or training for the job requirements of society—a set of criteria can be named: research grants, publications and citations, societal well-being, the stimulation of inquiry and reflection, the fostering of intellectual development, or job placement. Assigning weights to the roles or the criteria that describe them is an acid test of their relative importance. A respondent elaborates on the dilemma:

> A research university has as its chief role the creation of new knowledge and, as a corollary, its dissemination and application to the betterment of the human condition. But if we don't know anything new, then we don't have anything to apply, so at a university like ours, which is a research university and a land grant university, that means that research comes first. The taxpayers of the state might not agree with that, so the university has a number of different roles depending upon whom you talk to. It may well be that the often-heard complaint that research is more important at this institution than teaching is correct and that it should not be a complaint but an affirmation of the proper role of this kind of university as an institution of higher education.

The argument for maintaining the pre-eminence of research in research universities is simple. According to Pelikan (1992), anyone who would subordinate research to teaching bears the obligation to specify alternate venues for research and the advancement of knowledge. A larger challenge is the fact that a great deal of research is now being done outside the universities (Shils, 1983). Shils states that despite the erosions and arrogations, universities still remain the major centers of learning in their respective societies. The integration of research with teaching requires explicit coordination. Universities must also decide upon the kinds of steps that need to be taken institutionally to provide equal opportunity to learn.

> As far as policy issues are concerned, I think the most important one is reconciling issues of access and quality education, but that may have as much to do with the way we fund our institutions and the kinds of activities that we reward. In this country, the have's get and the have-not's generally don't get. When there are budgetary cuts, the flagship institutions in the public sector are generally protected to one degree or another. They are given greater protection than are the less prestigious institutions, those that are serving important segments of our population.
>
> In many respects, I am very hopeful about higher education. Difficult decisions can create a climate for change in a very positive way and should engender a philosophical discussion on the part of different groups. For example, over the last twelve years, the federal government has increased loans to the detriment of grants. That has meant that the poor are worse off in terms of college going, the upper class is better off, and the middle class is marginally affected. If that is true, is the philosophical statement, This country is committed to the principle of access? If we are, we will enable all students to go to college who desire a college education. That is a dramatic principle.

In response to the question of equal opportunity, universities need to make a series of coordinated decisions on (1) policy toward selection of the student body, (2) preparatory documentation and orientation to introduce students to their new learning tasks, (3) student services needed to deal with student adaptation, and (4) ways to monitor the process.

Another important issue is how to utilize instructional technology. Development time, resources, and in-service preparation for faculty to explore new media and technologies need to be recognized as part of the context in the learning community.

> The university has traditionally been a place where people come and spend four to ten years of their existence and either leave the academy and go elsewhere or else stay within the hallowed walls and go on with their existence. But technology is providing the opportunity to redefine that model. How should we redefine the model? I think in order to answer that question, we do not simply ask what technology is available, but we ask instead, What is it that we want our students to be able to do intellectually and how can we best help them achieve that? What kind of environments can we create? What kind of technologies do we adopt, and therefore, what kind of situation do we create for the students?
>
> We have to figure out how to use technology for information transmission, and it can do a lot more than that—simulations and so forth. The best scholarly minds have to embark on the process of designing those tools, which is very energy-intensive. Once that is done, it changes the role of the professor so dramatically from information transmission to the coaching, mentoring, exploring together for which many faculty are not suited. Then, we will have to learn how to perform well in those roles, in what could truly be a learning community where the bonds are much closer. What will change is the content that is available to everybody. In the information world, there is much

> more access to much more material, so the professor who wants to maintain the gatekeeping function won't be able to do that.

The variety of challenges is great, and attempting to respond to them will require proactive decision making. Assessment procedures that have originated external to postsecondary institutions provide a certain impetus for responding to the challenges.

The Effect of External Evaluation

Assessment procedures and indicators at program and institutional levels have commonly been developed in response to external demands that institutions be accountable or meet certain standards. The positive effect is that institutions are enjoined to broaden their perspective, to become aware of their own governance procedures, and to compare themselves with benchmark institutions and practices. The principal weakness of procedures and indicators developed for external audiences is that they provide limited information about *ways* to improve institutional functioning. To illustrate, of fourteen performance indicators described in the *Encyclopedia of Higher Education,* the eight indicators for teaching are student entry qualifications, degree results, cost per student or staff-student ratio, value added, rate of return, wastage or noncompletion rates, employment of students on graduating or after five years, and student and peer review (Cave and Hanney, 1992).

These indicators have more to do with students than with teaching, except for staff-student ratio, which may render instruction more difficult or easy, and student and peer review, which provide measures of satisfaction. The use of the indicators in program review would also be limited in terms of information about potential improvements that could be made. The six performance indicators for research are the number of research students, publications or patents, citation of publications, research income, peer review, and reputational ranking—oriented predominantly to evaluation of individual researchers. These indicators tell us little about steps that could be taken to improve the way in which programs function and students learn. As one respondent stated,

> Performance indicators are a growing phenomenon in this country. There are states that are already requiring their higher education systems to develop performance indicators. Most of the indicators are probably low-level and have been around for years, like student-faculty ratios or credit hours. Some states appear to be moving back to the Tennessee model of performance funding that will be based on institutional performance indicators more broadly, a kind of criterion-referenced funding. You get additional funds if you can demonstrate that your institution is performing at a given level or has increased its performance level by X percent on seven or eight specified criterion measures.

The Tennessee Performance Funding Program began in 1979 as an incentive for meritorious institutional performance, particularly in enhancing student learning outcomes (Banta, Rudolph, Van Dyke, and Fisher, 1996). A small budget supplement (up to 2 percent) is awarded to institutions that obtain accreditation for accreditable programs and ensure that graduates meet national averages in their major fields. Since 1979, the criteria on which performance funding is based have undergone four revisions. The most recent funding guidelines, as of 1993, represent a substantial movement in the direction of assessment for internal improvement rather than external reporting. In this revision, the number of performance standards doubled, from five to ten; peer review of unaccreditable undergraduate programs was added, and institutions were allowed to set their own goals in several areas.

To investigate the extent to which the performance standards were viewed as measures of the quality of higher education by those expected to use them, a survey was sent to the individuals responsible for compiling the annual performance funding reports at college and university campuses in Tennessee (twenty-three administrators, half of whom were faculty). Peer review was given the highest rating as a measure of quality, followed by accreditation, improvement plans, and student and alumni surveys. Thus, the most highly developed state performance funding program introduced internal review and improvement mechanisms into its accountability procedures. Although these measures are not specifically of the learning that takes place, they are closer to it than previous measures have been, and the measures received approbation from those responding to the assessment requirements.

At the four universities in this study, state or regional assessment for program or student accreditation purposes has been in place for the past two decades. Assessment for external purposes was not, however, a salient topic. One respondent expressed the opinion that the only regular reviews were those done for accreditation purposes. More concern was expressed that the accreditation process was becoming unglued and that people did not understand what was at stake.

> One of the unheralded areas in higher education in this country that is being maligned is accreditation. Slowly, quietly, without a lot of fanfare, the regional Associations of Colleges placed the expectation that you ought in your self-study to speak about the effects of the institution on the student in terms of what they have learned; you ought to have some congruence between what you say you are going to teach, how you teach, and so forth. The demise of the Council on Postsecondary Accreditation is a large landmark in the perceived failure of accreditation.
>
> What is lacking is any comparative base. If you get rid of accreditation, with what do you replace it? Europe is rapidly trying to invent self-study mechanisms. There is an advantage to having a visitor come in who is not on the same payroll, who is not necessarily a representative of an institution that is in the same political system as you are in, but has expertise in the area. When a country like Finland tries

> to invent a peer review system for programmatic accreditation, I fear that, with two dozen chemists in all of Finland, the kinds of accusations that are laid at the feet of accreditation here would play out in spades when you have twelve people looking at each other and commenting on each other's performance and the quality of the programs they have put together. We don't have that problem because of the large accrediting regions. We have far less propensity to inbreeding under those circumstances. There is also the potential for finding ready benchmarks, but what is unrealized is that Americans are reticent to criticize one another, so that renders the system of somewhat less impact than it might otherwise have.

Several important statements are made in this quotation. Accreditation or external review is a safeguard that other educational systems are now attempting to duplicate. In the United States, the system is sufficiently large to minimize political influence and to produce readily applicable improvements. The major drawback is that external evaluators tend to be insufficiently critical. In essence, accreditation serves a useful purpose, even if it does not fulfill all accountability needs. Other public measures of quality, for example surveys executed by national magazines, were perceived by the respondents to have limited validity, largely because the performance indicators used are not linked to learning.

> My problem with *U.S. News and World Report* is that they are focusing all of their energies on standardizing the data collection and closing loopholes so that institutions have less room to define how numbers are calculated and reported, but they are getting better and better at collecting information on the wrong sets of variables.

Magazine reports intended for the general public often use financial resources—the operating budget, scholarships and bursaries, residential spaces, and spending on nonacademic services per student—as indicators of quality (*Maclean's Magazine*, 1991). Other criteria frequently used are staff-student ratio, the number of research grants per professor, and the average grade of entering students. The principal effect of these reports is on application rates to various post-secondary institutions. They shed comparatively little light on the internal functioning of the institution. Overall, the effect of external assessments is to alert institutions to what must be done to maintain acceptable programs. They are thus bottom-line or remedial in their effect; their association with optimal functioning is minimal. Recent performance funding initiatives, on the other hand, appear to lead institutions to choose appropriate goals and work toward them, which does support institutional improvement.

Internal Institutional Assessment

In order to make decisions that will work in a university, goals and objectives at all levels, including the institution as a whole, must be understood. Cole (1994) points out that the fundamental problem of choice at research universities has more to do with basic ambiguity over governance than with the ability to articulate alternatives. He asks a series of difficult questions: Who has the operational authority to make choices? Who has the power to veto the choices made? What are the processes by which the choices of decision makers are legitimated within the university community? What is the role of faculty, students, administrative leaders, trustees, and alumni in making such choices? These questions highlight the fact that the problem universities have in making difficult decisions is not simply a matter of speed but of certain structural features that make reaching conclusions difficult.

Because universities tend to be organized in a collegial manner around a company of equals and because they rely on peer judgments of academic quality, consensus or unambiguous judgments are rare. Academic units may be unwilling to criticize others when the stakes are reductions in size or possible program elimination. Cole notes that since most academic deans anticipate rejoining the faculty, they are reluctant to make difficult decisions that cannot possibly please everyone. Muller (1994) uses the analogy of the university as a holding company to describe difficulties in decision making across units where decentralization has diluted any remaining respect for authority. In a response to the dilemma universities currently find themselves in vis-à-vis institutional governance, one administrator had decided to approach the problem from an organizational development perspective.

> In higher education, especially in large universities, one of the key issues if we are going to emerge in the twenty-first century as relevant, is to focus more on our employees. I don't think we have a tradition in most of our institutions of effectively promoting, valuing, rewarding, supporting, and training employees, and that includes faculty, administrators, and staff. Any management theory, especially those current right now, indicates that the knowledge reservoir on how to make things better is in the people that work in the institution. The complexities of the world, the speed at which everything is changing, and the unpredictability associated with all of it mean that it is not possible, as it used to be, for a CEO or even a couple of people to understand cognitively how an institution works or how an industry works or how anything works. That means that you have to rely on the collective wisdom of the people who work there in a much more central way. That means you have to empower and involve them and support them. We used to say that management is getting work done through others, and the emphasis was on the work and the others were kind of a nuisance. Now, the circle has come 180 degrees, and the emphasis has to be on the people; the work will get figured out by the people.

Assessment procedures that could be expected to improve institutional and program functioning received considerable attention from academic leaders in the four universities. Contrary to expectation, however, the process of program review in three of them appeared to have been superseded by institutional forms of evaluation or management. For example, at one of the two public universities, total quality management had been instituted, and at the other, strategic planning was the preferred stance. Of the private universities, one had a built-in institutional improvement team and its own version of quality management to guide continual improvement. The other, most collegial of the universities in its operation, had adopted a program review process. Across the four universities, institutional assessment had become a highly structured management process.

The demand for more efficient operation has led numerous institutions to apply total quality management (TQM), but it has usually been limited to administrative areas of the university. Others have pointed out, however, that TQM can be used in the classroom and that much of the data from student outcomes assessment can be applied to advantage within the TQM framework (Banta, 1996; Sims and Sims, 1995). At one university, for example, an attempt was made to use TQM in order to shift from historically based to data-based decision making.

> The core issue is data-based decision making. There has been a precedent here for historically based, politically based decision making, and the use of data has been more to serve protected needs than global needs. The idea in embracing total quality management, with its data orientation, is that we need to have data available all across campus, so that everyone's looking at the same data.

Teaching assignments and workloads were the first areas to come under scrutiny. The application of TQM has refocused attention on undergraduate teaching, partly in response to demands from government and the public.

> Data use is a big problem related to faculty evaluation, because getting accurate records on who is teaching what courses has proved to be a challenge. We may have TAs teaching several sections of a

> course, but the course record lists a faculty member who may never set foot in that classroom. Another area of assessment is workload assessment, based on concern about the proliferation of courses, vanity courses with fewer than ten students, tenure-track faculty not teaching enough lower-division undergraduates and introductory courses. Assessment in those areas is having some impact on faculty, reallocating their effort a little bit more toward undergraduate education.

Institutional assessment may thus open the door to changes in educational practice. What it does not supply is the analysis and definition of best practice. Moreover, perceptions of institutional efforts to improve quality may differ radically among faculty.

> The sense among faculty is that assessment efforts in the university are fragmented. We are beset by university planning, continuous organizational renewal and evaluation, total quality management, and program assessment, but what they really mean is a great deal of work for faculty members who are trying to do their job and barely have time to do that, much less participate in all of these procedures whose consequences are invisible. Assessment activities at this university include the monitoring of undergraduate teaching to determine if full professors are in contact with undergraduates. There are lots of us who are, but that is not usually known. So assessment appears in the three realms of institutional monitoring, student tracking, and surveys of students to capture the quality of student experience in order to determine how their experiences contribute to their success. Assessment also appears in the central administration's efforts of continuous organizational renewal and program review. The central administration thinks of this as being integrated, but that is not visible to us in the trenches.

An example of the limited participation in and understanding of institutional studies illustrates the inherent difficulty of using corporate management procedures in a decentralized university. In a case study of junior faculty conducted at another university, no faculty member of the sixty interviewed was knowledgeable about a major institutional study on the future of the university.

> I got comments like, "Is that the thing that is strategic planning, but they call it something different?" and "That's the thing that didn't change anything. I guess it was a success." Most junior faculty's frame of reference is the department and to a certain extent the college, but what does it mean that junior faculty never talk to the dean? I interviewed faculty who had been here from four to six years, and the only time they met with the dean was once at the social. They did not have meetings one-on-one, or group meetings; the deans did not think of calling them in periodically. When I interviewed the deans, they said they simply did not have time. If we leave aside the social justice aspect, the leader talking to the followers, the idea that we are making a multi-million-dollar decision, and that you don't talk with this individual, makes stupid economic sense. If a donor is at the door and says, "I am considering giving you a million dollars, do you have time to talk with that person?" The dean would spend an hour with that person, and the person might walk away and not give the million dollars. The junior faculty member may cost you a million dollars, and deans are saying that they do not have one hour in the year to talk with that person.

This quotation suggests, first, that institutional management roles may be ill-defined and overextended so that deans lack the resources to create a supportive environment in their colleges. Second, deans as representatives of their colleges are oriented to the larger academic community, to the detriment of knowing what is happening inside their colleges. Building a sense of community requires assigning priority to personnel administration. In organizational management, it is generally recognized that performance is a function of organizational and environmental factors and therefore is determined as much by the interaction of the parts in the organization as by the actions of individuals (Kurz, Mueller, Gibbons, and DiCataldo, 1989).

Performance must therefore be defined from a system maintenance perspective. This means taking into account how the academic setting is structured, characteristics of the process of work of its members, and outcomes, products, or services that result from the interaction of system structure and process. The kinds of assessment indicators needed to support intra- and interunit communication and decision making would have to be meaningful across units and yet sufficiently specific that they could be used to guide improvement within units.

One approach to addressing performance issues in an academic community is to create an institutional improvement team. In one university center, its members study all areas of the campus for potential improvements.

> We focus on finding out what is happening, how something is working or is not working; it could be on the bookstore, health services, residential life, or an academic program.

For example, studies on student retention provide data for program improvement and pinpoint where improvement is most needed to retain students. Another center member explains:

> Our retention studies look at overall retention rates of cohorts of students as they move through the university. Once we have that framework established, we can then look by school or college, by department, by students with various backgrounds, at GPA, who drops out. If they have less than 2.0, you are going to have a large proportion leaving, but then you look at those with good academic standing who leave to get a sense of why and when they leave.
>
> Six years ago, we ran an analysis of enrollment in programs over a three-year period to look for changes. We also looked at the assignment of full-time faculty to teaching responsibilities, teaching ratio,

> a lot of information that might be the basis for program review, and having people think about what their mission was and how they were going to deploy their resources.

In summary, to be useful within an institution, performance indicators should be meaningful across units yet sufficiently specific to guide improvement within. Program reviews, student and alumni surveys, and institutional improvement teams can be used to collect information for potential improvement across campus.

Assessment of Programs

The most common program review process begins with a unit self-study, which includes preparation or updating of a unit mission statement, the comparison of performance with the statement, and feedback from stakeholders in the unit (Donald, 1982). At one of the universities studied, a program review council evaluates all academic and administrative units within the university. According to a senior faculty member and previous chair of the council, the twelve members of the council, each of whom chairs a unit review subcommittee, learn a great deal from their participation in the process about how the university operates and the strengths and weaknesses of it. Academic units write a review of themselves, and the subcommittee poses a series of questions that the council wants answered. The program review council makes recommendations about the future of each unit in the university. The review process deals with the curriculum and attaches resources to the outcome but is still limited in the instructional and learning issues that are examined. As one respondent noted,

> The review process here is very important. The president has paid attention, and resources have flowed in response to the committee's recommendations, or the president has used the committee's recommendations to justify what he wanted to do. But it is the central administration who appoints those committees. While the process gathers information widely, it gathers virtually no information about

> the quality of instruction as we would think of it. They look at courses and curriculum and teaching load but not syllabi and course evaluations or assignments or evidence of learning.

Program reviews can be used to examine curriculum and instruction issues, but these issues do not tend to be a prominent part of program review. What is important is that the review procedure can be broadened or refocused to attend to learning issues. For example, in the first round of program reviews at my university, the emphasis was on research activities in the units. The second seven-year series of reviews was extended to include indices of teaching and the evaluation of instruction. Other learning issues may be approached by means of student and alumni surveys.

Student and Alumni Surveys

Given the investment of time and energy most students make in attending college, Astin (1993b) suggests that their perceptions of the value of their experience should be given substantial weight. He and others argue that satisfaction levels are much more susceptible to influence by the university environment and thus provide a clearer reading of its effects. Stakeholders in higher education agree. In the study of criteria and indicators of quality in postsecondary institutions, the two most important criteria of quality for an institution were clarity of mission and student satisfaction with the institution (Nadeau, Donald, Konrad, and Tremblay, 1990).

Administrators and academic department heads consider the degree of student satisfaction with their educational experiences an important dimension in the assessment of institutional effectiveness (Braskamp, Wise, and Hengstler, 1979; Cameron, 1981). Some have argued that better understanding of student satisfaction is fundamental to better understanding of educational process and quality (Hearn, 1985). Students experience the curriculum as designed by institutions and enacted in classrooms and are in the best position to describe how they interpret and experience the curriculum they are required to take (Pace, 1985; Twombly, 1992). Finding the appropriate place in the institution where data can be collected and utilized may be the greatest inhibitor. One venue that has proved useful for interviewing graduating students on their experiences while at university is the dean's office.

> Graduating students are interviewed in the dean's offices by the dean's staff, usually associate deans. The questions asked are about the quality of the program that would be appropriate for people who have not yet been on the job market. Occasionally, although I don't think this is specifically asked for, they hear anecdotes about particular faculty who have made a very positive impression, and sometimes negative information.

Other methods include senior surveys and surveys at graduation itself. For example, at one university, seniors were given a card to be handed back in when they picked up their gowns for graduation. On it, students were asked to provide their college with insight into their undergraduate education.

Alumni can also provide valuable insights, since they have the benefit of hindsight and can evaluate college and work experiences and their relative importance (Graham and Cockriel, 1990). Because graduates can report the actual significance in relation to their current employment or life status, the use of feedback from graduates in reviews of academic programs is increasing (Moden and Williford, 1988). Retrospective evaluations that relate undergraduate experience to subsequent employment or further study may provide more concrete and operational advice for improving undergraduate education than individual course evaluations. The suggestions that graduates provide through surveys are input for a broad range of decisions about the curriculum, course content, and major requirements, as well as faculty roles and teaching methods, student services, and resource allocation and institutional planning (Moden and Williford, 1988). The following example describes one administrator's strategy for improvement:

> When I became the professor in charge of the program, I sent a memo to the faculty that said, "To change things it takes two things, the desire to change and data. So, I am going to send a survey out to all past students, and I am going to have focus groups for all current students, I am going to interview each individual faculty member, I am going to have interviews with other people who have something to say about the program. We are going to assemble all the data. I want you to develop for me one question or one problem that you see in the program and offer a solution. I don't care how big or how small the problem is." I asked the graduate student association to do the same thing. I talked about this to a fellow who is chair of the center for total quality schools and he said, "You're doing TQM. That's what TQM is about."

In a more formal attempt to assess institutional program quality, graduates' perceptions of their undergraduate experience, their satisfaction with their program, teaching, and student life, and the relevance of their studies to experiences after graduation, were collected by means of a graduate survey (Donald and Denison, 1996a). Perceived quality of teaching was found to contribute significantly to graduates' rating of the overall quality of their academic program. The most frequently mentioned meaningful feature of their undergraduate education for alumni was the development of the ability to think.

This poses an interesting dilemma for university decision makers, who traditionally have focused on faculty and resources, when alumni focus more on learning and developmental outcomes. Earlier studies of graduates' perceptions of their undergraduate education have generally found that intellectual and cultural experiences are extremely important in determining alumni attitudes toward the colleges they attended (Pace, 1974; Spaeth and Greeley, 1970). Analyzing graduates' comments and advice provided us with a wider and fuller perspective of what engenders success in educational programs and institutions. Results were analyzed according to faculty, and a report to the dean was discussed in committee with senior administrators.

The program assessment methods reviewed here have different focal points—a comparison of program performance with program goals or mission, student and alumni satisfaction, and faculty and other stakeholders in the program. They bring assessment closer to program operation and at the same time are consistent with institutional quality procedures.

Using Institutional Assessment To Improve the Environment for Learning: A Synthesis

The underlying question that has guided this book is, *What characteristics of institutions of higher education enable students to learn?* Assessment is useful only if it used to improve practice. To do so, it must be consistent with the mission of the university and respond to its priorities, but it must also reflect the immediate tasks of individual units. Approaches to improving the learning climate at the broadest level include self-definition, clarifying the university mission and setting priorities, viewing postsecondary education as a multinational knowledge industry, reengineering procedures to reduce work, and using benchmarks or best practices that have been successful in other institutions. In determining the mission of the university, important conditions to be considered are whether another social agency can respond to the need, what the needs of the constituency are, the extent to which social equity issues will be taken into consideration, and how intellectual development will be fostered.

Because disciplines represent both knowledge bases and methods of inquiry, how they operate is critical in establishing the learning climate. Important for institutional improvement is an understanding of how learning goals vary across disciplinary areas and what this means in terms of student outcomes. Greater understanding across disciplinary boundaries is needed to aid the development of student competencies.

To ensure that students in postsecondary institutions have the opportunity to develop to their fullest potential, an important step is to identify what constitutes general academic preparedness and what student characteristics enable them to learn and develop. To do this, educational institutions must determine to what extent success is a matter of selection procedures, the fit of the student to the institution, student self-definition, procedures set in place to ensure that students are oriented to learning when they arrive, the curriculum and instruction offered at the institution, and the general learning milieu.

Administrative strategies that set the stage for learning involve informing students early about their role in the learning endeavor. Universities need to be clear about their admissions policy and what they expect of their students, as well as what help is available to guide students in their quest. Students should be alerted to the necessity of investing personally in learning and to be open to the changes that must take place in order to develop intellectually. Students need to be told about the potential of intrinsically oriented learning and their responsibility for regulating their learning.

Academic tasks that motivate learning have four characteristics: *choice*, *challenge*, *control*, and *collaboration*. At the institutional level, the most important way to foster student motivation for learning is to create a learning community, where students and their learning experiences are the focal point. Other steps include ensuring an advising system that works, rewarding faculty for effective advising, rewarding programs in which students and faculty interact more frequently, and inducing better learning by giving students opportunities for situated learning.

To help students become independent and self-regulating learners, first-year seminars and programs elucidate appropriate learning goals and how students can meet them. New media allow students to learn in a framework of situated cognition, where they develop a model within a context and then expand from it to other contexts. In-service preparation for faculty for media and technological changes in instructional strategies is essential.

To foster effective instruction, recognizing teaching in career decisions and teaching award programs is a favored strategy. Teaching can be honored in a variety of ways, through formal recognition, salary increases, development funds, release time, and by means of individual or group awards, grant competitions, or election to a teaching academy. Because teaching and learning are complex processes, longer-term improvement methods that aid reflection such as mentoring, faculty discussion groups, week-long workshops, and course design consultations are more effective in dealing with instructional issues. Programs for teaching assistants reflect their diverse needs for learning about course planning, teaching strategies, and evaluation procedures. Teaching centers engage in a variety of services and projects, serve as clearinghouses, and conduct research relevant to teaching and learning. Administrative strategies that support student learning include decreasing class size and establishing guidelines for class size.

Assessing student learning and development to improve learning, instruction, and program effectiveness has become increasingly important. Sources of data on learning outcomes include student administrative records of success in courses; averages in subsequent semesters; studies on retention; student evaluations of programs at graduation; and faculty, staff, and student opinions. To accommodate wide-scale assessment procedures, greater communication within and across institutions is vital. Classroom assessment techniques allow professors to enunciate teaching goals and reflect on how well they are achieving their teaching and learning goals. Student self-assessment is a powerful strategy for integrating students into the learning community, inducing student development, and assessing student learning outcomes.

A faculty reward system in which all professors are expected to excel in research, teaching, and service may lead to early burnout. Faculty research and student learning are symbiotic when faculty teach in their area of research. Attention to the scholarship of integration, concerned with interpreting and putting information in perspective, may link research and teaching more closely. Promotion and tenure criteria and annual reporting procedures that require evidence of effective teaching will lead to the improvement of teaching.

To improve institutional functioning, assessment must take into account the institution's mission, program objectives, measures of performance in meeting the objectives, and the collective wisdom of the learning community. Although external reviews may make institutions aware of program inconsistencies, an improvement process that is transparent, fair, and executed by the community will lead to optimum practice. Performance indicators should be selected by the academic community and should be meaningful across units yet sufficiently specific to guide improvement within. Peer review of programs becomes an opportunity to learn about how other units and the university as a whole operate. The review process is highly adaptable. Student surveys can be used to collect data on the quality of the program, while alumni surveys reveal the significance of programs in relation to graduates' employment or further study. An institutional improvement team can investigate areas for potential improvement across campus.

The perceptions and strategies that the respondents in the four universities have described are diverse and can be applied at many levels. They can therefore be useful to institutions with different histories and missions searching for improvement procedures that fit their own environments. Some benchmark practices may be readily adopted; others may serve to provoke new species of benchmark practices. The innovative practices suggested by colleagues in the four universities and the research results surrounding them are testament to the creativity and intellectual strength available, and undoubtedly needed, to respond to the challenges we face.

References

Abrami, P. C. (1985). Dimensions of effective college instruction. *The Review of Higher Education*, 8(3), 221–228.

Adams, M. (1992). Editor's notes. In M. Adams (Ed.), *Promoting diversity in college classrooms: Innovative responses for the curriculum, faculty and institutions* (pp. 1–5). New directions for teaching and learning, no. 52. San Francisco: Jossey-Bass.

Albright, M. J., & Graf, D. L. (1992). Editor's notes. In M. J. Albright & D. L. Graf (Eds.), *Teaching in the information age: The role of educational technology,* (pp. 1–6). New directions for teaching and learning, no. 51. San Francisco: Jossey-Bass.

Alverno College. (1989). *Ability-based learning program*. Milwaukee, WI: Alverno College Productions.

American Council on Education. (1986). *Campus trends, 1986*. Washington, DC: Author.

American Psychological Association. (1994). *Publication manual of the American Psychological Association* (4th ed.). Washington, DC: Author.

Angelo, T. A., & Cross, K. P. (1993). *Classroom assessment techniques: A handbook for college teachers* (2nd ed.). San Francisco: Jossey-Bass.

Arizona Board of Regents. (1982). *Arizona university system mission and scope statements*. Phoenix, AZ: Author.

Arizona Board of Regents. (1990). *Toward the year 2000: Arizona Board of Regents' strategic plan*. Phoenix, AZ: Author.

Ashworth, A., & Harvey, R. (1994). *Assessing quality in further and higher education*. London: Jessica Kingsley.

Association of American Colleges. (1985). *Integrity in the college curriculum: A report*. Washington, DC: Author.

Association of American Colleges. (1991). *Liberal learning and the arts and science major: The challenge of connecting learning*. (Vol. 1). Washington, DC: Author.

Astin, A. W. (1984). Student involvement: A developmental theory for higher education. *Journal of College Student Personnel, 25*, 297–308.

Astin, A. W. (1985). *Achieving educational excellence: A critical assessment of priorities and practices in higher education*. San Francisco: Jossey-Bass.

Astin, A. W. (1993a). An empirical typology of college students. *Journal of College Student Development*, *34*, 36–46.

Astin, A. W. (1993b). *What matters in college? "Four critical years" revisited*. San Francisco: Jossey-Bass.

Astin, A. W., Green, K. C., & Korn, W. S. (1987). *The American freshman: Twenty year trends*. Los Angeles: Cooperative Institutional Program of the American Council on Education and the University of California.

Astin, A. W., & Henson, J. (1977). New measures of college selectivity. *Research in Higher Education*, 6, 1–9.

Astin, A. W., & Panos, R. (1969). *The educational and vocational development of college students*. Washington, DC: American Council on Education.

Austin, A. E. (1992). Faculty cultures. In B. R. Clark & G. R. Neave (Eds.), *The encyclopedia of higher education* (pp. 1614–1623). Oxford, England: Pergamon Press.

Baird, J. R. (1988). Quality: What should make higher education "higher"? *Higher Education Research and Development*, *7*(2), 141–152.

Banta, T. W. (1992). Student achievement and the assessment of institutional effectiveness. In B. R. Clark & G. R. Neave (Eds.), *The encyclopedia of higher education* (pp. 1686–1697). Oxford, England: Pergamon Press.

Banta, T. W. (1996). Using assessment to improve instruction. In R. J. Menges, M. Weimer, & Associates (Eds.), *Teaching on solid ground: Using scholarship to improve practice* (pp. 363–384). San Francisco: Jossey-Bass.

Banta, T. W., Rudolph, L. B., Van Dyke, J., & Fisher, H. S. (1996). Performance funding comes of age in Tennessee. *Journal of Higher Education*, *67*(1), 23–45.

Barefoot, B. (1995, February). *The freshman seminar: A flexible fixture in American higher education*. Paper presented at the annual national conference on the freshman year experience, Columbia, SC.

Barnett, F. G. (1977). *A study of ego development of teacher interns as a result of membership in an elementary education teacher training program*. Unpublished master's thesis, McGill University, Montreal.

Barron's Profiles of American Colleges: 21st edition (1996). College Division of Barron's Educational Series. Hauppage, NY: Barron's Educational Editors.

Barzun, J. (1993). *The American university: How it runs, where it is going* (2nd ed.). Chicago: University of Chicago Press.

Bateman, D. (1990). *A longitudinal study of the cognitive and affective development of Cegep students*. Unpublished doctoral dissertation, McGill University, Montreal.

Bateman, D., & Donald, J. G. (1987). Measuring the intellectual development of college students: Testing a theoretical framework. *Canadian Journal of Higher Education, 17*, 27–45.

Baxter Magolda, M. (1992). *Knowing and reasoning in college: Gender-related patterns in students' intellectual development*. San Francisco: Jossey-Bass.

Becher, R. A. (1989). *Academic tribes and territories*. Milton Keynes: Open University Press.

Becher, R. A. (1992). Disciplinary perspectives on higher education: Introduction. In B. R. Clark & G. R. Neave (Eds.), *The encyclopedia of higher education* (pp. 1763–1776). Oxford, England: Pergamon Press.

Bentham, J. (1948). *Introduction to the principles of morals and legislation*. Oxford, England: Hafner Press.

Bergquist, W. H., Gould, R. A., & Greenberg, E. M. (1981). *Designing undergraduate education: A systematic guide*. San Francisco: Jossey-Bass.

Bess, J. (1982). *University organization: A matrix of the academic profession*. New York: Human Sciences.

Biggs, J. B. (1988). The study process questionnaire (SPQ): User's manual. Hawthorn, Victoria: Australian Council for Educational Research.

Biggs, J. B. (1993). What do inventories of students' learning processes really measure? A theoretical review and clarification. *British Journal of Educational Psychology, 63*, 3–19.

Biggs, J. B., & Collis, K. F. (1982). *Evaluating the quality of learning: The SOLO taxonomy*. New York: Academic Press.

Biglan, A. (1973). The characteristics of subject matter in different academic areas. *Journal of Applied Psychology, 57*(3), 195–203.

Blackburn, R., Knuessel, R., & Brown, R. (1988, April). *Attributes of valued faculty members*. Paper presented at the annual meeting of the American Educational Research Association, New Orleans, LA.

Blaisdell, M. L. (1993). Academic integration: Going beyond disciplinary boundaries. In Richlin, L. (Ed.), *Preparing faculty for new conceptions of scholarship* (pp. 57–69). New directions for teaching and learning, no. 54. San Francisco: Jossey-Bass.

Bloom, B. S. (1976). *Human characteristics and school learning.* New York: McGraw-Hill.

Blumenstyk, G. (1993, September 1). Colleges look to "Benchmarking" to measure how efficient and productive they are. *Chronicle of Higher Education*, pp. A41–A42.

Bonwell, C. C., & Eison, J. A. (1991). *Active learning: Creating excitement in the classroom.* (ASHE-ERIC Higher Education Report No. 1). Washington, DC: The George Washington University, School of Education and Human Development.

Bowen, H. R., & Schuster, J. H. (1986). *American professors, a national resource imperiled.* New York: Oxford University Press.

Boyer, E. L. (1990). *Scholarship reconsidered: Priorities of the professoriate.* Princeton, NJ: Carnegie Foundation for the Advancement of Teaching.

Braskamp, L. A., Brandenburg, D. C., & Ory, J. C. (1984). *Evaluating teaching effectiveness: A practical guide.* Beverly Hills, CA: Sage.

Braskamp, L. A., Wise, S. L., & Hengstler, D. D. (1979). Student satisfaction as a measure of departmental quality. *Journal of Educational Psychology, 71*(4), 494–498.

Broudy, H. S. (1977). Types of knowledge and purposes of education. In R. C. Anderson, R. J. Spiro, & W. E. Montagne (Eds.), *Schooling and the acquisition of knowledge* (pp. 1–17). Hillsdale, NJ: Erlbaum.

Brown, J. S., Collins, A., & Duguid, P. (1989). Situated cognition and the culture of learning. *Educational Researcher, 18*(1), 32–42.

Brown, L. T. (1983). Some more misconceptions about psychology among introductory psychology students. *Teaching of Psychology, 10*, 207–210.

Brown, L. T. (1984). Misconceptions about psychology aren't always what they seem. *Teaching of Psychology, 11*(2), 75–78.

Bruce, J. (1995, August). *Developing an information strategy: The role of technology.* Paper presented at the annual forum of the European Association for Institutional Research, Zurich.

Cabal, A. B. (1993). *The university as an institution today.* Ottawa, ON: International Development Research Centre; Paris: United Nations Educational, Scientific and Cultural Organization.

California Postsecondary Education Commission. (1988). *Eligibility of California's 1986 high school graduates for admission to its public universities.* Sacramento, CA.

Calvino, I. (1968). *Cosmicomics.* San Diego: Harcourt Brace.

Cameron, K. S. (1981). Domains of organizational effectiveness in colleges and universities. *Academy of Management Journal, 24*(1), 25–47.

Cashin, W. E., & Downey, R. G. (1995). Disciplinary differences in what is taught and in students' perceptions of what they learn and how they are taught. In N. Hativa & M. Marincovich (Eds.), *Disciplinary differences in teaching and learning* (pp. 81–92). New directions for teaching and learning, no. 64. San Francisco: Jossey-Bass.

Cave, M., & Hanney, S. (1992). Performance indicators. In B. R. Clark & G. R. Neave (Eds.), *The encyclopedia of higher education* (pp. 1411–1423). Oxford, England: Pergamon Press.

Center for the Study of Higher Education view book. (1992). University Park: Pennsylvania State University, Author.

Centra, J. (1979). *Determining faculty effectiveness.* San Francisco: Jossey-Bass.

Centra, J. (1993). *Reflective faculty evaluation: Enhancing teaching and determining faculty effectiveness.* San Francisco: Jossey-Bass.

Chickering, A. W. (1984). *Commuting vs. residence students: Overcoming the educational inequalities of living off-campus.* San Francisco: Jossey-Bass.

Clark, B. R. (1987a). *The academic life: Small worlds, different worlds.* Princeton, NJ: The Carnegie Foundation for the Advancement of Teaching.

Clark, B. R. (Ed.). (1987b). *The academic profession: National, disciplinary and institutional settings.* Berkeley, CA: University of California Press.

Clark, B. R. (1995, August). *Institutional structure and management.* Paper presented at the annual forum of the European Association for Institutional Research, Zurich.

Clifford, M. M. (1991). Risk taking: Theoretical, empirical and educational considerations. *Educational Psychologist, 26,* 263–297.

Cohen, P. A. (1981). Student ratings of instruction and student achievement: A meta-analysis of multisection validity studies. *Review of Educational Research, 51,* 281–309.

Cole, J. R. (1994). Balancing acts: Dilemmas of choice facing research universities. In J. R. Cole, E. G. Barber, & S. R. Graubard (Eds.), *The research university in a time of discontent* (pp. 1–36). Baltimore: The Johns Hopkins University Press.

Cranton, P., & Smith, R. (1990). Reconsidering the unit of analysis: A model of student ratings of instruction. *Journal of Educational Psychology, 82*(2), 207–212.

Delillo, D. (1985). *White noise.* New York: Viking Press.

Diamond, R. M. (1993). Changing priorities and the faculty reward system. In R. M. Diamond & B. E. Adam (Eds.), *Recognizing faculty work: Reward systems for the year 2000* (pp. 5–22). New directions for higher education, no. 81. San Francisco: Jossey-Bass.

Diamond, R. M., & Adam, B. E. (1995). *Syracuse University revisited: Changing priorities*. Syracuse, NY: Center for Instructional Development.

Dinham, S. M. (1996). *What college teachers need to know*. In R. J. Menges, M. Weimer, & Associates (Eds.), *Teaching on solid ground: Using scholarship to improve practice* (pp. 297–313). San Francisco: Jossey-Bass.

Donald, J. G. (1982). A critical appraisal of the state of evaluation in higher education in Canada. *Assessment and Evaluation in Higher Education*, *7*(2), 108–126.

Donald, J. G. (1984). Quality indices for faculty evaluation. *Assessment and Evaluation in Higher Education*, 9(1), 41–52.

Donald, J. G. (1985). The state of research on university teaching effectiveness. In J. G. Donald & A. M. Sullivan (Eds.), *Using research to improve teaching* (pp. 7–20). New directions for teaching and learning, no. 23. San Francisco: Jossey-Bass.

Donald, J. G. (1986). Knowledge and the university curriculum. *Higher Education, 15*(3), 267–282.

Donald, J. G. (1987a). Learning schemata: Methods of representing cognitive, content and curriculum structures in higher education. *Instructional Science, 16*, 187–211.

Donald, J. G. (1987b). *Report on the research project: The learning task in the university: Introductory psychology at Stanford University*. Montreal: McGill University, Centre for University Teaching and Learning.

Donald, J. G. (1990). University professors' views of knowledge and validation processes. *Journal of Educational Psychology*, 82(2), 242–249.

Donald, J. G. (1991). The Commission of inquiry on Canadian university education: The quality and evaluation of teaching. *Revista Interamericana de Gestion y Lederazgo Universitario, 1*, 157–173.

Donald, J. G. (1992a). The development of thinking processes in postsecondary education: Application of a working model. *Higher Education*, 24(4), 413–430.

Donald, J. G. (1992b, August). Learning psychology: Ethnographic studies of professors' and students' perceptions. In *Learning, thinking, and problem solving: Issues in teaching and transfer*. Symposium conducted at the meeting of the American Psychological Association, Washington, DC.

Donald, J. G. (1994). Science students' learning: Ethnographic studies in three disciplines. In P. R. Pintrich, D. Brown, & C. Weinstein (Eds.), *Student motivation, cognition and learning:Essays in honor of Wilbert J. McKeachie* (pp. 79–112). Hillsdale, NJ: Erlbaum.

Donald, J. G. (1995). Disciplinary differences in knowledge validation. In N. Hativa & M. Marincovich (Eds.), *Disciplinary differences in teaching and learning* (pp. 7–17). New directions for teaching and learning, no. 64. San Francisco: Jossey-Bass.

Donald, J. G. (1996, April). *Professors' and students' perceptions of teaching and learning: Postsecondary students' orientation to learning*. Paper presented at the annual meeting of the American Association of Educational Research, New York.

Donald, J. G. (1997). Higher education in Quebec: 1945–1995. In G. Jones (Ed.), *Higher education in Canada* (pp. 159–186). New York: Garland.

Donald, J. G., & Denison, D. B. (1996a). Evaluating undergraduate education: The use of broad indicators. *Assessment and Evaluation in Higher Education, 21*(1), 23–39.

Donald, J. G., & Denison, D. B. (1996b, May). *Assessment criteria for university students: A study of students' perceptions of criteria of student quality*. Paper presented at the annual meeting of the Canadian Society for the Study of Higher Education, St. Catherines, ON.

Donald, J. G., Flanagan, D., & Denison, D. B. (1993). *The potential of selected teaching improvement practices to improve the quality of teaching: A survey of the views of deans and department heads at McGill University*. Montreal: McGill University, Centre for University Teaching and Learning.

Donald, J. G., & Penny, M. (1977). *Instructional analysis kit*. Montreal: McGill University, Centre for University Teaching and Learning.

Dressel, P., & Mayhew, L. (1974). *Higher education as a field of study*. San Francisco: Jossey-Bass.

Dunkin, M. (1992). Teaching: University and college. In B. R. Clark & G. R. Neave (Eds.), *The encyclopedia of higher education* (pp. 1750–1760). Oxford, England: Pergamon Press.

Eaton, M., & Pougiales, R. (1993). Work, reflection and community: Conditions that support self-evaluations. In J. MacGregor (Ed.), *Student self-evaluation: Fostering reflective learning* (pp. 5–14). New directions for teaching and learning, no. 56. San Francisco: Jossey-Bass.

Eble, K. E. (1986, July/August). A group portrait. *Change*, 21–23.

Eble, K. E., & McKeachie, W. J. (1985). *Improving undergraduate education through faculty development: An analysis of effective programs and practices*. San Francisco: Jossey-Bass.

Edgerton, R. (1993). The re-examination of faculty priorities. *Change, 25*(4), 10–25.

El-Khawas, E. (1993). *Campus trends 1993* (Higher Education Panel Report No. 83). Washington, DC: American Council on Education.

English, H. B., & English, A. C. (1958). *A comprehensive dictionary of psychological and psychoanalytic terms*. New York: David McKay.

Entwistle, N. J., & Ramsden, P. (1983). *Understanding student learning*. London: Croom Helm.

Entwistle, N., & Tait, H. (1990). Approaches to learning, evaluations of teaching, and preferences for contrasting academic environments. *Higher Education, 19*, 169–194.

Ericksen, S. C. (1984). *The essence of good teaching: Helping students learn and remember what they learn*. San Francisco: Jossey-Bass.

Erwin, T. D. (1991). *Assessing student learning and development: A guide to the principles, goals, and methods of determining college outcomes*. San Francisco: Jossey-Bass.

Ewell, P. T. (1987). Establishing a campus-based assessment program. In D. F. Halpern (Ed.), *Student outcomes assessment: What institutions stand to gain* (pp. 9–24). New directions for higher education, no. 59. San Francisco: Jossey-Bass.

Ewell, P. T. (1991). To capture the ineffable: New forms of assessment in higher education. In G. Grant (Ed.), *Review of Research in Education, 17* (pp. 75–125). Washington, DC: American Educational Research Association.

Feldman, K. A. (1976). The superior college teacher from the students' view. *Research in Higher Education, 5*, 243–288.

Feldman, K. A. (1989). Instructional effectiveness of college teachers judged by teachers themselves, current and former students, colleagues, administrators, and external (neutral) observers. *Research in Higher Education, 30*, 137–194.

Feldman, K. A. (1996). Identifying exemplary teaching: Using data from course and teacher evaluations. In M. D. Svinicki & R. J. Menges (Eds.), *Honoring exemplary teaching* (pp. 41–50). New directions for teaching and learning, no. 65. San Francisco: Jossey-Bass.

Fox, P. W., & LeCount, J. (1991, April). *When more is less: Faculty misestimation of student learning*. Paper presented at the annual meeting of the American Educational Research Association, Chicago, IL.

Franklin, J., & Theall, M. (1995). The relationship of disciplinary differences and the value of class preparation time to student ratings of teaching. In N. Hativa & M. Marincovich (Eds.), *Disciplinary differences in teaching and learning* (pp. 41–48). New directions for teaching and learning, no 64. San Francisco: Jossey-Bass.

Fransson, A. (1977). On qualitative differences in learning. IV: Effects of motivation and test anxiety on process and outcome. *British Journal of Educational Psychology, 47*, 244–257.

Frederiksen, N. (1984). Implications of cognitive theory for instruction in problem solving. *Review of Educational Research*, 54(3), 363–407.

Garcia, T., & Pintrich, P. (1992, August). Critical thinking and its relationship to motivation, learning strategies, and classroom experience. In *Learning, thinking, and problem-solving: Issues in teaching and transfer.* Symposium conducted at the annual meeting of the American Psychological Association, Washington, DC.

Goldman, R. M., Schoner, P. G., & Pentony, D. E. (1980). *The vocabulary of a discipline: The political science concept inventory.* Santa Barbara, CA: Clio Books.

Gordon, V. N. (1984). *The undecided college student: An academic and career advising challenge.* Springfield, IL: Charles C. Thomas.

Gordon, V. N. (1995). Resources for academic advising. In A. G. Reinarz & E. R. White (Eds.), *Teaching through academic advising: A faculty perspective* (pp. 103–111). New directions for teaching and learning, no. 62. San Francisco: Jossey-Bass.

Graham, S. W., & Cockriel, I. (1990). An assessment of the perceived utility of various college majors. *NACADA Journal, 10*(1), 8–17.

Gray, P. J., Froh, R. C., & Diamond, R. M. (1992). *A national study of research universities on the balance between research and undergraduate teaching.* Syracuse, NY: Center for Instructional Development.

Gross, E., & Grambsch, P. (1968). *University goals and academic power.* Washington, DC: American Council on Education.

Guthrie, D. S. (1992). Faculty goals and methods of instruction: Approaches to classroom assessment. In J. Ratcliff (Ed.), *Assessment and curricular reform* (pp. 69–80). New directions for higher education, no. 80. San Francisco: Jossey-Bass.

Halliday, A., & Resnick, R. (1988). *Fundamentals of physics.* New York: Wiley.

Harter, S. (1981). A new self-report scale of intrinsic versus extrinsic orientation in the classroom: Motivational and informational components. *Developmental Psychology, 17,* 300–312.

Hearn, J. C. (1985). Determinants of college students' overall evaluations of their academic programs. *Research in Higher Education, 23*(4), 413–437.

Higher Education Research Institute. (1991). *The American college teacher: National norms for the 1989–1990 H.E.R.I. faculty survey.* Los Angeles: University of California.

Hildebrand, M., Wilson, R. C., & Dienst, E. R. (1971). *Evaluating university teaching.* Berkeley: University of California, Center for Research and Development in Higher Education.

Hirst, P. (1974). *Knowledge and the curriculum: A collection of philosophical papers.* London: Routledge & Kegan Paul.

Irby, D. M. (1978). Clinical faculty development. In C. Ford (Ed.), *Clinical education for the allied health professions*. St. Louis: Mosby.

Jones, E. (1992). How faculty promote cognitive development in their students. In J. Ratcliff (Ed.), *Assessment and curricular reform* (pp. 81–90). New directions for higher education, no 80. San Francisco: Jossey-Bass.

Kahn, S. (1996). Awards to groups: The University of Wisconsin system's departmental teaching award. In M. D. Svinicki & R. J. Menges (Eds.), *Honoring exemplary teaching* (pp. 11–16). New directions for teaching and learning, no. 65. San Francisco: Jossey-Bass.

Katchedourian, H. A., & Boli, J. (1985). *Careerism and intellectualism among college students*. San Francisco: Jossey-Bass.

Kells, H. R. (1992). *Self-regulation in higher education*. London: Jessica Kingsley.

Kennedy, D. (1994). Making choices in the research university. In J. R. Cole, E. G. Barber, & S. R. Graubard (Eds.), *The Research university in a time of discontent* (pp. 85–114). Baltimore: The Johns Hopkins University Press.

Keohane, N. O. (1994). The mission of the research university. In J. R. Cole, E. G. Barber, & S. R. Graubard (Eds.), *The research university in a time of discontent* (pp. 153–177). Baltimore: The Johns Hopkins University Press.

Kimball, B. A. (Ed.). (1988). *Teaching undergraduates*. Buffalo, NY: Prometheus Books.

King, A., & Brownell, J. (1966). *The curriculum and the disciplines of knowledge*. New York: Wiley.

King, P. M., & Baxter Magolda, M. B. (1996). A developmental perspective on learning. *Journal of College Student Development*, *37*(2), 163–173.

Kitchener, K. S., & King, P. M. (1990). The reflective judgment model: Ten years of research. In M. L. Commons, & others (Eds.), *Adult development, 2: Models and methods in the study of adolescent and adult thought*. New York: Praeger.

Kremer, J. (1990). Construct validity of multiple measures in teaching, research and service and reliability of peer ratings. *Journal of Educational Psychology*, *82*(2), 213–218.

Kruytbosch, C. (1992). Academic disciplines: Physical sciences. In B. R. Clark & G. R. Neave (Eds.), *The encyclopedia of higher education* (pp. 2329–2331). Oxford, England: Pergamon Press.

Kuh, G. D. (1992). Administration: Student affairs. In B. R. Clark & G. R. Neave (Eds.), *The encyclopedia of higher education* (pp. 1329–1338). Oxford, England: Pergamon Press.

Kuh, G. D., Schuh, J. H., Whitt, E. J., & Associates (1991). *Involving colleges: Successful approaches to fostering student learning and development outside the classroom*. San Francisco: Jossey-Bass.

Kuhn, T. S. (1970). *The structure of scientific revolutions*. Chicago: University of Chicago Press.

Kulik, J. S., & McKeachie, W. J. (1975). The evaluation of teachers in higher education. *Review of Research in Education*, *3*, 210–240.

Kurz, R. S., Mueller, J. J., Gibbons, J. L., & DiCataldo, F. (1989). Faculty performance: Suggestions for the refinement of the concept and its measurement. *Journal of Higher Education*, *60*(1), 43–58.

Kusniac, E., & Finley, M. L. (1993). Student self-evaluation: An introduction and rationale. In J. MacGregor (Ed.), *Student self-evaluation: Fostering reflective learning* (pp. 5–14). New directions for teaching and learning, no. 56. San Francisco: Jossey-Bass.

Lane, J. E. (1992). Local communities and higher education. In B. R. Clark & G. R. Neave (Eds.), *The encyclopedia of higher education* (pp. 946–956). Oxford, England: Pergamon Press.

Lattuca, L. R., & Stark, J. S. (1993, November). *Modifying the major: Extemporaneous thoughts from ten disciplines*. Paper presented at the annual meeting of the Association for the Study of Higher Education, Pittsburgh, PA.

Leary, D. E. (1992). Psychology. In B. R. Clark & G. R. Neave (Eds.), *The encyclopedia of higher education* (pp. 2136–2150). Oxford, England: Pergamon Press.

Levinson-Rose, J., & Menges, R. (1981). Improving college teaching: A critical review of research. *Review of Educational Research*, *51*, 403–434.

Levy, D. (1992). Private institutions of higher education. In B. R. Clark & G. R. Neave (Eds.), *The encyclopedia of higher education* (pp. 1183–1195). Oxford, England: Pergamon Press.

l'Hommedieu, R., Brinko, K. T., & Menges, R. J. (1990). Methodological explanations for the modest effects of feedback from student ratings. *Journal of Educational Psychology*, *82*(2), 232–241.

Linstone, H. A., & Turoff, M. (1975). *The Delphi method: Techniques and applications*. Reading, MA: Addison-Wesley.

Lipset, S. M. (1994). In defense of the research university. In J. R. Cole, E. G. Barber, & S. R. Graubard (Eds.), *The research university in a time of discontent* (pp. 219–224). Baltimore: The Johns Hopkins University Press.

Litten, L. H., & Hall, A. E. (1989). In the eyes of our beholders: Some evidence on how high school students and their parents view quality in colleges. *Journal of Higher Education*, *60*(3), 302–324.

Maclean's Magazine. (1991, October 21). *Special report: A measure of excellence*. Maclean-Hunter: Toronto, ON.

Marchesani, L. S., & Adams, M. (1992). Dynamics of diversity in the teaching-learning process: A faculty development model for analysis and action. In M. Adams (Ed.), *Promoting diversity in college classrooms: Innovative responses for the curriculum, faculty, and institutions* (pp. 9–19). New directions for teaching and learning, no. 52. San Francisco: Jossey-Bass.

Marsh, H. W. (1984). Students' evaluations of university teaching: Dimensionality, reliability, validity, potential biases and utility. *Journal of Educational Psychology, 76*, 707–754.

Mcgregor, H. C. (1992). Biological sciences: Introduction. In B. R. Clark & G. R. Neave (Eds.), *The encyclopedia of higher education* (pp. 2181–2183). Oxford, England: Pergamon Press.

McKeachie, W. J. (1979). Student ratings of faculty: A reprise. *Academe, 62*, 384–397.

McKeachie, W. J. (1990). Research on college teaching: The historical background. *Journal of Educational Psychology, 82*(2), 189–200.

McKeachie, W. J., & Lin, Y. (1978). A note on validity of student ratings of teaching. *Educational Research Quarterly, 4*, 45–47.

McKeachie, W. J., Lin, Y., & Mann, W. (1971). Student ratings of teacher effectiveness: Validity studies. *American Educational Research Journal, 8*, 435–445.

McKeachie, W. J., Pintrich, P., Lin, Y., & Smith, D. (1986). *Teaching and learning in the college classroom: A review of the research literature*. Ann Arbor: University of Michigan, National Center for Research to Improve Postsecondary Teaching and Learning.

Mentkowski, M., & Chickering, A. W. (1987). Linking educators and researchers in setting a research agenda for undergraduate education. *The Review of Higher Education, 11*(2), 137–160.

Mentkowski, M., & Loacker, G. (1985). Assessing and validating the outcomes of college. In P. T. Ewell (Ed.), *Assessing educational outcomes* (pp. 47–64). New directions for institutional research, no. 47. San Francisco: Jossey-Bass.

Mentkowski, M., & Strait, M. J. (1983). *A longitudinal study of change in cognitive development and generic abilities in an outcome-centered liberal arts curriculum*. (Final Report No. 6). Milwaukee, WI: Alverno College Productions.

Meyer, J.H.F., Parsons, P., & Dunne, T. T. (1990). Individual study orchestrations and their association with learning outcome. *Higher Education, 20*, 67–89.

Milem, J. F., & Astin, H. S. (1994, April). *Scientists as teachers: A look at their culture, their roles, and their pedagogy*. Paper presented at the annual meeting of the American Educational Research Association, New Orleans, LA.

Mill, J. S. (1863). *Utilitarianism*. London: Longmans Green.

Moden, G. O., & Williford, A. M. (1988). Applying alumni research to decision making. In Melchiori, G. S. (Ed.), *Alumni research: Methods and applications* (pp. 67–76). New directions for institutional research, no. 60. San Francisco: Jossey-Bass.

Morstain, B. R. (1973). *Student Orientation Survey: Form D, Preliminary Manual.* Newark: University of Delaware, Office of Academic Planning and Evaluation.

Muller, S. (1994). Presidential leadership. In J. R. Cole, E. G. Barber, & S. R. Graubard (Eds.), *The research university in a time of discontent* (pp. 115–130). Baltimore: The Johns Hopkins University Press.

Murray, H. G. (1985). Classroom teaching behaviors related to college teaching effectiveness. In J. G. Donald & A. M. Sullivan (Eds.), *Using research to improve teaching* (pp. 21–34). New directions for teaching and learning, no. 23. San Francisco: Jossey-Bass.

Murray, H. G., & Renaud, R. D. (1995). Disciplinary differences in classroom teaching behaviors. In N. Hativa & M. Marincovich (Eds.) *Disciplinary differences in teaching and learning* (pp. 31–39). New directions for teaching and learning, no. 64. San Francisco: Jossey-Bass.

Nadeau, G. G., Donald, J. G., & Konrad, A. (1992, April). *Criteria and indicators of quality and excellence in Canadian colleges and universities*. Paper presented at the annual meeting of the American Educational Research Association, San Francisco.

Nadeau, G. G., Donald, J. G., Konrad, A., & Tremblay, L. (1990, June). *Criteria of quality and excellence in Canadian colleges and universities: Results of the first Delphi study*. Symposium conducted at the Canadian Society for the Study of Higher Education, Victoria, BC.

National Association of Student Personnel Administrators. (1987). A perspective on student affairs. Iowa City, IO: American College Testing Program.

National Center on Postsecondary Teaching, Learning, and Assessment. (1993). Penn State Department of Publication U. Ed. EDU 91–24.

Newell, W. H. (1994). Designing interdisciplinary courses. In J. T. Klein & W. G. Doty (Eds.), *Interdisciplinary studies today* (pp. 35–51). New directions for teaching and learning, no. 58. San Francisco: Jossey-Bass.

Newman, F. (1988). Rewarding excellent teaching. In B. A. Kimble (Ed.), *Teaching undergraduates: Essays from the Lilly Endowment workshop on liberal arts* (pp. 185–197). Buffalo, NY: Prometheus.

Newman, J. H. (1976). The idea of a university (I. T. Ker, Ed.). Oxford, England: Clarendon.

Noel, L. (1985). Increasing student retention: New challenges and potential. In L. Noel, R. Levitz, & D. Saluri (Eds.), *Increasing student retention: Effective programs and practices for reducing the dropout rate* (pp. 1–27). San Francisco: Jossey-Bass.

Northwestern Observer. (1991, April). The evaluation and improvement of teaching. Evanston, IL: Northwestern University: Author.

Nyquist, J. D., Abbott, R. D., Wulff, R. D., & Sprague, J. (1991). *Preparing the professoriate of tomorrow to teach: Selected readings in TA training*. Dubuque, IA: Kendall/Hunt.

Organization for Economic Cooperation and Development. (1982). *The university and the community*. Paris: Cedex.

Pace, C. R. (1974). *The demise of diversity? A comparative profile of eight types of institutions*. Berkeley, CA: Carnegie Foundation for the Advancement of Teaching.

Pace, C. R. (1985). Perspectives and problems in student outcomes research. In P. T. Ewell (Ed.), *Assessing educational outcomes* (pp. 7–18). New directions for institutional research, no. 47. San Francisco: Jossey-Bass.

Pace, C. R. (1988). *Measuring the quality of college student experiences*. Los Angeles: UCLA Center for the Study of Evaluation.

Pace, C. R. (1990). *The undergraduates: A report of their activities and progress in college in the 1980s*. Los Angeles: UCLA Center for the Study of Evaluation.

Palmer, P. (1993). Good talk about good teaching: Improving teaching through conversation and community. *Change*, 25(6), 8–13.

Paris, S. G., & Turner, J. C. (1994). Situated motivation. In P. Pintrich, D. Brown, & C. Weinstein (Eds.), *Student motivation, cognition, and learning: Essays in honor of Wilbert J. McKeachie* (pp. 213–237). Hillsdale, NJ: Erlbaum.

Pascarella, E. T., & Terenzini, P. T. (1991). *How college affects students: Findings and insights from twenty years of research*. San Francisco: Jossey-Bass.

Pascarella, E. T., Terenzini, P. T., & Wolfle, L. (1986). Orientation to college and freshman year persistence/withdrawal decisions. *Journal of Higher Education*, *57*, 155–175.

Pelikan, J. (1992). *The idea of the university: A reexamination*. New Haven, CT: Yale University Press.

Penn State catalogue, 1994–95 (1994). University Park: Pennsylvania State University.

Penney, M. (1977). *Self-evaluation for teaching improvement*. Unpublished master's thesis, McGill University, Montreal.

Perry, R. P. (1985). Instructor expressiveness: Implications for improving teaching. In J. G. Donald & A. M. Sullivan (Eds.), *Using research to improve teaching* (pp. 35–49). New directions for teaching and learning, no. 23. San Francisco, Jossey-Bass.

Perry, R. P. (1990). Instruction in higher education. Introduction to the special section. *Journal of Educational Psychology*, *82*(2), 183–188.

Perry, W. G. (1970). *Forms of intellectual and ethical development in the college years: A scheme*. Troy, MI: Holt, Rinehart & Winston.

Perry, W. G. (1981). Intellectual and ethical development. In A. W. Chickering & Associates, *The modern American college: Responding to the new realities of diverse students and a changing society* (pp. 76–116). San Francisco: Jossey-Bass.

Peterson, M. (1995, August). *Institutional structure and management*. Paper presented at the annual forum of the European Association for Institutional Research, Zurich.

Peterson's competitive colleges 1996–1997 (1996). (15th ed.) Princeton, NJ: Author.

Pfinster, A. O. (1992). Liberal arts colleges. In B. R. Clark & G. R. Neave (Eds.), *The encyclopedia of higher education* (pp. 1146–1156). Oxford, England: Pergamon Press.

Pintrich, P. R. (1987, April). *Motivated learning strategies in the college classroom*. Paper presented at the annual meeting of the American Educational Research Association, Washington, DC.

Pintrich, P. R. (1988). A process-oriented view of student motivation and cognition. In J. S. Stark & L. A. Mets (Eds.), *Improving teaching and learning through research* (pp. 55–70). New directions for institutional research, no. 57. San Francisco: Jossey-Bass.

Pintrich, P. R. (Ed.). (1995). *Understanding self-regulated learning*. New directions for teaching and learning, no. 63. San Francisco: Jossey-Bass.

Pintrich, P. R., Brown, D., & Weinstein, C. (Eds.). (1994). *Student motivation, cognition and learning: Essays in honor of Wilbert J. McKeachie*. Hillsdale, NJ: Erlbaum.

Pintrich, P. R., Cross, D. R., Kozma, R. B., & McKeachie, W. J. (1986). Instructional psychology. *Annual Review of Psychology*, *37*, 611–651.

Pintrich, P. R., & DeGroot, E. (1990). Motivated and self-regulated learning components of classroom academic performance. *Journal of Educational Psychology*, *82*, 41–50.

Pintrich, P. R., Marx, R. W., & Boyle, R. A. (1993). Beyond cold conceptual change: The role of motivational beliefs and classroom contextual factors in the process of conceptual change. *Review of Educational Research*, *63*(2), 167–199.

Piper, D. W. (1993). *Quality management in universities*. Canberra: Department of Employment, Education and Training.

Pollock, G., Bowman, R. J., Gendreau, P., & Gendreau, L. (1975). An investigation of selection criteria for admission to an Ontario university. *Canadian Journal of Higher Education*, *5*(3), 1–16.

Ramsden, P. (1992). *Learning to teach in higher education*. London: Routledge.

Ratcliff, J. (1992). Reconceptualizing the college curriculum. *Perspectives*, *22*, 122–137.

Ratcliff, J. L., & Yaeger, P. M. (1994, April). *What are the coursework patterns most associated with the development of quantitative abilities of college students with low math skills?* Paper presented at the annual meeting of the American Educational Research Association, New Orleans.

Rees, A., & Smith, S. P. (1991). *Faculty retirement in the arts and sciences*. Princeton, NJ: Princeton University Press.

Rhodes, F.H.T. (1994). The place of teaching in the research university. In J. R. Cole, E. G. Barber, & S. R. Graubard (Eds.), *The research university in a time of discontent* (pp. 179–189). Baltimore: The Johns Hopkins University Press.

Rose, R. (1986). Disciplined research and undisciplined problems. In D. E. Chubin, A. L. Porter, F. A. Rossini, & T. Connolly (Eds.), *Interdisciplinary analysis and research: Theory and practice of problem-focused research and development*. Mt. Airy, MD: Lomond.

Rosenberg, C. (1979). Towards an ecology of knowledge: On discipline, context, and history. In A. Oleson & J. Voss (Eds.), *The organization of knowledge in modern America, 1860–1920* (pp. 440–455). Baltimore: Johns Hopkins University Press.

Rosenzweig, R. M. (1994). Governing the modern university. In J. R. Cole, E. G. Barber, & S. R. Graubard (Eds.), *The research university in a time of discontent* (pp. 299–308). Baltimore: The Johns Hopkins University Press.

Rothman, M. A. (1992). Physics in higher education. In B. R. Clark & G. R. Neave (Eds.), *The encyclopedia of higher education* (pp. 2388–2398). Oxford, England: Pergamon Press.

Russell, D. (1982). The causal dimension scale: A measure of how individuals perceive causes. *Journal of Personality and Social Psychology*, *42*(6), 1137–1145.

Ryan, C. C. (1995). Professional development and training for faculty advisers. In A. G. Reinarz & E. R. White (Eds.), *Teaching through academic advising: A faculty perspective* (pp. 35–42). New directions for teaching and learning, no. 62. San Francisco: Jossey-Bass.

Ryan, M. P. (1984). Monitoring text comprehension: Individual differences in epistemological standards. *Journal of Educational Psychology*, *76*(2), 248–258.

Schmitz, C. C. (1993). Assessing the validity of higher education indicators. *Journal of Higher Education*, *65*(5), 503–521.

Scott, R. A. (1992). Social sciences: Introduction. In B. R. Clark & G. R. Neave (Eds.), *The encyclopedia of higher education* (pp. 2071–2080). Oxford, England: Pergamon Press.

Seldin, P. (1980). *Successful faculty evaluation programs*. Crugers, NY: Coventry.

Shils, E. (1983). *The academic ethic*. Chicago: University of Chicago Press.

Silberman, M. (1996). *Active learning: 101 strategies to teach any subject*. Boston: Allyn & Bacon.

Sims, S. J., & Sims, R. R. (Eds.). (1995). *Total quality management in higher education: Is it working? Why or why not?* Westport, CT: Praeger.

Skolnikoff, E. B. (1994). Knowledge without borders? Internationalization of the research universities. In J. R. Cole, E. G. Barber, & S. R. Graubard (Eds.), *The research university in a time of discontent* (pp. 333–360). Baltimore: The Johns Hopkins University Press.

Snow, C. P. (1959). *The two cultures and the scientific revolution*. Cambridge, England: University Press.

Spaeth, J. L., & Greeley, T. M. (1970). *Recent alumni and higher education. A survey of college graduates*. Berkeley, CA: Carnegie Foundation for the Advancement of Teaching.

Spendolini, M. (1992). *The benchmarking book*. New York: AMACOM.

Sporn, B. (1995, August). *Developing an information strategy: The role of technology*. Paper presented at the annual forum of the European Association for Institutional Research, Zurich.

Stadtman, V. (1992). National systems of higher education: United States. In B. R. Clark & G. R. Neave (Eds.), *The encyclopedia of higher education* (pp. 777–788). Oxford, England: Pergamon Press.

Stark, J. S. (1975). The relation of disparity in student and faculty educational attitudes to early student transfer from college. *Research in Higher Education*, 3(4), 329–344.

Stark, J. S., & Morstain, B. R. (1978). Educational orientations of faculty in liberal arts colleges: An analysis of disciplinary differences. *Journal of Higher Education*, 49(5), 420–437.

Stark, J. S., Shaw, K. M., & Lowther, M. A. (1989). *Student goals for college and courses*. Report No. 6. Washington DC: School of Education and Human Development, The George Washington University.

Steele, J. (1986, April). *Assessing reasoning and communication skills of postsecondary students*. Paper presented at the annual meeting of the American Educational Research Association, San Francisco.

Stralser, S. (1995). Benchmarking: The new tool. *Planning for Higher Education*, 23, 15–19.

Suter, L. (1994, April). *Developing national indicators of the condition of undergraduate education in science, mathematics and engineering*. Paper presented at the annual meeting of the American Educational Research Association, New Orleans.

Sutton, F. X. (1994). The distinction and durability of American research universities. In J. R. Cole, E. G. Barber, & S. R. Graubard (Eds.), *The research university in a time of discontent* (pp. 309–332). Baltimore: The Johns Hopkins University Press.

Svinicki, M. D., & Menges, R. J. (Eds.). (1996). *Honoring exemplary teaching*. New directions for teaching and learning, no. 65. San Francisco: Jossey-Bass.

Taylor, A. L., & Schmidtlein, F. A. (1995, August). *Changing higher education environments: The new status quo for research universities' management and planning*. Paper presented at the annual forum of the European Association for Institutional Research, Zurich.

Terenzini, P. T., Springer, L., Pascarella, E. T., & Nora, A. (1995). Academic and out-of-class influences on students' intellectual orientations. *The Review of Higher Education, 19*(2), 23–44.

Thomas, A. (1989). Further education staff appraisal. *Assessment and Evaluation in Higher Education, 14*(3), 149–157.

Thomas, A. (1990, April). *The basis of student judgment on teaching quality in different academic areas*. Paper presented at the annual meeting of the American Educational Research Association, Boston.

Thompson, J. D., Hawkes, R. W., & Avery, R. W. (1969). Truth strategies and university organization. *Educational Administration Quarterly, 5*, 4–25.

Tinto, V. (1982). Limits of theory and practice in student attrition. *Journal of Higher Education, 53*(6), 687–700.

Tinto, V. (1985). Withdrawal from college. In L. Noel, R. Levitz, & D. Saluri (Eds.), *Increasing student retention* (pp. 28–43). San Francisco: Jossey-Bass.

Tinto, V. (1987). *Leaving college: Rethinking the causes and cures of student attrition*. San Francisco: Jossey-Bass.

Tobias, S. (1990) *They're not dumb, they're different: Stalking the second tier.* Tucson, AZ: Research Corporation.

Toulmin, S. (1972). *Human understanding*, Vol. 1. Oxford, England: Clarendon Press.

Trutmann, A. (1995, August). Opening address, *Dynamics in higher education: Traditions challenged by new paradigms*, Annual forum of the European Association for Institutional Research, Zurich.

Twombly, S. B. (1992). Student perspectives on general education in a research university: An exploratory study. *Journal of General Education, 41*, 238–272.

Van Note Chism, N., Fraser, J. M., & Arnold, R. L. (1996). Teaching academies: Honoring and promoting teaching through a community of expertise. In M. D. Svinicki & R. J. Menges (Eds.), *Honoring exemplary teaching* (pp. 25–32). New directions for teaching and learning, no. 65. San Francisco: Jossey-Bass.

Vaughan, E. D. (1977). Misconceptions about psychology among introductory psychology students. *Teaching of Psychology*, *4*, 138–141.

Volkwein, J. F. (1989). Changes in quality among public universities. *Journal of Higher Education*, *60*(2), 136–151.

Watson, C., & Gill, M. (1977, June). *An evaluation of the Grade 13 marks which are the major criterion of admissions into Ontario universities*. Paper presented at the annual conference of the Canadian Society for the Study of Higher Education, Fredericton, NB.

Weber, M. (1958). *The Protestant ethic and the spirit of capitalism*. New York: Scribner.

Weiland, J. S. (1992). Humanities: Introduction. In B. R. Clark & G. R. Neave (Eds.), *The encyclopedia of higher education* (pp. 1981–1989). Oxford, England: Pergamon Press.

White, R., Gunstone, R., Elterman, E., Macdonald, I., McKittrick, B., Mills, D., & Mulhall, P. (1995). Students' perceptions of teaching and learning in first year university physics. *Research in Science Education*, *25*(4), 465–478.

Whitehead, A. N. (1929). *The aims of education*. New York: Macmillan.

Williams, T. R., & Schiralli, M. (1991). *Canadian university presidents' perceptions of campus life issues*. Paper presented at annual conference of the Canadian Society for the Study of Higher Education, Kingston, ON.

Willingham, W. W. (1985). *Success in college: The role of personal qualities and academic ability*. New York: College Entrance Examination Board.

Willis, D. (1993). Academic involvement at university. *Higher Education*, *25*, 133–150.

Wilshire, B. (1990). Professionalism as purification ritual: Alienation and disintegration in the university. *Journal of Higher Education*, *61*(3), 280–293.

Wingspread Group on Higher Education. (1993). *An American imperative: Higher expectations for higher education*. Racine, WI: Johnson Foundation.

Winkler, A. M. (1992). The faculty workload question. *Change*, July/August, 36–41.

Woodhouse, D. (1995). Efficient quality systems. *Assessment and Evaluation in Higher Education*, *20*(1), 15–24.

Zukav, G. (1979). *The dancing Wu Li masters: An overview of the new physics*. New York: Bantam.

Index